LABOUR AND SOCIALIST MOVEMENTS IN EUROPE BEFORE 1914

Edited by
Dick Geary

BERG

Oxford / New York / Munich
Distributed exclusively in the US and Canada by
St. Martin's Press, New York

First published in 1989 by
Berg Publishers, Inc.
Editorial offices:
165 Taber Avenue, Providence, RI 02906, U.S.A.
150 Cowley Road, Oxford OX4 1JJ UK

Paperback edition 1992
© Berg Publishers, Inc.

British Library Cataloguing in Publication Data
Labour and socialist movements in Europe before 1914.
1. Europe. Labour movements, history
I. Geary, Dick
335'.0094
ISBN 0-85496-200-X   ISBN 0-85496-705-2 (paperback)

Library of Congress Cataloging-in-Publication Data
Labour and socialist movements in Europe before 1914 / edited by Dick Geary
p.   cm.
Bibliography: p.
Includes index.
1. Labor and laboring classes—Europe—History. 2. Trade-unions—
Europe—History. I. Geary, Dick. II. Title: Labor and socialist movements in
Europe before 1914.
HD8376.1.23   1989   322'.2'094- dc19
ISBN 0-85496-200-X   ISBN 0-85496-705-2 (paperback)   88-21418

CONTENTS

LIST OF TABLES

INTRODUCTION

Dick Geary

Since the 1960s there has been an enormous outpouring of works on
the labour history of most European countries. Traditional studies
of socialist ideology and national organisations (trade unions and
political parties) have been supplemented by local and regional
studies, a point of considerable significance, given the fragmented
history of labour, even in individual nations. Generalisations about
the working class have been further undermined by the analysis of
individual trades and crafts, and of conflicts within them: conflicts
as often between skilled and unskilled, male and female, as between
workers and their employers. The study of everyday life, of practices on the shop-floor and in the community, at work and at play,
has enriched our understanding of the complexity of those factors
which enable certain groups of workers to organise and engage in
successful collective action, whilst others rarely figure in the pages
of the history books on account of their *apparent* docility and
passivity.

 In the light of the above one might assume that the time was well
past for another collection of 'survey essays' such as this, in which a
group of relatively young historians write about the country of their
interest and expertise. But such an assumption appears decidedly
wrong to this editor for a number of reasons. The very mass of
monographic research pursued in the last few years demands some
attempt to integrate it into an overall and less specialised perspective, especially as even the professional historian, let alone the
average student or layman, has scarcely the time or energy to absorb
all the newly discovered data and reinterpretations. Furthermore,
much of the most important work on European labour history of

recent origin has appeared in languages not at the disposal of most English readers. Thus the following chapters incorporate the results of research otherwise unavailable to many. A final justification for this volume is that the individual authors do not merely survey the work of others but produce the fruits of their own research and make their own intervention in areas of controversy.

A collection such as this cannot hope to be comprehensive: obviously some important cases are omitted, as, for example, those of Belgium, Austria-Hungary and Scandinavia. The following chapters do, however, deal with several of the most important labour movements in Europe before the outbreak of the First World War, namely those of Britain, France, Germany, Italy, Spain and Russia. The inclusion of British material in works on 'Europe' has not been too common in publications on this side of the Atlantic, but is something that here requires not the slightest justification. Britain was the world's first industrial nation and the mother of the world's oldest labour movement. As early as the 1830s there already existed within these shores trade associations (unions) of some permanence; and by 1914 the British trade unions had a membership which far outnumbered that of any other European nation. British workers had already lived through a series of conflicts, not least in the stormy days of Chartism, that were to engulf the continent at a later date with the onset of industrialisation. Their organisations and aspirations became for some Europeans a model to be emulated and were followed with great interest by no lesser a personage than Karl Marx. For others the trajectory of the British labour movement, especially the predominant reformism after the middle of the nineteenth century, demonstrated precisely what was to be avoided. Yet perhaps the most important reason for including a study of British labour in this volume is precisely because of the way in which the British case differed from developments across the channel: the relative liberalism and non-interventionism of the British state, the willingness of many British employers to deal with trade unions, the continuing strength of liberal/constitutionalist values amongst sections of the population *outside* the working class — all of these factors go some way towards explaining the relative moderation of British workers, the dominance of trade-union rather than radical political strategies, and the relatively small support achieved by explicitly socialist organisations. In fact there seems to exist a dynamic interaction between middle-class and working-class politics. Where a national bourgeoisie is weak or tied to an existing and authoritarian state, as in Russia before the First World War, or in countries in which the middle class increasingly abandons liberal values and comes to support semi-authoritarian political systems, as was to some extent the case in Imperial Germany and pre-war Spain, there the prospects of working-class liberalism appear to be weaker, whilst political radicalism on the part of labour becomes more marked. Conversely the Republican traditions of at least some sections of the French bourgeoisie and the buoyant liberalism of the British middle class enabled a fair proportion of workers to remain in the liberal camp.

The authors of the individual chapters in this volume have not been tied to an identical timespan for the obvious reason that the onset of industrialisation and the subsequent emergence of a modern labour movement varied so enormously from country to country, with Britain at one end of the spectrum, as it were, and — with certain regional exceptions — Spain and Russia at the other. What the chapters try to do is to provide an overview of and explanation for the development of the various national labour movements in the period before the outbreak of the First World War; to examine what kinds of workers became involved in different forms of collective action (skilled or unskilled, male or female, urban or rural, those in small or large concerns, those living in different kinds of communities and localities) and why; and to account for the differing ideologies and values that did as much to divide as to unite labour in this period. A necessary consequence of this is that the emphasis in each individual chapter is not necessarily the same but rather reflects both national peculiarities and the preoccupations of recent historiographical controversy. If any generalisation can be made, it is that generalisations about the European 'working class' are best avoided. Revolutionary socialism found a large audience in Tsarist Russia but scarcely any in Edwardian England. In France, Germany and Italy there did develop socialist parties of some significance before 1914; but in all these cases, these parties were riven with internal conflicts, some personal, some ideological and others determined by the different economic and social situation of various groups of workers. The pre-war socialist parties in France, Germany and Italy encompassed radicals and reformists, revolutionaries and non-revolutionaries, Marxists and non-Marxists; and to some extent the split of the socialist movement into social-democratic and communist camps in the inter-war years was a consequence not only of new economic developments or the intervention of the Russian Bolsheviks (via the Third International), but also of these deeply rooted pre-war divisions.

The different ideological identities of national labour movements before the First World War obviously reflect the different economic and social structures of the various countries. Revolutionary fervour in Russia and millenarian anarchism in Spain may at first sight seem to correlate with appallingly low living standards, whilst the political moderation of labour in Victorian Britain has understandably been seen as a result of the relative affluence of the British worker, and especially that of the skilled 'labour aristocrat'. However, any attempt to reduce levels of working-class radicalism to such crude economic variables is fraught with all kinds of difficulty. Imperial Germany produced a large and ostensibly Marxist socialist movement at a time of *rising* living standards. The rank and file of that movement, as also applies to the socialist organisations in France and Italy, were not the unskilled and lowly paid but precisely the kind of 'labour aristocrats' (printers, skilled engineering and building workers) who in Britain remained loyal to liberalism. This suggests that to a very large extent the differing ideological identities of national labour movements are to be explained more by political factors than by purely industrial developments. In fact, all the following chapters identify the nature and role of the *state* as crucial in explaining different levels of working-class radicalism. Genuinely parliamentary states had much less difficulty in incorporating the working class into the body politic (and, for that matter, in mobilising its support in wartime) than did authoritarian or discriminatory regimes. Also important in determining the attitudes of labour was the behaviour of employers in the field of what these days is known as industrial relations. This becomes quite clear when one contrasts the British case, in which a significant percentage of employers were either willing or forced to recognise trade unions and conclude collective wage agreements, in which they were strongly encouraged by Liberal governments after the turn of the century, with that of Imperial Germany, where larger employers, especially in heavy industry, refused to abandon an authoritarian attitude to their labour force or to deal with unions. In this respect, however, it should be noted that it is the British case which is atypical: in no other European country had anything resembling a system of collective bargaining come into existence before 1914.

What also becomes clear is that the nature and values of workers varied not just from one country to another but also *within* national boundaries. In Spain anarchism found a foothold in some places, according to both local tradition and economic structure (Andalusia, Catalonia), whilst the significantly weaker socialist movement developed in others (Madrid and the northern Basque provinces). Yet even Spanish anarchism was far from monolithic in its structure: the union-based anarcho-syndicalism of Catalan textile workers was of a very different kind from the protests of Andalusian rural labourers, as Paul Heywood's contribution to this volume makes clear. In France different organisations and traditions separated the factory labour of the northern textile towns and the miners from the artisanate of Paris. In Germany the Social Democratic Party in the relatively liberal south-western state of Baden — significantly the Second Reich was a federal state — was much less radical than the party organisations in repressive Prussia. John Davis, in his chapter on the Italian labour movement, stresses the importance of regional differences if anything to an even greater degree.

To some extent, as we have seen, these differences can be ascribed to the varying local political situation or the attitude of the local bourgeoisie. Many of the internal conflicts within the national labour movements reflected the contrasting priorities of trade unionists on the one hand and socialist politicians on the other, as the chapter on Germany seeks to demonstrate. In some cases conflicts were a consequence of personal rivalries, as in the early days in France, Germany and Spain; but such rivalries often overlapped with different ideological traditions such as those which Roger Magraw depicts in the extremely fragmented development of French socialism between 1880 and 1905. Such personal and historical divisions were also, however, a consequence of a central aspect of European industrialisation, both between and within individual nations: *uneven development*. Even within national economies the pace of change varied enormously. Nowhere was this more evident than in Russia: amidst a sea of inefficient peasant agriculture there developed in St Petersburg one of the most technically advanced and concentrated munitions industries in the world. In Spain the long-established textile industry of Catalonia and the more recent development of heavy industry around Bilbao contrasted with the backwardness of rural Spain, as well as setting the areas apart from one another in their industrial structures. Imperial Germany witnessed the massive industrial expansion of Leipzig, Dresden,

Chemnitz, Berlin and Hamburg, as well as of the newer towns of the Ruhr; but much of Germany south of the River Main remained untouched by industrialisation, as did the vast eastern provinces of Posen and Pomerania. The proletariat of industrial Italy, concentrated in the Milan–Genoa–Turin triangle, had perhaps something in common with those employed in nearby capitalist agriculture but little or nothing in common with the peasants who worked the large estates of Southern Italy.

The obvious result of such uneven development was the heterogeneous nature of the 'working class' in all industrial countries, with artisan crafts or cottage industry dominant in some areas, and large-scale factory production characteristic of others. Furthermore, industrialisation did not necessarily create a more homogeneous labour force. Even within one industrial sector, for example engineering, the pace of technological modernisation varied enormously from branch to branch, even from factory to factory. Nowhere before the First World War had pay and skill differentials been completely eroded, and in some sectors they actually increased in this period. Small-scale production not only survived but was actually stimulated by new inventions, such as gas and electric motors and the sewing machine, and by the need to maintain and repair more modern machinery. Conditions for workers could also vary enormously outside the factory. Those who lived in company housing were normally better provided for than those who had to pay rent in the private sector, and they often displayed specific attitudes which separated them from other workers, as in the German case. Workers crowded into the tenement blocks of Berlin, and for that matter those of Liverpool and Glasgow, experienced problems of a quite different nature from those of 'workers' who nonetheless still dwelt in villages or small provincial towns. And it is important to realise that, Britain apart, there were a great many of these. In 1914 approximately one half of those Germans categorised as 'workers' in the Imperial census still lived in small towns and villages of under 10,000 inhabitants; and in such places unions and socialist organisations were usually conspicuous by their absence.

Yet even within a single locality the working class remained divided in a number of ways which rendered solidarity and collective action at best difficult and in some places impossible. Ethnic tensions set Irish against English, Pole against German, even when they lived and worked side by side — though often they did not, for immigrants often moved into areas already densely settled by their fellow countrymen, whilst in the German case mining employers deliberately built separate housing colonies for Polish and German labour. Ethnic minorities were themselves often divided internally: Loyalist Irish confronted Republican with manifest hostility, whilst Poles and Masurians were equally divided along confessional lines, with the Protestant Masurians loyal to the Imperial crown of Germany and the Catholic Poles often supporting Polish nationalist organisations. But the tensions were even more complicated than the above might suggest: the religious practices of Protestant Masurians had little in common with those of German Protestants, whilst Polish Catholics revealed a hostility not only to the German authorities but also to German Catholics.

The confessional variable was one of which contemporaries were very aware but which has often been lost sight of in our more secular age. Confessional allegiance did play a major role in determining the choices of many industrial workers and could act as a hindrance to socialist mobilisation: in Germany, for example, Social Democracy was much more successful at winning support in Protestant than Catholic areas, not least because Catholicism spawned its own industrial and social organisations (trade unions and workers' clubs) to counter the socialist menace. In France, Italy and perhaps most obviously Spain working-class radicalism often overlapped with anti-clerical traditions: areas of high religious observance tended to be areas where the political left was weak. The profoundly different industrial and political behaviour of women may also relate to religion.

Perhaps the greatest dividing line within the European working class on the eve of the First World War was that of sex. Women formed a significant part of the labour force in all European countries but were grossly under-represented in virtually all trade-union and socialist organisations. They could and did engage in strike action from time to time. Indeed they were on occasion the initiators of some of the largest textile strikes in continental Europe: but for the most part of the permanent organisation of female labour was the exception rather than the rule. Working-class women were primarily concentrated in the low-wage sectors of the economy: agriculture (in continental Europe), domestic service, cottage industry, and the less skilled jobs in textiles, chemicals and food-processing. In the main they had neither the time, the money nor the energy to sustain organisation, especially where they were additionally landed with household chores. They lacked bargaining power and were easily replaced. In this sense the female worker was the archetype of the unskilled. She may also have been put off by the aggressive masculinity of working-class culture, even in its organised form; and she often remained closer to the churches than did her male counterpart.

Skill differences also continued to be of huge significance within the male labour force. The infamous 'sectionalism' of skilled labour in Britain, the refusal of skilled workers to treat their less skilled colleagues as their equals, has been a major area of comment and historical investigation. But almost everywhere before 1914 it was skilled workers who initiated labour organisation and continued to predominate within that organisation. Admittedly things were beginning to change with the advent of 'new unionism' in Britain between 1889 and 1892, and especially between 1911 and 1914, when some less skilled and previously unorganised groups of workers displayed an unprecedented proclivity to strike and to join unions. It is also true that industrial, as distinct from craft, unions, attempting to recruit all skill levels, came to characterise part of trade union scene in Germany after 1890. Yet the skilled still remained numerically and politically dominant within organised labour in 1914; and the mobilisation of the unskilled was characterised by a series of setbacks generated by downturns in the business cycle and employer counter-offensives. For the most part the unskilled lacked bargaining power in the market place, had low expectations and no, or few, organisational traditions on which solidarity could be founded. A newly constituted industrial labour force, recruited from different regions, different social and trade backgrounds, and different traditions (some rural, some urban) took time to form a cohesive whole that was capable of collective action. This does not mean they were happy with their lot; and they might express their dissatisfaction by taking to the bottle (not very common), absenteeism or changing firm or job. But before 1914 it was invariably a minority of the work-force that found itself in working-class industrial and political organisations, even in that most urban and industrial of all European countries, Great Britain. In societies still largely agrarian the problems of labour organisation were even greater, though in some places, such as Provence in southern France and certain rural areas of capitalist agriculture in northern Italy, socialist and trade union organisations did make headway amongst the local peasantry, as did anarchism in Spanish Andalusia. No less important, argues Christopher Read in his contribution on Russia, was the peasant background of many Russian factory workers, who carried collectivist rural traditions from the village into their new urban environment. Conversely, German socialists always found it heavy going in the countryside, where a land-owning peasantry tended to align itself with the political right, even if the peasants were no mere dupes of aristocratic manipulation, as recent research has demonstrated.

It was not only peasants who were mobilised by or mobilised themselves in non-socialist and often explicitly anti-socialist organisations. Many industrial workers who did organise before 1914 joined precisely such groups. Company unions, formed by the employers, subsidised by them and often providing pension benefits and housing, could be found in several industrial countries, most notably in German heavy industry. Such 'yellow unions' disavowed industrial conflict and were 'loyal' to their supposedly paternalistic employers. Rarely before the First World War did white-collar workers identify with their manual, blue-collar workmates. Closer to management, enjoying pension, holiday and seniority entitlements, often performing supervisory tasks, this increasingly large section of the labour force remained largely distant from the labour movement; whilst in the German case some white-collar workers who did organise joined a body (the German National Union of Commercial Employees) that was imperialist, anti-socialist and anti-Semitic. On the other hand many skilled British manual workers continued to support Liberalism, whilst the French Radical Party could rely on a not unimportant reservoir of proletarian support. Thus the growth of independent labour and socialist parties was no unambiguous or constant forward march before the First World War. More often it was discontinuous and fragmented. But by 1914 it had become a major factor in most of the industrial nations of Europe, one remarked upon by innumerable commentators from all walks of life and one which in certain countries such as Imperial Germany and Tsarist Russia terrified the living daylights not only out of the authorities but also out of increasingly large numbers of the middle class. In some countries — most notably Britain, though also to a lesser extent in France and Italy too — the presence of an organised labour movement led to significant constitutional and some welfare reforms; whilst the failure of other countries to integrate their working class into the body politic led to cataclysm at the end of the First World War, as witnessed by the two Russian Revolutions of 1917 and the upheavals which engulfed

Germany between 1918 and 1923.

BIBLIOGRAPHY

Each of the following chapters contains a list for further English-language reading on the individual country discussed in that chapter. Here are some more general works:

C. Colhoun, *The Question of Class Struggle* (Chicago, 1982)

D. Geary, *European Labour Protest, 1848–1939* (2nd edn, London, 1984)

E. Hobsbawm, *Labouring Men* (London, 1968)

——, *Worlds of Labour* (London, 1984)

J. Joll, *The Second International, 1889–1914* (London, 1966)

I. Katznelson and A. Zollberg (eds), *Working-Class Formation* (Princeton, 1986)

J. Kuczynski, *The Rise of the Working Class* (New York, 1967)

A.J. Lindemann, *A History of European Socialism* (New Haven, Conn., 1983)

H. Mitchell and P.N. Stearns, *Workers and Protest* (Ithaca, NY, 1971)

J.B. Moore, Jnr, *Injustice* (White Plains, NY, 1978)

P.N. Stearns, *Lives of Labour* (London, 1975)

C. Tilly, L.A. Tilly, R. Tilly, *The Rebellious Century, 1830–1930* (Cambridge, Mass., 1975)

L.A. Tilly and C. Tilly (eds), *Class Conflict and Collective Action* (Beverly Hills, Calif., 1981)

E.O. Wright, *Classes* (London, 1985)

1

THE BRITISH LABOUR MOVEMENT BEFORE 1914

Gordon Phillips

Working-class structure and working-class attitudes in the early industrial period

Looked at through bourgeois eyes, the British labour scene of the late nineteenth century appeared, in a European setting, reassuringly peaceful. Though unusually well-organised, the wage-earning class was conspicuously unrevolutionary in its outlook. 'Trade unionists', wrote the *Times* in 1883,

> have little or none of the wild fancies and subversive schemes and idle rhetoric which are too commonly the stock in trade with their French and German fellows. There is no trace now of a deep-rooted antagonism to the capitalist class as such, no belief whatever in a millenium to follow from a general overthrow of the existing institutions of the country . . . When we remember how vast the power is which they wield already, we may well rejoice at the moderate use they seem prepared to make of it.[1]

Much the same complacency had reigned ever since the Second Reform Act of 1867 had conferred the franchise upon the majority of urban working-class householders. To a conservative French *literatteur* like Taine, who witnessed a march of the brickmakers of Oldham around 1870,

> It is a remarkable fact that these unions do not deviate from their original

1. Quoted in R. Davidson, *Whitehall and the Labour Problem* (London, 1985), p. 52.

object: they have no other aim but wage increases, and do not think in terms of seizing political power, which they most certainly would do in France. They are in no way political, are not even social; they envisage no Utopias, do not dream of reforming society, putting down usury, abolishing the hereditary principle, of equal pay for all or of making every individual a partner in the State.[2]

Such generalisations have a superficial air; but they were, in essentials, incontrovertible. And they are endorsed, as it were, by witnesses from the left. Marx, in his long English exile, entertained high hopes of an indigenous proletarian revolution during the Chartist agitation of the 1840s, and even at the heyday of the first International. Britain was, he still believed in 1870, 'the only country in which the material conditions for this revolution have developed up to a certain degree of maturity'. But he was rapidly and thoroughly disillusioned by the timid coda of the next two decades. His pessimism was shared, and perhaps encouraged, by Engels, who wrote to Bebel in 1883:

> Do not on any account whatever let yourself be bamboozled into thinking there is a real proletarian movement going on here. . . . The elements at present active may become important. . . . but only if a spontaneous movement breaks out here among the workers and they succeed in getting control of it. Till then they will remain individual minds, with a hotch-potch of confused sects, remnants of the great movements of the forties, standing behind them, and nothing more.[3]

The question of why the archetypal Marxist proletariat developed so unrevolutionary a physiognomy, is a familiar and persistent one. It is also, of course, highly contentious. It will not be possible to review this historical controversy here, without neglecting many of the themes and variations which have enriched it. Without undue distortion, however, it is possible to place the debating historians in two camps, according to whether their perspective is of longer or shorter term. On the one side stand those who argue, by and large, that the British working class was consistently moderate in its politics, almost incapable of being mobilised as a force for social

2. *Notes on England* (English trans. London, 1971), p.232.
3. *Marx and Engels on Britain* (Moscow, 1962), p.561; also G. Stedman Jones, 'Some Notes on Karl Marx and the English labour movement', *History Workshop* (1984) 18, pp.124–37.

disruption or reconstruction. At its birth, so to speak, it was already domesticated. The problem of explaining this peaceful disposition is therefore that of identifying the primordial influences, political, social and cultural, which shaped its character *ab initio*. Those influences were not necessarily fixed and immutable, but they were at any rate cumulative and consistent. In Britain, class was made and matured in a milieu which inhibited class war.

On the other side stand the historical exponents of discontinuity: those who see British labour history as changing course at certain critical junctures, and who thus focus attention upon such moments of transition. In the first half of the nineteenth century a native labour movement displays signs, from this viewpoint, of repudiating industrial servitude and political oppression. It accommodated itself to, and is accommodated by, the established order only after the decline of Chartism. In this account, the historical problem to be addressed concerns the nature of that relatively rapid and decisive transition, when labour acquired a new and stable identity. Those who accept the transition theory, themselves disagree on how to account for it. There is less disagreement upon, and consequently less shape to, the interpretation of working-class history later in the century. But since the origins of the social détente are disputed, there remains some room for dissension as to its security, and as to the potential for labour rebellion which it contained.[4]

This essay will be found to owe more to the first of these perspectives, though deriving some benefit from the second. It will present the British labour movement as a creature of conservative habit, whose character changed with time, but changed slowly and unevenly. Its revolutionary attributes were never very pronounced. The relationships of this movement with other sections of society altered, at times, more sharply, and in this respect a mid-century discontinuity in labour history is more clearly manifest. It must be admitted, however, that the choice between opposing interpretations of this broad and comprehensive kind is necessarily somewhat arbitrary. The 'working classes' of Britain, however designated, were always heterogeneous; their experience and capacity for collective action varied markedly from trade to trade, locality to

4. Much of the debate here rehearsed centres upon E.P. Thompson's *The Making of the English Working Class* (London, 1968). A historiographical summary may be found in F.K. Donelly, 'Edward Thompson and his critics', *Social History* (1976) 2, pp.219–38. A recent statement of the 'continuity' thesis is given by Alan Fox, *History and Heritage* (London, 1985).

locality, decade to decade — dependent upon economy fluctuations, technological innovations, and demographic trends. Moreover, the evidence from which this complex past has to be reconstructed is seriously defective. It is concentrated at the points where labour activity is greatest and social conflict most intense, leaving the inert and passive elements of the work-force in obscurity. It records the opinions and perceptions of political élites, whether of the governing class or of popular movements, while affording only fleeting and restricted glimpses of the minds of wage earners at large. The controversial nature of working-class history thus reflects, in large part, these problems of method and resources — or, more precisely, reflects the way in which historians of differing outlook and temperament seek to rise above them.

By European standards, Britain already possessed a large industrial sector at the beginning of the nineteenth century, together with an increasingly commercialised agricultural system. Of roughly five and a half million occupied in 1801, probably around two-thirds were wage earners, or at least partly dependent upon wage labour. Upwards of one quarter of these were employed in manufacturing and mining, and over 10% in trade and transport. Even the large agricultural population had a foothold in the industrial sector, for farm labourers themselves might have secondary and seasonal occupations, and their wives and children were commonly recruited for domestic industry.

This labour force was diverse in character and unequal in status. Even if we leave aside agriculture, and the numerically quite substantial body of personal servants, we may still distinguish at least four broad categories of wage earners. The journeyman artisan or mechanic possessed some recognised skill, often by virtue of apprenticeship, he served one or several small masters, and regarded his usual place of employment as a town workshop. The domestic outworker was more often located in a rural setting, produced goods with members of his family, for a merchant or middleman, and was more likely to be dependent on static and cumbersome machinery. Day labourers, common in building and transport, performed the relatively routine and unskilled jobs which rendered them part of the labouring poor, and on the margin of subsistence. Finally, by the 1790s, there had already come into being a significant class of factory or mill worker, notably in cotton and iron manufacture, deeply stratified by skill, sex and age, though sharing the constraints and disciplines associated with large-scale production and the operation of power-driven machinery.

This classification is necessarily makeshift, exaggerating some distinctions and eliding others, while leaving certain trades like miners and seamen in hazy border zones. It indicates, however, from one aspect, the necessary limitations of collective consciousness within this working population. At the same time, the nuances of social differences in eighteenth-century Britain should not disguise the existence of group loyalties. Men of the same trade were conscious of a common allegiance, at least within the local community. The well-established pattern of regional economic specialisation thus gave an added vigour to occupational consciousness and culture, especially among artisans and some outworkers. The textile villages of the South West, the silk weavers of Spitalfields, the file makers of Sheffield and the shipwrights of the Thames exhibited strong ties and sometimes strong antagonisms. These were not communities of wage earners alone, but they were communities in which wage earners, and wage earning, were predominant; and their cultural identity testified to this fact. Here were to be found men with a clear awareness of the customs and traditions of their occupations. Having practised a trade for much of their lives, they were apt to regard it as a form of property, a livelihood to be left in their possession and passed on to their sons. The remuneration of labour and the price of its product were thought to reflect some intrinsic worth in the artificer, and properly to afford a standard of comfort well above that of the poor and degraded, those without a trade. Materials and methods of work, stints and hours of activity, were at least in some measure matters for wage earners to decide. Styles of dress, modes of speech, initiation ceremonies and shared amusements or indulgences were embodied in an ordered, if probably not an orderly, way of life.

The social outlook of these groups of wage earners was parochial, and was in many respects shared by neighbours with different vocations and similar status: small employers and shopkeepers, freeholders and even those on the margin of the established professions. Workers from a craft background were, on the other hand, far removed from the vagrants, paupers and even the day labourers who stood at the bottom of the social hierarchy. It is clearly inappropriate to speak of an eighteenth-century working class, in either political or economic terms. The kind of distress which engendered popular protest in this setting was liable to be fairly localised, but also to be fairly indiscriminate in its incidence within a local community. Alternatively, like the crisis which overtook Spitalfields in the 1790s, it was largely confined to a particular trade. The most common form of unrest encountered in the eighteenth century reflected the heterogeneity of 'plebeian' society: the riot, whether precipitated by excise taxes, food prices, the infringement of English liberties or religious animosities, was likely to involve men and women from widely different occupations and income levels.

Already, however, certain kinds of protest and collective action were peculiar to wage earners. Adam Smith, in the 1770s, was quite familiar with the phenomenon of the strike, a term which was indeed derived from the trade argot of one group of craftsmen, the hatters. Nearly four hundred such labour disputes occurring in Britain and Ireland between 1717 and 1800 left some kind of record, while probably many others left no trace. One-third of the known stoppages took place in the various branches of the textile and clothing industries, while shipbuilding and water transport, building and mining all accounted for significant numbers. Most of these conflicts were small, though in the woollen trade of the West Country, dominated by merchant capitalists, they might extend across a whole county. They were always exposed to legal retribution, even before the passage of the general Combination Acts of 1799 and 1800 (which were themselves designed to obviate the need for private legislation covering particular occupations). Both the expense and inconvenience of litigation made these sanctions less formidable, however, and in some instances at least employers were found ready to settle with the malcontents, or to agree to some mode of arbitration.

There was, it is true, sometimes little to separate the strike and the riot. Wage earners resorted readily to the latter, to combat the threat of machinery or to reinforce their demands for the legal control of wages, just as strikers might engage in intimidation or the destruction of property in furtherance of an industrial conflict. In these cases, however, the form of protest was clearly one specific to workers, dependant for their livelihood on employment in an ailing trade. And it manifested the existence of combinations, formal or informal, confined to such groups. Trade clubs and trade societies, indeed, flourished among the mechanics and artificers of eighteenth-century industry, and sought, by whatever means seemed appropriate, to protect a recognisable sectional interest. They strove, accordingly, not just to maintain acceptable standards of pay, but to prevent overwork, and especially to restrict access to their trade to 'legal' and 'honourable' men. The preoccupation of these early combinations with the problem of an excess of labour was reflected, accordingly, sometimes in a hostility to mechanisation, and sometimes in the measures they took to organise and facilitate tramping, the migration of members seeking work. While domestic workers were largely concerned with wage issues in this period, the principal goal of the embryonic unions of craftsmen was to establish themselves as the source of labour for their trade. In the larger centres, particularly London, they acted as houses of call where both journeymen and masters could apply to find employment and workmen. The contacts opened between such institutions marked the first stage of the transition from the trade club to the trade union.

The wage earners of this industrial system were thus well able to articulate demands and to achieve a limited measure of organisation. Social conflict was, however, restrained by the moral assumptions which governed economic behaviour, and by the paternalist guise assumed by social relationships. In the sphere of wages, of prices, of the labour market and the productive process, custom and tradition prevailed and were expected to prevail over change and innovation. In so far as these were upheld, no basis existed for any general animosity between masters and servants, capital and labour. Where they ceased to do so, men looked to government, in some form, for redress. For all the inequalities of wealth which separated the élite and the mass in eighteenth-century Britain, a remarkable level of communication was maintained. The respectable journeyman and outworker felt no inhibitions in bringing his grievances before the judiciary, the magistracy, or the legislature. Social politics were transacted through suits, appeals and petitions, and even combination was tolerated where it had recourse to these instruments. The popular protest expressed in strike or riot was characteristically an attempt to reinforce an appeal to authority, or to signal the anger aroused by its neglect. And such appeals were given audience, if somewhat capriciously, at all levels of government: magistrates did on occasion regulate food prices and mediate disputes over wages; courts entertained the pleas of workmen against their employers; parliament enacted legislation to prevent industrial distress and disorder in the tailoring trade (in 1721 and 1766), in silk weaving

(1773), and in the coal trade of the Thames (1757).

This social scene was not, however, static or rigid. The pace of economic growth quickened perceptibly from the 1760s, and with it the rate of technological advance. To some extent, even in earlier years, the industrial communities of Britain can be seen adjusting to change, even as they tried to regulate it. Wage standards, for instance, whatever their 'customary' content, were flexible; market forces, and combinations of employers, could propel them up and down, even if it took time for a new norm to be accepted. Similarly the hostile response which sometimes, though by no means always, greeted mechanical improvements, testified to an awareness of the unpredictability of employment and earnings. The real value of eighteenth-century paternalism is also a matter of dispute. The industrial regulations promulgated from time to time were enforced only briefly, if at all; while by the end of the century senior judges, albeit sympathetic to the claims of the poor, asserted a growing reluctance to involve the law in trade disputes. Hence the social conflict of this period contained elements of the theatrical and the real, reflecting both an injured morality and a deeper enmity felt towards the rich by the poor. Most riots might be dismissed, even in 1801, as 'the tuppenny squabbles of every market day'; but the Gordon riots of 1780 had attained a scope and intensity which were far more alarming, and prompted the first serious discussion in government of the idea of a professional police.

Is the historian justified, on this evidence, in ascribing to British artisans, and to the plebeian class at large, some qualities which already set them apart from their European counterparts? It is clearly difficult to make comparisons between methods of production, patterns of work and labour supply on this scale. Given the weight of custom and tradition in all artisan cultures, however, it may well be possible to discover a worker mentality transcending national boundaries. The craftsman's sense of skill and status, his attitudes to trade and to family, his social relationships and aspirations, may well exhibit frequent parallels. What must also be emphasised, on the other hand, is the extraordinary size and density of the industrial work-force of Britain. Nowhere on the Continent, at the turn of the nineteenth century, were two-fifths of the occupied population to be found in the sectors of manufacturing, trade and transport. It is the early and gradual development of enterprise in mining, shipbuilding, and above all textiles, which sets British economic history apart, as much as the 'revolutionary' advances of the years after 1780. As early as 1815, moreover, a Swiss visitor could be struck by the multitudes of Britons already entirely cut off from the land: a divorce as yet atypical even of most handicraft workers elsewhere in Europe. Johann Caspar Escher wrote in his diary on 20 August 1814, from Manchester: 'In England a heavy fall in the sale of manufactured goods would have the most frightful consequences. Not one of all the many thousand English factory workers has a square yard of land on which to grow food if he is out of work and draws no wages.'[5]

This precocious industrial expansion had considerable significance in the shaping of working-class history. It marked, and enhanced, the general prosperity of the British economy during the seventeenth and eighteenth centuries. Coupled with agricultural rationalisation and commercial expansion, it increased personal incomes and consumption. Wage earners shared in this improvement of living standards, if to a variable and uncertain extent; average wages in Britain probably surpassed those of any other European country except Holland on the eve of the Industrial Revolution. Furthermore, the dimensions of the labour force outside agriculture facilitated its subsequent growth. The recruitment of labour to an enlarged industrial sector, in the first half of the nineteenth century, relied surprisingly little upon its transference from agriculture. If the considerable factor of Irish immigration is left out of account, only about one in five of the new hands in manufacturing, during 1780–1850, were drawn from agrarian occupations. This in itself may indicate a degree of continuity between the labour of the manufacturing and the modern period (in Marx's sense of those terms). However radically the industrial environment changed in Britain, it certainly did not entail putting peasants, or their equivalent, into factories. Even in areas of rapid transformation, like the North West, the practise of domestic manufacture as a by-occupation had been widespread in the century before the Industrial Revolution. Finally, the extent of wage labour in the pre-industrial period made concerted action, and an embryonic organisation, more common. The kind of pre-history of the labour movement sketched above would be a meagre affair if written in

5. See W.O Henderson (ed.), *Industrial Britain under the Regency, 1814–18*, (London, 1968), p.34. The theme was a recurrent one, especially in French accounts of the British scene: cf. L. Faucher, *Manchester in 1844: its Present Condition and Future Prospects* (English trans. 1844, reproduced London, 1969), p.110; and Taine, *Notes on England*, p.230.

other European contexts. The *compagnonnages* and *fraternités* of France and Germany remain mysterious and intangible, by comparison with the combinations of Gloucestershire weavers or London tailors. And no other city could boast the two hundred Friendly Societies which London artisans had formed by the 1820s, many probably of much earlier foundation.

It would be hazardous, no doubt, to conclude from their numerical importance that wage earners in Britain had an awareness of their social and economic importance which their Continental counterparts lacked. What they had acquired, however, at least in England, was a sense of sharing constitutional rights and liberties handed down from a distant past. The popular radicalism of the eighteenth century, in which artisans already played a part, was steeped in this antiquarian tradition, patriotic but suspicious of monarchical power, legalistic but unruly, disjointed but resting upon a widespread political awareness. In this political culture wage earners, or some among them, acquired a distinct notion of freedom and civil rights before they conceived any idea of class. When the latter entered their rhetoric, the former remained intact, to shape, modify and at times confuse its meaning.

The experience of the Industrial Revolution

Even before the end of the eighteenth century, the settled world of the old artisanate was exposed to unfamiliar and disruptive forces of change. The effects were not uniform, and certainly not immediate. What is conveniently termed 'the Industrial Revolution' in Britain followed divergent paths, some advancing to modernity much more rapidly than others. The destruction of the older world of labour was still incomplete, even on the eve of the First World War. This irregularity in the progress of modern capitalism allowed some working men to adapt to its demands more readily and more successfully than others. Only in the long run did the sheer persistence of the economic transformation overtake the whole of society.

As early as the 1790s, however, the process of proletarianisation was claiming its first victims. Workmen of high status and relatively comfortable circumstances were menaced by the very growth of the market for goods and for labour, and by the more ruthless behaviour of those who, trading in any commodity, bought cheaply to sell most profitably. But proletarianisation might mean a number of social reconstructions. It resulted from the relocation of industries in new, often rural or semi-rural areas, facilitating the use of low-wage outworkers. The decline of London as a manufacturing centre, evident before the mid-nineteenth century, was the leading instance of the economic decay of the corporate environment of artisan production. This dispersion was frequently accompanied by a subdivision of the labour process, the use of cheaper materials and perhaps of larger manual machines, which permitted a scale of production appropriate to a mass market, whether at home or abroad. The simplification of work was, however, to be found even in the former urban strongholds of the artisan, where large sectors of the clothing and woodworking trades were taken over by garret masters and sweating workshops. Even where the journeymen preserved some of their skills, they suffered some loss of status as the prospect of promotion to the ranks of master and employer diminished. Finally, the spread of the factory, in textiles, chemicals, pottery and elsewhere, and of the large-scale capitalist enterprise which formed its counterpart in metallurgy and mining, signified the emergence of a proletariat graphically depicted by Engels in 1844, and saluted by the heroic prophecies of the Communist Manifesto.[6]

These industrial changes gave rise to a vastly enlarged wage-earning class. The labour force of Britain, five to six million strong at the beginning of the century, had risen to 9.4 million by 1851, of which just over two million remained in agriculture, forestry and fishing. An industrial working class, broadly defined, numbered at least five million. But to portray this stratum as economically unified, or even as tending to become so, is clearly misleading. The analysis of 'proletarianisation' itself suggests the diversity of experience of its members, and possible conflicts of interest among them. Some artisans were partially or wholly insulated from new techniques and forms of organisation: shipwrights, watchmakers, hatters, wheelwrights. In rural Britain, a host of traditional crafts were to flourish down to the end of the century. Other mechanics, including smiths and millwrights, Birmingham metal workers and Sheffield tool makers, could with some effort and ingenuity adapt their skills to an expanding market and, if required, to a factory

---

6. J. Rule, 'Artisan Attitudes: a comparative survey of skilled labour and proletarianization in Britain before 1848', *Bulletin of the Society for the Study of Labour History* (1985) 50.

regime. Even in the trades most vulnerable to over-expansion and debasement, élites survived to cater for the bespoke market of a wealthy clientele. On the other hand, those groups who suffered most from industrial innovation were at least partly cut off from the rest of the workforce: country outworkers from urban craftsmen; domestic workers from factory recruits, immigrant populations from the indigenous, casual and seasonal from permanent hands.

These contrasts were apparent even in a modern manufacturing centre, such as Manchester. Leon Faucher, a perceptive though not unprejudiced observer, surveyed the workers of cottonopolis a year later than Engels, and with considerably more discrimination. In his eyes a gulf existed, not just between the Irish and English communities of the city, but between the stable core of the work-force and the transient periphery. An equally striking difference, of living conditions if not of income, distinguished the Manchester proletariat from that of the neighbouring industrial villages, to which the more paternalist of the textile entrepreneurs resorted. To Faucher, moreover — whatever doubts he felt about the social animosities of an industrial society — the economic condition of the best-placed cotton operatives already seemed markedly preferable to that of 'the common labourer' of the countryside.[7]

To view the working class in this fashion is to predicate of it a sectional, and for the most part a conservative, outlook. It assumes that protest and, where it arose, organisation, would reflect the interests of particular trades, communities and cultural or ethnic groupings. And it anticipates a popular movement still concerned mainly to defend its known way of life against disruption, settled living standards against erosion, prized distinctions of status against extinction. Such an interpretation is, however, patently and even absurdly one-sided. For all its variety, the Industrial Revolution did in some respects create problems that were shared by workers of different grades and occupations. Faucher himself points to two elements of this shared economic experience. Firstly, the fluctuations of the trade cycle, of commercial expansion and contraction, imposed themselves upon almost every sector of the national economy. Though discernible as a commercial phenomenon only from the 1820s, the trade cycle had in a sense manifested itself already in the inflationary crisis of the 1790s, and the employment crisis which followed the return to peace in 1815. The sustained and unparalleled

7. Faucher, *Manchester in 1844*, pp.60–2.

rise in prices after 1793 pressed upon the living standards of all wage earners. It found some more able to respond effectively than others; but it demanded, on all sides, a questioning of custom and of the sanctity of the moral economy as the basis of economic behaviour. The slumps of 1815, 1819, 1829 and 1842 were, by the measure of the protest they evoked, of larger importance. In a crisis year like 1842, when industrial depression was accompanied by a deficient harvest, it was difficult to discover any occupation in any region which escaped the consequences of distress. To some wage earners, this meant a further instalment in a downward wage spiral. To some, it brought a sudden and devastating transition from relative comfort to near penury, as money earnings were subjected to vicious cuts. Faucher remarked, in a passage which seems to anticipate Marx, how such recurrent depressions served to widen the gulf between the capitalist employer and his workmen: 'The small capitalists are a class unknown; the middle capitalists are disappearing gradually; the large capitalists alone resist the violence of the storm, and make around them a desert.'[8] To some it brought unemployment, so widespread as to be inescapable, and a loss of income which could be replaced only by hard-pressed kin, meagre charity or the hateful Poor Law. Distress of this kind, as has often been urged, did not automatically engender class feeling; but where spasmodic and general privation alternated with conditions of well-being, or succeeded a past of roseate affluence, its contribution to collective consciousness was more marked.

The other, and more imponderable, outcome of industrial development, for Faucher, was 'overwork'. Exploitation, the tightening of industrial discipline, was seen by social commentators from Cobbett to Owen as a symptom of contemporary commercialism. Like proletarianisation, it took various forms. It can, indeed, be seen as the everyday economic expression of that long-run process of social degradation. Where it was perceived, or even half-perceived, it fostered a resentment of authority in industry, an aversion to the arbitrariness of employers and their agents, of wide though indeterminate extent. Such grievances against 'driving' and petty tyranny could be felt alike by the workmen of general building contractors, by domestic workers *vis-à-vis* middlemen, by agricultural labourers against profiteering farmers, as well as by factory hands. Wherever men were required to work harder, for

8. Faucher, *Manchester in 1844*, p.126.

what they felt was an inadequate reward, they might acquire a feeling of common enmities, if not of comradeship, which had been absent in the past.

Above all, however, class consciousness was the product of political experience, of the changing aspect of government. From the onset of those local alarms and disturbances which arose with the French Revolution, the state regarded popular protest with a new anxiety, at times bordering on panic. Much of the old equanimity and sang-froid which the ruling class had displayed in the face of civil commotion was dissipated. The public trials of English and Scottish radicals in 1793 signalled the beginnings of a series of political prosecutions extending down to the Chartist years. The two acts of 1794 inaugurated a legislative attack upon all forms of subversion. The Combination Acts of 1799 and 1800, designed to outlaw organised strikes, were preceded by measures to suppress the activities of radical Corresponding Societies. Public order was enforced by a much readier use of the military, as in the Luddite outbreaks of 1811–12. Troops could be reinforced, if necessary, by the volunteer forces of the yeomanry, or similar bodies of armed auxiliaries of local government, whose most notorious achievement was the bloody dispersal of the political rally at Manchester in 1819, known thereafter as 'Peterloo'. A more disciplined controller of crowds was furnished by the Metropolitan Police Act of 1829, establishing a professional force widely used outside London, to supplement the less reliable provincial police established in piecemeal fashion after 1835. The judicial system was toughened by the increase of stipendiary magistrates; while in an emergency like that of the agrarian violence of 1830 special judicial commissions were set up to ensure exemplary sentencing. At the same time, the state seemed to acquire a hardened attitude to social want. Though it took some care to secure the adequacy of food supplies, in other respects it would no longer countenance the regulation of markets. It steadily resisted the demands of impoverished domestic workers for minimum wage statutes from the 1790s onwards. The general powers of magistrates to regulate conditions of employment were curtailed when the Elizabethan Act of Apprentices was repealed in 1814. Restrictions on the use of machinery were similarly removed. The prohibition of cropping machinery in the woollen industry, for instance, was excised in 1809. The Poor Law, the last refuge of the distressed, had been modified by the initiative of local guardians in response to price inflation and under-employment during the Napoleonic wars. Thereafter, however, its administration grew more parsimonious. And the amending Act of 1834 sought to abolish outdoor relief for the able-bodied pauper, by extending and standardising a custodial institution, the workhouse, as a kind of social penitentiary.

None of this can be said, without serious qualification, to have made an English working class. Vulnerable as they might be to commercial crises, wage earners remained, in other respects and at other times, economically heterogeneous. 'The labouring population has hitherto been spoken of as if it formed only one class', wrote William Thornton in 1846, 'but it is really divided into several, among which the rates of remuneration are far from being uniform'.[9] While discipline and authority in industry were perceived as an incubus, they were encountered in different degrees, resisted with varying effect, and accepted by some more readily than others. State repression, too, was neither systematic nor constant. The enforcement of laws against collective protest and subversive propaganda was sometimes difficult. At best, such measures drove the resilient rebels underground. The taxation of newspapers, for example, brought into being an illegal but scarcely clandestine unstamped press. The Combination Acts achieved even less, with neither unions nor industrial stoppages being eradicated. The Acts were repealed in 1824. The movement for Catholic Emancipation in Ireland in 1827–8, and for parliamentary reform in 1830–32, demonstrated alike that popular agitation, if large in scope, could not be extinguished by official threat and intimidation. It had somehow to be contained, and not crushed.

Economic protest and political action c. 1800–1850

The impact of economic and political change, complex and uneven as it might be, was sufficient to produce working-class protest on an unparalleled scale. It gathered force from about 1811, and reached a climax during the early years of the Chartist movement in 1837–42. Vast in extent, this protest was, not surprisingly, diffuse, both in ideology and mode of action. It exhibited both extreme and moderate, violent and non-violent forms. It engaged adversaries, em-

9. W.T. Thornton, *Over-population and its Remedies*, quoted in R. Glenn, *Urban workers in the Early Industrial Revolution* (Beckenham, 1984), p.284.

ployers and governments, on two fronts; and though at times these came close together, they did not merge. In a sense, the whole history of popular struggle represented a continuous and unplanned search for solutions to the immediate problems of insecurity and oppression, rather than the pursuit of any known and accepted remedy. Progress, if recorded, was by trial and error.

Any simple schema will necessarily distort the labour history of this period. To achieve clarity and brevity, however, we shall make a rough distinction between workers who were economically weak and those who were economically strong: that is, between those for whose labour the long-run market demand was declining, and those in occupations that were stable or expanding. The classification is highly imperfect, but it offers some insight into two forms of collective action. Machine-breaking was, primarily, a recourse of the former; while trade unionism developed as the agency, *par excellence*, of the latter. Two other modes of protest will be considered, however, which made some attempt to involve both groups: the 'general unionism' of the early 1830s, closely connected with the ideas and practice of co-operation; and the popular electoral reform movement culminating in Chartism.

Machine-breaking represents, in one manifestation, the most direct line of action by workers against the threats of industrialism. In another, it is no more than a secondary method of extracting from employers limited economic concessions — 'collective bargaining by riot', in Eric Hobsbawm's celebrated phrase. In both it occurs, spasmodically, throughout the eighteenth and early nineteenth centuries. As a large-scale and convergent movement, however, it is quite short-lived. It appears first in the guise of Luddism in 1811–16; later, and with somewhat changed character, as the Swing riots among agricultural labourers in the south of England in 1830.

In both these instances, machine-breaking is, in its immediate purpose and underlying morality, a repudiation both of commercial capitalism and of the politics of *laissez-faire*. In 1811–16 it involves three categories of wage earner, alike faced by a catastrophic drop in living standards. Midlands hosiery workers confronted employers intent on cutting wages, but some in addition engaging cheap unapprenticed labour and larger machines, swamping the market with inferior goods. Yorkshire wool croppers and shearmen were directly menaced by the use of machinery which could displace handicraft skills. Lancashire handloom weavers saw their livelihood endangered less, as yet, by the factory power-loom than by the growing resort of mill owners and merchants to rural, Irish and female labour. In all these areas, attacks on property were directed selectively against maleficent employers. And these outbreaks followed, significantly, unavailing efforts to secure the redress of grievances by legislation, through petitions to parliament and sometimes to local magistrates. Violence was as much a protest against the liberal state as against the capitalist employer.

The action of the agricultural labourers reflected a similar dual perspective on their situation. Worsening seasonal unemployment and declining wages were exacerbated by mechanisation and the use of casual labour; while the relief afforded by the parochial Poor Law was curtailed by retrenching authorities. Again, the response was partly a destruction of the labour-saving threshing machines, partly a campaign directed against the most unfeeling of the farmers, and occasionally against local magistrates or overseers. In this case, however, the farm-hands were seeking an increase of wages, not as the handloom weavers had done, by legislative means, but by confronting their employers directly. To this extent, although the labourers clearly retained an attachment to an agrarian old regime, they had already taken a considerable step towards the formulation of economistic, trade-union objectives.

These movements of impoverished outworkers, degraded artisans and downtrodden labourers could achieve little for their participants. The conditions of these groups did not improve in their aftermath. Yet the outbreaks, though informed by a powerful sense of social wrong, were transient and unrepeated. For this, there were perhaps three main reasons. Firstly, the economically weak, just because they were driven to an extreme protest by their circumstances, were largely isolated from other groups of workers. Though receiving sympathy and support within their own communities, they gained no support from outside. Secondly, they were confronted by a determined and repressive government, keen to deter further breaches of public order. The Luddites were liable to capital penalties, and overawed by a large military presence. The leading Swing rioters received harsh terms of transportation at the hands of specially appointed judicial commissions, and within a few years were further cowed by the new disciplinary apparatus of the reformed Poor Law. Finally, at least for the industrial victims of capitalism, in these conditions, a political radicalism directed to parliamentary reform came to seem a preferable option. Bringing them into association with a larger campaign, and challenging the oppressive state more prudently but no less determinedly, the advantages of this form of popular politics were obvious.

Trade unionism was not a device peculiar to the economically strong workers, but it was all but impossible for others to sustain such organisations for any length of time. The outworkers in textiles and clothing who had formed substantial combinations in the eighteenth century were increasingly incapable of doing so in subsequent years. For the most part the trade societies of the early nineteenth century were still the preserve of urban artisans. Some of these, it is true, like tailors, shoemakers and carpenters, were in trades subject to labour dilution, and where habits of combination owed something to tradition as well as to economic power. Others, including the building trades, the shipwrights, the compositors and the metal trades, enjoyed a greater measure of bargaining power even in face of larger employers, advancing technology and wider markets. What is most notable, however, is the development of unionism among some of the élite occupations of the factory system: the foundry workers, the steam engine makers, the cotton mule spinners, the potters all had developed trade societies, more or less enduring, before the 1830s.

It is, of course, almost impossible to make any numerical assessment of the strength of industrial combination before mid-century. Clearly, however, organisation extended rapidly between the repeal of the Combination Acts in 1824 (followed by a wave of strikes in 1825), and the collapse of the Grand National Consolidated Trades Union in 1834. In the main stronghold of that association, London, constituents from twenty-nine trades were affiliated. Unionism was growing again in London and the provinces from the mid-1840s; probably almost two hundred local organisations were to be found in the capital, some of them linked in federal structures, and up to forty unions had some claim to national status. Even the largest of these 'unions' remained diminutive, however. The masons, among the largest, commanded a subscribing membership of under 2,000 in 1834, rising to 5,500 by 1851 — though it seems certain that many more workmen were enlisted without maintaining contributions. Even on this restricted platform, the leading societies had begun to appoint full-time officers, to hold delegate conferences and develop formal constitutions and rules.

The persistent themes of union policy were still those of an earlier era: to protect the status of those within the trade, and thereby their economic independence. That independence was, no doubt, more narrowly conceived. It came gradually to have more to do with standard wages, and less with the freedom of artisans to change masters. It still signified, however, some degree of control over the work process by the workers themselves. And it still entailed, by whatever mechanism, the restriction of entry into an occupation for unqualified outsiders. Finally, to an indefinite extent, it necessitated efforts to limit production. In the past such restrictions had been implicit in the journeyman's insistence on opportunities for leisure; now they were conceived more deliberately as a solution to the problem of unemployment within the ranks of recognised tradesmen. 'Previous to the union', stated the leader of the Thames shipwrights in 1825,

> it was nothing uncommon for men to take such a quantity of work that many men were left destitute; but I am sure many a man died a premature death from want of sustenance, because the greater part of this employ was engrossed by a few hands. The union provides against this. . . . that no man is to engross or take to himself a greater quantity of work than what he can accomplish. The result is it throws it open for other people to come in.[10]

The limitation of work stints, the prohibition of overtime and piecework or taskwork, the curtailment of hours, were all demands which, in one occupation or another, had achieved prominence by the 1830s. They supplemented and reinforced, in this regard, the time-honoured strategy of 'tramping' which had, more than anything, brought the old trade clubs together into larger and closer unions.

Trade unionism, though its existence depended on a measure of economic strength, was also a product of economic vulnerability. Especially in the brief interval from 1825 to 1842, it exhibited not only a mood of militancy but a receptivity to radical, anti-capitalist ideas and a sense of class solidarity. 'It is all the workers of England against a few masters at Bradford', claimed one trade journal in the woolcombers' dispute of 1825; and unions were indeed often willing to lend financial, if rarely physical, support to others under attack.[11] This sense of cohesion and social isolation fed upon and

10. Quoted in J. Rule, *The Experience of Labour in the Eighteenth Century* (London, 1981), p.196.

11. Quoted in I. Prothero, *Artisans and Politics in Early Nineteenth-century London* (Folkstone, 1979), p.160.

itself nourished the hostility of employers, who in these years
appeared strongly disposed to proscribe union membership and
condemn union practices. Yet industrial association was never
fashioned simply as an instrument of class war. While some organisations were attracted to the syndicalist vision of general unionism
others, like shipwrights, printers and tool-makers, held aloof (as
they were to do, largely, from Chartism). While combinations
engaged more frequently in strikes, they retained their function of
friendly societies, preaching and disseminating provident habits.
While they confronted capitalist masters, they may well have appreciated the benefits of that mutual toleration which had often
prevailed even a decade earlier. By 1845, the National Association
of United Trades was calling for the legal arbitration of disputes and
enforcement of wage agreements, loosely connecting in this formula
a version of eighteenth-century paternalism with a perception of
mid-Victorian collective bargaining.

The relatively exclusive character of trade unionism was briefly
cast off in the years between 1829 and 1834. Though 'general'
unionism was by no means an assertion of proletarian unity, it did
seek to accommodate new groups of wage earners, with no acknowledged skill or status. The textile federations established in the
North and Midlands sometimes associated outworkers with factory
workers, and 'aristocratic' spinners with plebeian operatives in the
weaving and finishing branches. The builders' union, formed in
Birmingham in 1833, sought to recruit unskilled labourers. The
Grand National Consolidated Trades Union established branches
for women workers and shop assistants, while one of the causes it
embraced was that of the agricultural labourers at Tolpuddle, trans-
ported for the alleged oath-taking by which they engaged themselves to their own abortive union. What further distinguished this
movement, however, was its link with co-operation, and with
Robert Owen, its most famous progenitor. Among the objects of
the GNCTU was the creation of funds for investment in co-
operative communities. And many other trade societies in these
years either associated themselves with Owenite schemes for co-
operative production and exchange, or set up their own experimen-
tal schemes to undertake collective contracts and to oust capitalist
middlemen.

The co-operative principle had, potentially at least, a wider appeal
than artisanal trade unionism. It promised economic salvation to all
capitalism's casualties and plaintiffs. It offered something to the

landless labourer, the under-employed craftsman, the factory hand. It combined a millenarian vision for the religious, a plausible scientific paradigm for the autodidact, a pragmatic means of subsistence for the needy and an opportunity for the penurious entrepreneur. The GNCTU was, accordingly, not merely a trade combination, embracing also benefit clubs and retail co-operative societies. Its missionaries were probably willing, under Owen's prompting, to recruit allcomers, working-class or not, who subscribed to a co-operative ideal.

Co-operation could enlist a mass following, however, only by diversifying its objectives to a point of incoherence. Co-operative production attracted established trade unions as a way of affording temporary relief to members unemployed or on strike; but to Owenites' *pur sang* it formed the basis of an alternative society. The GNCTU aimed, ultimately, to conduct a general strike for the eight-hour day, and thereafter to assume control of industry through its own lodges. But it was also committed to assist constituents in dispute, and dissipated its funds in support of the struggles of silk weavers, builders and others to withstand the attempts of employers to eradicate combination. Owen's lack of sympathy with these sectional, class-oriented confrontations led to divisions within the leadership of the movement, and its rapid collapse. Thereafter, co-operators largely dissociated themselves from other forms of radical activity, and concentrated their efforts upon propaganda, education and 'rational recreation'. The practice of co-operative retailing, which revived in the 1850s, preserved a communitarian ideal; but the chief legacy of Owenism was to be an intellectual one.

The movement for democratic electoral reform gathered broader support than co-operativism, and, down to 1850, enjoyed a longer active life. A radical political ideology based on the restraint of executive power, the elimination of political corruption, and the extension of the franchise had already taken shape by the 1770s. All the six points of the People's Charter of 1837 (manhood suffrage, secret ballot, removal of qualifications for MPs, their official remuneration, the creation of equal constituencies, annual parliaments) had been articulated before the end of the eighteenth century. Down to the 1790s, this had been the credo of a class of British *sans-culottes* of small trades, marginal professional men, shopkeepers and independent artisans. At least from the end of the Napoleonic war, however, it became, more and more, the ideology of a multifarious mass of wage earners. Even in the Chartist years, members of the 'middling class' or 'urban peasantry' remained a significant element in the movement. But in almost all regions they were by now greatly outnumbered by men of lower status: outworkers, craftsmen of both higher and lower grade, miners and factory workers.

How far the influx of workers into the reform campaign altered the nature of its political beliefs is a contentious issue. What can be asserted safely, however, is that between 1815 and 1839 (the first climax of Chartism's career), a growing body of industrial workmen came to see some kind of salvation in parliamentary reform. They did so, it seems plausible to suggest, partly because they discerned a bias in legislation against their own interests, regardless of whether they perceived those interests as common to a class. In part, too, they were drawn to political radicalism by the failure of other forms of collective resistance and protest. Finally, though least significantly, they were educated in such doctrines by a bourgeoisie, commercial and intellectual, which itself entertained some hostility towards aristocratic and agrarian rulers.

Popular radicalism, once established, passed through three main phases. In 1815–20 it grew out of the economic distress which followed the French wars. It depended heavily upon an inspirational national leadership, especially that of Henry 'Orator' Hunt, MP, able to attract and arouse mass audiences. A local organisation existed, in the form of radical and Hampden clubs, but of a fairly rudimentary and *ad hoc* character. A greater maturity was already visible by the Reform Bill crisis of 1830–32. Although, in some areas, the mobilisation of a working-class movement still required some external direction, from bourgeois and professional men of reformist temper, in other instances a distinctive and autonomous ultra-radicalism drew primarily upon the support of wage earners and artisans. The National Union of the Working Classes in London, which endorsed a variety of social and political causes on behalf of this constituency, was paralleled by the political unions and associations of the industrial North, in Manchester, Leeds, Oldham, Halifax and elsewhere, which had overtly rejected middle-class tutelage. The movement remained fragmented, however, and its objectives indeterminate. The existence of a reform measure before Parliament, although it wholly excluded the working class from the electorate, diverted a good deal of attention from causes more naturally its own. Certainly the independent working-class movement had no influence upon the course of political events; its role was, in this sense, less significant than that of either the socially mixed Political Union of Birmingham, or the unorganised popular riots in Bristol and Nottingham.

By the Chartist period, the political issues had clarified. The limitations of the electoral settlement of 1832 had been emphasised by the behaviour of the government it had issued in: the introduction of a deterrent Poor Law, the refusal of legislation on working hours, the prosecution of trade unionists and working-class newspapers. What emerged after 1837 was thus a campaign with more formidable support, and within its limits addressed to well-defined objectives. Though weak in rural and non-industrial areas, and in certain particularist enclaves like the tin-mining districts of Cornwall, Chartism also achieved an impressive nationwide coverage. And though fluctuating with the advent and departure of economic crises, in 1839, 1842 and 1848, it maintained a high level of continuous activity for more than a decade.

The attempts of the Chartists to unite so large and disparate a following were, however, necessarily fraught with difficulties. Chartism's principal problem was simply lack of political power. Though it could muster support for its demands in the form of mass meetings and petitions, when these proved insufficient to overawe the government, its leadership was unable to deploy effective 'auxiliary measures'. It is debatable whether this failure resulted from a lack of social and economic unity in the working class, and those strata closest to it. What can be more confidently stated is that Chartism did not have the capacity to impose a political unity upon its following. It had not, in the first place, an organisation adequate for this purpose. Though it created, more than any previous popular movement, an extensive local structure as well as a national leadership, the two were only tenuously linked. The National Charter Association boasted nearly three hundred branches in 1841; but these engaged in whatever activities they pleased, were very reluctant to furnish finance for central bodies, and probably communicated with them infrequently and ineffectively. These local units, in turn, had a fragile relationship with the mass of workers who turned out to Chartist orations or took part in the 'general strike' of 1842. The account of the French diarist, Flora Tristan, afforded a sympathetic but revealing description of a Chartist national convention in 1842, meeting at a Fleet Street public house, and numbering only some thirty delegates.[12] An even smaller convention decided to

12. Jean Hawkes (ed.), *The London Journal of Flora Tristan* (London, 1982),

launch the Chartist land company in 1845 (on whose funds activity at national level relied heavily but illegally thereafter). Constrained by the law, and struggling to retain a stable core of activists, Chartism was ill-fitted to concert any national strategy.

The nature of that strategy, moreover, was a source of internal dispute. A determined and reactionary state could, ultimately, be coerced only by a popular uprising, or perhaps by some form of political strike. Both measures were discussed. Both fostered disagreement, however, not only within the leadership but more deeply within the working class itself. While some insurrectionaries could be found among the adherents of the movement, others were clearly averse even to a rhetoric of violence. Faucher observed that the cotton spinners at the Edgeworth mill in Burton were both Chartists and Methodists, and in some cases disciples of teetotalism. The strike wave of 1842, which represented the most serious attempt to augment moral pressure, produced a like discordance. For some participants the turnout remained, as it had begun, a form of resistance to wage cuts; for others it was an opportunity to force acceptance of the six points. And while in a few areas, where employers had been most overbearing in the past, the stoppages gave rise to violence, in the majority they remained peaceful. The confusion in which this episode ended, and the official retribution which accompanied it, led to a substantial exodus of moderate supporters. Though Chartism achieved a further climax in 1848, it was never again to be so comprehensive of the whole working class as in its early years.

This aura of respectability, orderliness and restraint had thus already come to distinguish important sections of the British working class before mid-century. It was by no means unambiguous, or simple to delineate. It was certainly not confined to an 'aristocracy' of the labour force, rarely coinciding with occupational boundaries. The 1844 strike of Durham pitmen had none of the violence of the 'Scotch cattle' in Wales in 1839; cotton operatives in Preston attacked property and persons in 1842, whereas those of South Lancashire were commended for restraint. The provenance of these respectable values is likewise difficult to trace. They may owe something to the religious evangelicalism, embodied especially in popular Methodism, which enlisted many workers, particularly in rural areas, during the first thirty years or so of the century. They

---

pp.47–51.

were encouraged, in some cases, by the experience of organisation, for Friendly Societies, trade unions and co-operatives could not be sustained without some absorption of habits of discipline and regularity. They were, no doubt, values inculcated by the industrial system itself, in so far as sobriety and virtue earned a premium of steady employment. And they reflected in some a conviction that the admission of the working class into the political nation was aided by its proven rationality and moral worth. Whatever the explanation, the establishment of such behaviour patterns was not to breed deference, but a desire for, even an expectation of, social esteem. After attending a camp meeting of Primitive Methodists near Newcastle, the French traveller Deichtal wrote of the 'lower class' participants,

> since they are accustomed to join together for every kind of purpose they like the same independence in their worship, and since they feel just as capable as their priests of discussing Heaven and Hell and interpreting the prophecies, they give themselves the satisfaction of discoursing rather than hearing someone else do it.[13]

Chartism receded as it was found unable to claim that wider social esteem.

The final flourish of Chartism in 1848 highlighted the peculiarity which British politics had already assumed in a European context. Radicalism here offered up no martyrs, and few victims. The state, whatever tremors it suffered, was not in the end forced into whole-sale repression — or, for that matter, indoctrination. 'Cheap bread, plenty of potatoes, low-priced American bacon, a little more Dutch cheese and butter', wrote the Tory Home Secretary in 1842, 'will have a more pacifying effect than all the mental culture which any government can supply'.[14] This economism had, indeed, been expressed by cooler politicians for a quarter of a century. And it informed, more or less directly, a series of industrial and financial reform measures from the 1820s on: the repeal of the Combination Acts, the Truck Act, the Commutation of Tithes, the Allotments Act, the Mines Act. These culminated in the repeal of corn protec-

13. B. Ratcliffe and W.H.Chaloner (eds.), *A French Sociologist Looks at Britain* (Manchester, 1977), p.72 (the journal entry for 7 September 1828).

14. Quoted by D. Gadion, 'Class formation and class action in North-west industrial towns, 1830–50', in R.J. Morris (ed.), *Class, Power and Social Structure in British Nineteenth-century Towns* (Leicester, 1986), pp.57, 58.

tion in 1846, following in the wake of other cuts in indirect taxation; and in the application of a ten-hours law to women and children in textile factories in 1847 — 'the first time', according to Marx, 'that in broad daylight the political economy of the middle class succumbed to the political economy of the working class'. The view of the statute's author, Shaftesbury, in 1851, was no more partisan, and perhaps no less justified: 'Chartism is dead in these parts', he announced in Manchester, 'the Ten Hours Act and cheap provisions have slain it outright.'

Trade unionism in Britain, 1850–1914

Between 1850 and 1914 the British labour movement was centred upon the trade unions. Their membership in the late 1850s stood at about 600,000. It was highly dispersed in a myriad small societies; even the greatest of the amalgamations encompassed no more than ten to twenty thousand men (the largest in 1860, the Amalgamated Society of Engineers, had 21,000). It remained restricted to the skilled: that is, to workers who, by apprenticeship or otherwise, underwent some form of training or preparation before entering an adult occupation. Thereafter, the union movement underwent three periods of rapid expansion: in the early 1870s; between 1888 and 1892; and in the pre-war years of 1910–14. There were no officially compiled membership figures before 1892, and earlier estimates are accordingly unreliable. But successive membership peaks were achieved, of about 1.3 to 1.6 million briefly in 1876, about 1.6 million again, more durably, in the 1890s, and (on the Board of Trade's authority) 4 million by 1914. The number of organisations remained large: over 1,200 throughout the period 1892–1914. The degree of concentration increased, however, so that at the outbreak of war three-quarters of the membership was enrolled in the hundred principal societies. From the 1870s, too, recruitment had begun to extend outside the ranks of the skilled — at first only insecurely, but by the twentieth century with a stronger impetus. By 1914 combination had gained relative stability among a range of non-apprenticed machine operatives, some workers in transport and local government, and some women factory workers.[15]

15. H.A. Clegg, A. Fox and A.F. Thompson, *A History of British Trade Unions since 1889*, vol. i (Oxford, 1964), p.2.

In mid-century, the union movement rarely embraced more than 10% of an occupation's work-force, even in the crafts. By the end, it still covered only a minority of wage earners, though now extending to some 40% of adult males. Density had always been comparatively high among cotton spinners, printers and some groups of metal workers (notably the boilermakers in shipbuilding and engineering). It increased rapidly from the late 1880s especially among miners and railwaymen. The pattern reflects, by and large, an effective adaptation of the movement to industrial growth and modernisation; though this success was not to be maintained in the inter-war years. In less dynamic sectors like clothing, furniture and hardware, in which factory technology was introduced only slowly, combination tended to stagnate or decline.

To regard the unions as the dominant medium of collective working-class activity is, in statistical terms, misleading. Friendly and Benefit Societies boasted a larger membership of over 4.4 millions (in England and Wales) in 1872, and probably 7 millions by 1914. Their organisation was, however, often centralised and undemocratic (though it had been much less so prior to the 1870s). Furthermore, their recruitment was by no means confined to wage earners, and the officers of the leading societies usually came from a higher social class. Most important, though they were by no means apolitical, the Friendly Societies made no serious attempt to mobilise their mass support for any purpose other than insurance and convivial entertainment. The co-operative movement, commanding a known membership of some 350,000 in the early 1870s, and 2.4 million by 1905, was more ambitious in its aspirations for its working-class supporters. The Women's Co-operative Guild, for example, provided almost the only body attempting to represent the interests of working-class housewives. But only in their retailing functions did the co-operatives involve the bulk of their membership. And in this sphere they engaged in economic and political conflict only on a narrow front, with the capitalist shopkeepers and wholesalers.

Trade unionism, whatever its limitations, was implicated in a larger battle. Yet its growth was by no means simply the outcome of industrial conflict. It can be attributed, at least in some measure, to the external factor of economic change: to the enlargement of the industrial population itself, and to the modernisation of its economic environment. The occupied population in Britain doubled in size, from 9.4 million to 18.4 million, between 1851 and 1911. The proportion engaged in agriculture fell, during these years, from about 22 to 8.2%. On the other hand the numbers engaged in the metal industries and in mining expanded more than fivefold between 1841 and 1911, accounting for some 3.2 million workers by the latter census. Yet in these and other advancing industries the rate of technological and organisational progress was, in general, steady rather than dramatic. Only in a few instances did it tranform the labour process so completely as to eliminate established skills, or supersede manual effort. And within this work-force the predominant position of adult men no longer seemed threatened: the presence of children was somewhat lessened by the establishment of a national elementary education system after 1870; and the activity of women remained heavily concentrated within a narrow and separate sphere, of textiles, clothing and domestic service.

The unions had, of course, to exert themselves in order to recruit this potential mass membership. Two phases of organisational development were important in this respect. In the 1840s and 1850s the existing craft societies acquired a more integrated structure, a wider geographical sphere, and a sounder financial base. They set out, deliberately, to recruit on a national, or at least a regional, scale; and full-time officers were appointed, for the first time, partly to undertake the task of publicising and proselytising to this end. From the late 1880s especially, a new generation of unions adopted these procedures in order to embrace a much wider constituency. The 'general' unions were constructed so as to be able to accommodate a variety of occupational groups, both unskilled and semi-skilled, and to allow for their volatility and relatively low involvement in union government by a much expanded bureaucracy of paid organisers and agents. It was also these 'open' unions, and the large industrial organisations of miners and railwaymen, which set out to secure from employers an explicit endorsement of the closed shop, establishing the union card as a ticket of employment.

Unionism would have gained far fewer adherents, however, had it not been afforded substantial legal recognition by the state. The restricted legality conceded in 1824 was strengthened by the Friendly Societies Act of 1855, and more decisively by a series of labour statutes dealing with contracts, strikes and the protection of funds, passed between 1868 and 1875. These measures conferred a kind of official approval of trade combination which had pointedly been refused to Chartism in the 1840s. They coincided, moreover, with the governmental persecution of communards, socialists and all alleged sympathisers then in full flood on the continent. To British governments, it appeared that conflicts between labour and capital occurred within an autonomous zone, into which the executive should not intrude except as a neutral intermediary. In the latter role, however, it appeared with a new conviction in the years before 1914. And in doing so it confirmed a belief, which had already been tacitly held by 1868: that the extension of industrial organisation could give promise, not of more strikes and stoppages, but of a stable and settled machinery for preserving industrial peace.

The tolerance with which government and parliament came to regard trade unionism in Britain owes a good deal, no doubt, to the extension of the national franchise in 1867. Although the vote was extended at this juncture to only a minority of the working class (that is, to rather less than three in five of the urban wage earners), the object of reform was specifically to incorporate that class within the polity. Since both the principal political parties acknowledged the need to attract electoral support from this quarter, some competition to promote labour interests was predictable. But in a sense the passage of the reform measure was itself an extension of that larger political strategy, already noted — of seeking, by cautious but concrete offerings, to ensure the allegiance of workers to the existing order. It was the apparent success of that strategy in the years since 1846 which guaranteed its continuance.

The state gave a lead which industrial employers ultimately followed. Shortly before the First World War, one amateur investigator of Euro-American economies noted the exceptional equanimity with which British businessmen viewed combination:

Nothing has struck me more in the course of this investigation than the remarkable difference in attitudes towards trade unions displayed in private by employers in this country and in the others. I have not heard a single word in favour of trade unions by employers in Germany or America . . . Employers there hate and dread the unions. In England I have met with no such feeling at all. I have heard the unions unfavourably criticised and sometimes condemned, but without bitterness; I have far more often heard from employers and managers fair and even friendly expressions of opinion[16]

Such attitudes were by no means prevalent in the mid-nineteenth

16. Quoted in R. McKibbin, 'Why was there no Marxism in Great Britain?', *English Historical Review* (1984) 99.

century. Even in the 1850s and 1860s, however, some employers were echoing the views of the unions' intellectual allies: that organisation tended to promote reliability and good conduct among workmen; that it restrained disputes rather than fomenting them; that it inhibited unfair competition where labour conditions were concerned. In an industrial system which remained relatively atomistic, employers could henceforth rarely co-ordinate, for any length of time, a policy of eradicating union organisation. And in these circumstances the benefits of corporate collective bargaining became steadily more attractive. In one locality and industry after another, over the years 1850–1914, joint institutions were set up to discuss and adjudicate grievances, negotiate wages and conditions of employment, define working practices and spheres of authority. In textiles and building from the 1850s, in engineering between 1870 and 1900, in mining from the 1880s, on the railways by the eve of war, negotiating media were formed, never to be dissolved.

How far did this social acceptance involve a concomitant change of outlook and behaviour on the part of the unions? On the one hand, it is possible to detect some moderation of language, some relinquishment of more visionary purposes like producer co-operation, and a greater pragmatism in industrial tactics. On the other hand their public avowal of the precept 'a fair day's wage for a fair day's work' was far from a simple submission to capitalist exigencies. There was no consensus about what constituted fairness. Clearly unions remained concerned to safeguard employment, to regulate the labour market in their own interests, and therefore, as in the past, to prevent overproduction. Particularly among skilled men, the jealous defence of job rights and trade customs was a constant preoccupation. The Comte de Paris conveyed this social perspective in terms which might have been almost equally applicable to the eighteenth-century craftsman:

The artisan, late apprentice, looks upon the knowledge which he has purchased by so many years of unpaid toil as his actual property; he considers as an intruder and a counterfeit not only any workman who has not gone through the same training as himself, but even anyone who, having been apprenticed to a different branch of the trade, should attempt to join that to which he belongs, or even to encroach, in the merest trifle, on what he considers as his special department.[17]

17. Comte de Paris, *The Trades Unions of England* (English trans. London, 1869), p.59.

In the years of full employment which characterised the mid-Victorian boom, unions and employers could reach a measure of agreement which respected these labour predilections. The former gave up at least some of the traditional elements of craft autonomy, accepted a higher measure of discipline and regularity, and in some industries adapted themselves to the demands of piece-work. Employers, for their part, accepted a shorter working day, and more or less tight controls on the entry of new workmen into skilled or privileged occupations. This *modus vivendi* was never wholly stable, however; and by the 1880s, the resurgence of unemployment and the pressure of commercial competition from abroad weakened it further. Between 1888 and 1914 two major strike waves occurred, the first in 1888–93, the second in 1910–14, which in part at least reflected the efforts of old and new labour organisations to ensure their influence in the productive process. The attempts of employers to increase output and lower labour costs on their own terms were, fairly effectively, resisted. The union movement entered the war in a confident and assertive frame of mind.

The origins of the Labour Party

How far this industrial militancy modified the political outlook of unionists, leaders and members, is unclear. It is certainly plausible to claim that working-class political activity in Britain receded after the climax of Chartism, and revived only with the foundation of the Labour Representation Committee in 1900 (renamed the Labour Party in 1906). Furthermore, the eclipse of Chartism was marked by a withdrawal of union involvement in radical campaigns, at least those not under their predominant control; while the rise of the Labour Party followed the strike wave and the 'employers' offensive' of the previous ten years. During the long interval, only a few insubstantial political organisations had sought to identify themselves with labour and its interests: the secularist societies which upheld an Owenite ideal between the 1850s and the 1880s; some of the working men's clubs which were formed, especially in London, from the 1870s, and the socialist societies originating in the 1880s.

To suggest that trade unionists eschewed politics in these years would, however, be misleading. It ignores their role in the First International: though this was, admittedly, marginal and somewhat superficial, even in the case of the building and clothing trades which dominated the British representation. More importantly, it depreciates the extent and vitality of popular Liberalism. Among a sample of 144 labour leaders in the North West in the third quarter of the century, 130 are known to be identified with Liberalism. While the proportion was probably lower in the case of ordinary co-operative and union members, the strength of the tie is unquestionable. Nor should the growth of this attachment be seen simply as a displacement of radical and class politics; it marks, equally, the adaptation of Liberalism itself to working-class opinions and moods. Those wage earners who combined radicalism with respectability, at any rate, could find here a natural home. Liberalism, in the Gladstonian period, was not so remote from Chartism as to repel its former devotees; Chartist banners were, indeed, still to be seen at its election rallies in the 1890s. While not, of course, a party of the working class for itself, it was capable (at its urban base) of combining a thorough and vigorous notion of democratic government, a hatred of social privilege and an objection to monopolistic wealth, a disposition to prefer civil liberties to strenuous law enforcement, a strong leaning towards land reform, and an approval of at least some collectivist legislation on questions like factory hours, workmen's trains and the control of the drink trade. The weakness of Liberalism, as compared to Chartism, was its failure to embrace that large mass of wage earners who remained more or less beyond the reach of union, co-operative and Friendly Society. But this was to be a weakness, likewise, of socialism and of the early Labour Party.

Although socialist organisations were established in Britain in the 1880s and 1890s, they were neither confined to the working class nor, more importantly, extended to any kind of mass support. The Social Democratic Federation (SDF), which espoused a fairly vulgar Marxism from 1883, formed active enclaves in East London and Lancashire; the Independent Labour Party (ILP), established ten years later, and propagating a much more reformist 'ethical' doctrine, built its strongholds in the industrial North and Scotland. Prior to 1900 the subscription membership of the SDF never exceeded about 3,250, and that of the ILP 10,720; and these were not significantly augmented by the various schismatic and independent societies which appeared alongside them.

It was easy, therefore, for a European observer to discount the socialist threat in its British manifestation. In so far as this creed attracted the working class, de Rousiers suggested in 1896, it testified to the existence of economic difficulties that were sectional and, sometimes, transient:

> Socialism, with its apparently easy solutions, may fascinate bodies of men who are well-disciplined but confronted with insurmountable difficulties, like the plumbers, typographers, and all the other trades in which the members are capable of good organization, but the conditions of which have been changed by the pressure of circumstances too strong for them. It has an equal fascination for groups without cohesion, hastily organized and incapable of self-direction. To the first Socialism seems a means of constraint fitted to supplement their means of defence, while to the second it seems a ready-made system fitted to supply their incapacity for self-organization. In both cases a leaning towards Socialism is an evidence of inferiority.[18]

This judgement carries weight, inasmuch as socialism did create a following among workers made insecure by new technology, like the boot and shoe operatives; and those to whom collective bargaining rights were denied, like railwaymen or Yorkshire woollen workers. But it understates the influence, or at least the potential influence, of the movement in a number of ways. Firstly, the circulation of socialist ideas was far wider than the membership of socialist parties. A popular text like Blatchford's *Merry England*, and papers like the *Clarion* and the *Daily Herald* enjoyed a wide readership. Moreover, the parties themselves, like the new unions, enrolled many more recruits than they retained. Some of the causes which they took up, especially their agitation on behalf of the unemployed, extended their popular following very considerably. Above all, they achieved a disproportionate influence among union officials and activists. To an increasing number within this cadre of industrial leaders, at national and local level, socialism represented a convincing interpretation of their own experience of capitalism, an ideological support for organisational solidarity, and sometimes a creed around which to rally opposition to an older generation of union oligarchs wedded to Liberalism. The industrial base of socialism thus grew naturally with the passage of time, as a younger cohort of union notables inherited place and patronage.

It was not, however, to further socialist policies that the unions sought direct labour representation at the end of the century. The TUC's decision to set up a Labour Representation Committee

18. P. de Rousiers, *The Labour Question in Britain* (London, 1896), p.362.

(LRC) in 1899, for the purpose of nominating and supporting parliamentary candidates from their ranks, had scarcely any doctrinal significance. It stemmed, rather, from the enlarged scope of union organisation, and the political ambitions which growth fostered. These aspirations the Liberal Party was unable and unwilling to fulfil, in a period when its electoral fortunes were low. More immediately, the TUC resolution was prompted by the desire to reinstate the legal rights laid down in the 1870s, curtailed and undermined by a series of adverse judicial decisions in the 1890s. Nonetheless, the emergence of the LRC indicated the advance of socialism, in that the unions now proposed to promote labour candidatures in alliance with socialist societies. While the latter could not exact any commitment to principle or programme in return, they could impose the price of a formal severance from Liberalism. Organically, the Labour Party was to be independent, free to decide what measures it would support, promote or resist.

The Labour Party secured thirty parliamentary seats at the election of 1906, and raised this tally to forty-two by the end of 1910, thanks primarily to the affiliation of the mining unions, bringing some coalfield constituencies as dowry. It is a matter of debate whether this record signified that a pattern of continued growth had been established. Much was owed to an electoral understanding with the Liberal Party, originating in 1903, which withdrew Liberal opponents in certain working-class seats in order to avoid dividing the progressive vote, and on the assumption that Labour's electoral front would remain narrow. In fact the latter did not put up more than seventy-nine candidates at any pre-war election, and at best received fewer than 8% of the popular vote. When the Labour Party sought to enter Liberal strongholds, its poll was not impressive; and the party strife which arose was largely responsible for a fall in its Commons strength to thirty-seven at the outbreak of war. Even in areas preponderantly industrial the unions could not readily mobilise a vote on its behalf. On the other hand, party organisation was steadily consolidated, and the rise in union membership in itself gave the party greater resources. For better or worse, it had unquestionably become the channel through which union élites sought access to political power. At local level, moreover, the party's advance seemed somewhat more consistent: it had won over 400 council seats in urban England and Wales (outside London) by 1914, already achieving parity with the older parties in cities like Leeds and Leicester.

What held Labour in check was not its own shortcomings, or the still restricted franchise, but the political and social culture which it inhabited. The British working class had adjusted to the demands of industrial and urban life gradually, and in a myriad ways. Neither political alignment nor even trade unionism was a central feature of that process of adjustment — although both could, in time, become part of it. In this way of life, whether we consider skilled or unskilled, rough or respectable, workers, the place of the state and its agents was inconspicuous; and so, accordingly, was the battle for power within it. De Rousiers made the point, in an implicit comparison, after visiting the family of a Lothian collier:

> He does . . . pay a very small sum [in taxes], included in his rent, but that is all. No octroi, hardly any duties, and no conscription. Neither the hand of the state nor the hand of the county nor the hand of the parish exert any sensible pressure[19]

In the British context, a labour movement dominated by trade unionism had established a secure place for itself during the second half of the nineteenth century. Such a movement could be approved, not only by the leaders of progressive 'public opinion', but by the liberal state. This is not just the outcome of a union 'pragmatism' which eschewed the revolutionism and utopianism of working-class political parties. It also reflects the longevity of industrial organisation, and the gradual acquisition, by employers and statesmen, of a clearer understanding of its nature. Yet it was also true, at root, that unionism was acceptable because it posed a less direct challenge to the structure of political authority than a proletarian party. And inasmuch as it was militant or combative, the interests for which it fought were primarily sectional. These interests were not merely pragmatic, but even so they could be accommodated. The Austrian parliamentarian Baernreither suggested such a distinction in the 1890s:

> The higher habits and requirements of the working classes, the higher 'standard of life' on which they are insisting, are far from being the simple result of favourable conditions in respect of wages; but, on the contrary, these habits and requirements constitute a limit which the combined will of the working-man is seeking to impose on a reduction of his wages.

19. Ibid. p.184.

But this perspective, he argued, was not peculiar to the unions.

> The [wage] question is no longer regarded as one simply economic, but social and ethical. Not only do science and the legislature fearlessly deduce the logical results of this change, but the very classes, who some twenty or thirty years ago selfishly endeavoured to resist them, now readily accept the consequences of their new position. In this manner the relations between capital and labour have unquestionably drawn closer together in England than in any other country in Europe.[20]

This insular privilege was patently bought at a price. Old-established as the union movement was, it remained, even in 1914, relatively narrow in extent. The great majority of women, of white-collar workers, and even many of the unskilled (including the agricultural labour force) remained beyond its reach. Without attempting to identify a cohesive aristocracy, moreover, the labour historian is bound to emphasise the breadth of the economic fissures within the industrial working class. Baernreither himself acknowledged the scale of poverty prevailing among the urban 'residuum'. As for the benefits which trade unionists enjoyed, and helped to preserve, these were obviously dependent on the continued prosperity and expansiveness of a national and international capitalist economy. When this vitality diminished, as it already showed signs of doing before 1914, the position of a movement which concentrated upon a discrete industrial sphere became far more vulnerable.

BIBLIOGRAPHY

K.D. Brown, *The English Labour Movement, 1700–1951* (London, 1982)

C. Calhoun, *The Question of Class Struggle* (Oxford, 1982)

H.A. Clegg, A. Fox and A.F. Thompson, *History of British Trade Unions since 1889* (2 vols), (Oxford, 1964 and 1985)

H. Collins and C. Abramsky, *Karl Marx and the British Labour Movement* (London, 1965)

C.R. Dobson, *Masters and Journeymen: a Prehistory of Industrial Rela-*

20. *English Associations of Working Men* (London, 1893), pp.79, 22.

tions, 1717–1780 (London, 1980)

J. Epstein and D. Thompson (eds.), *The Chartist Experience* (London, 1982)

A. Fox, *History and Heritage* (London, 1985)

W.H. Fraser, *Trade Unions and Society* (London, 1974)

R. Glenn, *Urban Workers in the Early Industrial Revolution* (Beckenham, 1984)

E.J. Hobsbawm, *Labouring Men* (London, 1964)

——*Worlds of Labour* (London, 1984)

D. Howell, *British Workers and the Independent Labour Party, 1888–1906* (Manchester, 1983)

N. Kirk, *The Growth of Working-class Reformism in Mid-Victorian England* (London, 1985)

R. McKibbin, *The Evolution of the Labour Party, 1910–23* (Oxford, 1974)

W. Mommsen and H.-G. Husunng (eds), *The Development of Trade Unionism in Great Britain and Germany, 1880–1914* (London, 1985)

H. Pelling, *The Origins of the Labour Party* (London, 1954; Oxford, 1965)

S. Pollard, 'Labour in Great Britain', in *Cambridge Economic History of Europe*, vol.vii (Cambridge, 1978)

I. Prothero, *Artisans and Politics in Early Nineteenth-century London* (Folkstone, 1979)

J. Rule, *The Experience of Labour in Eighteenth-century Industry* (1st edn London, 1963; 3rd edn London, 1980)

E.P. Thompson, *The Making of the English Working Class* (London, 1968)

2

SOCIALISM, SYNDICALISM AND FRENCH LABOUR BEFORE 1914

Roger Magraw

The emergence of the French working class

The rallying of French workers to national defence in 1914 has been taken to prove that underneath the class-war rhetoric which coloured the political discourse of the *belle époque* lay the deeper reality of broad national consensus. Had the once 'alienated' working class of 1848 and 1871 been successfully 'integrated' into Republican bourgeois-democracy? Was the 'revolutionary' rhetoric of syndicalists simply a verbal smokescreen thrown up in unavailing efforts to obscure the fact that a 'mature" working class was learning to accept industrial capitalism, to play the rules of trade union bargaining to win economistic gains, a share of the 'cake'? From such a perspective even evidence of increased working-class mobilisation (a rising socialist vote; increased union membership) can be reinterpreted to suggest institutional 'integration' into the electoral system or into 'modern' industrial relations (Stearns, 1971). This essay will discuss the extent to which a shift towards pragmatic reformism is indeed the dominant characteristic of the French working class in these years.

Characteristics of national labour movements are largely determined by some combination of three factors:[1]

(1) The structure and composition of the work-force
(2) The nature of the State

1. See G. Eley, 'Combining Two Histories: The SPD and the German Working Class before 1914', *Radical History Review* (1984) 28–30, pp.13–44.

(3)   The availability to workers of alternative, radical, ideologies. Thus, historians of Russia may 'explain' '1905–17' by reference to the peasant links of a highly concentrated working class combined with the repressive nature of Tsarism and the diffusion of Populist and Marxist ideologies by a radicalised intelligentsia. The contrast between the 'liberal' Victorian State and Wilhelmine authoritarian democracy helps explain the contrast between pragmatic British Labourism and the ambiguous blend of Marxism and reformism within the 'negatively integrated' subculture of the SPD (German Social Democratic Party). Six features help define the specific character of the French labour movement.

Firstly, the working-class grew only slowly, remaining a *minority* class in a society where over 60% of the population were 'rural' in 1914. (As T. Judt[2] emphasises, neat distinctions between 'workers' and 'peasants' are frequently inappropriate. At least until the Great Depression of the 1870s, much industry remained located in the countryside to utilise wood-fuel, water-power and cheap labour: textile weaving in Normandy, the Lyonnais and other regions relied on rural outworkers; coal-mines employed 'peasant miners' who disappeared at harvest-time; the building industry employed migrant Limousin peasant masons. Although some such groups (e.g. Yonne wood-floaters) acquired a reputation for militancy, the capacity for collective self-defence in scattered rural workers was generally low. This persistent rural–industrial symbiosis complicates neat distinctions between 'artisans' and 'factory proletarians'.) There were some four million industrial employees in 1890, five million in 1914. Political power through the ballot-box remained impossible for any purely proletarian party.

Secondly, household and handicraft production using 'artisanal' labour persisted to a much greater extent than in Victorian Britain. As late as 1896, 36% of French workers were employed in those 88% of French establishments which had five workers or less. Only 36% worked in establishments of more than fifty employees.

Thirdly, the 'new' proletariat of the post-1880 Second Industrial Revolution was recruited disproportionately from recent migrants, women and immigrants.

Fourthly, in contrast to the 'archaism' of her socio-economic structures France was precocious in achieving universal (male) suffrage (1848) and a 'democratic' Republic (1871). Political/

2. T. Judt, *Marxism and the French left* (Oxford, 1986).

ideological 'modernisation' *preceded* rapid technological/economic change.

Fifthly, popular insurrection — urban *and* rural — contributed to both achievements, as indeed to the bourgeoisie's defeat of feudalism (1789–1830). However, some of the goals of the popular movement were thwarted. In 1830 the Orleanist *grande bourgeoisie* reaped the rewards of the defeat of the aristocracy. In 1848–51 attempts of artisans and radicalised peasants to found a 'Social and Democratic Republic' were defeated by Bonapartism. Nevertheless, a variety of radical ideologies — Jacobinism, Blanquist insurrectionism, Proudhonist mutualism, the vision of a 'social' Republic which would nurture producer co-operatives — achieved currency among a politicised popular vanguard, challenging the embryonic industrial bourgeoisie's control of State power.

And finally: trade union development, conversely, was belated and slow. Unions remained illegal until 1884 and formal membership remained modest down to 1914. In contrast to the pragmatic reformism of their larger British counterparts many French unions proclaimed a revolutionary syndicalist ideology.

The French economy was marked by uneven development, with widening regional disparities between an expanding North and East and a de-industrialising South and West. Large enterprises remained islands in a sea of small firms. In 1872 the St Etienne region contained 16,000 miners, 5,000 workers in large armaments factories — alongside 45,000 artisanal ribbon weavers and 8,000 gun and hardware workers. Sluggish growth rates in the Great Depression (c. 1875–1896) exposed structural weaknesses. Agricultural price collapse cut rural purchasing power. In the Lyonnais crisis in the traditional industries was compounded by problems in newer sectors (coal, metal). Falling profits and rising unemployment revived protectionism, designed to buy social peace by shielding petty producers, prompted the quest for colonial markets and encouraged cost-cutting strategies — new technologies and new techniques of labour discipline.

However, French 'backwardness' should not be exaggerated. Bursts of railway construction (1850s, 1880s) drew peripheral regions into the national economy. France outperformed Britain in some 'new' sectors (e.g. cars, electricals) in 1896–1914, when overall growth rates were impressive. Above all, emphasis on 'quality' goods reflected not 'Malthusian' archaism but rational decisions to concentrate on markets not dominated by British mass-production.

Limoges porcelain, Grenoble gloves and Paris furniture utilised traditions of skill and design. 'Flexible specialisation' permitted small craft firms to produce a range of non-standardised goods sensitive to market changes.

The silk industry exhibited a capacity for self-renewal — adopting Jacquard looms, new dyestuffs, durable Asiatic silks then, later, electrified looms and artificial fibres. Though some silk factories emerged, most silk production remained within workshops or households, co-ordinated by merchants not by industrialists. Marx's prediction that capitalist development involved propertyless wage-labour recruited from dispossessed craftsmen appeared premature. In 1860, 60% of French industrial goods were made by handicraft-household production, employing 75% of 'industrial' workers. Entrepreneurs benefited from having less capital tied up in plant and machinery during cyclical slumps. However, 'artisan' survival came at the price of increasing subordination to merchant capitalists who controlled raw materials and orders. Master silk-weavers (canuts) needed to buy Jacquard looms to remain competitive, yet many fell into debt to merchants in borrowing money for this purchase. They were 'squeezed' by merchants who moved cheaper and coarser weaving out to rural outworkers or mechanised mills. They worked longer hours for lower rates to meet such competition. By the 1860s Lyons silk-masters retained only 'quality' weaving — and survived only by laying off male journeymen in favour of cheaper female workers (Sheridan, 1981). Division of labour and the growth of a 'ready-made' standardisation for department stores threatened tailors, hatters, shoemakers and the like. 'Capitalist' masters tended to separate themselves off from the bulk of their fellow craftsmen, employing more workers and new work organisation. Artisans survived only by jettisoning traditions, cutting apprenticeships. Journeymen retained their own tools. But power over productive forces had altered, and labour had been subordinated in various ways, even though the 'bourgeoisie' tended to be, as yet, financial and mercantile rather than industrial.

Many craftsmen viewed such changes in class relations as a threat to their skills, culture and community. (Of course, not all artisans were 'threatened'. There was no *unilinear* trend towards industrial concentration and proletarianisation; indeed it is possible that in the 1850–60s there was something of an Indian summer for many craft-trades. Equally, industrialisation itself generated new categories of skilled occupations, such as railway mechanics and boilermaking.) Although masters did clash with journeymen, the principal battle-lines were drawn up with a master/journeyman coalition on one side and merchant capitalists on the other. In 1831 and 1834 Lyons *canuts* rose in insurrection as merchants reduced pay *tarifs* and shifted work to lower-paid rural weavers (Bezucha, 1974). Mutual Aid Societies and surviving journeymen's *compagnonnages* provided a cloak for an illegal proto-unionism. However, the militancy of the July Monarchy (1830–48) cannot be explained simply in structural terms related to the economic threat to skilled artisans. Popular participation in the 1830 Revolution raised political expectations which ensuing *grand bourgeois* political dominance rapidly disappointed. Bourgeois élites had wooed workers' support to oust the aristocratic Restoration, only to leave workers exposed to the chill winds of free market economics. Repression smashed immediate popular protest but failed to uproot the new consciousness. The language of protest had changed dramatically since the 1820s when, despite sporadic strikes or Luddism, there existed no real vocabulary for workers' political protest. The 'capitalist' was now portrayed as the enemy. *Work*, both a 'duty' and a 'right', became the source of all authentic value. Appeals were made to 'working-class solidarity' — often by artisans who were moving beyond narrow craft-corporatism to assert their support for the wider labour force. Technological and economic changes, still very gradual, cannot in themselves explain this sudden *prise de conscience*. Labour militancy cannot be reduced to the job-control concerns of artisans; rather, it grew out of workers' experience of bourgeois control of State power. It was a *democratic* demand for wider political and social rights, a demand for dignity and social equality as urban citizens not simply in the workshop (Sewell, 1980).

During the Second Republic militant workers, supported by indebted cash-crop peasants in Central and Southern France, voted for a Democratic-Socialist party which championed an 'associationist' Republic in which the State would provide cheap credit and orders for producer co-operatives. The repression which followed the Bonapartist *coup d'état* (1851) had important long-term consequences for the labour movement by exposing hitherto latent internal divisions. The outlawing of open working-class politics pushed sectors of the artisanal élite into a 'Proudhonist' stance — hitherto espoused only by a small minority — which responded to the authoritarian State by arguing that 'politics' were irrelevant and by giving priority to economic activities in Mutual Aid Societies and co-operatives. However, whereas advocates of producer co-operatives before 1851 had been in the vanguard of labour politics, arguing that co-operation could rescue the entire working class from the capitalist wage system, those of the 1850–60s became more defensive, exclusivist, and suspicious of 'dilution' by unskilled and female workers. Conversely, when labour militancy revived in 1867–70, to play a role in destabilising the regime, socialist leaders who advocated *political* action aimed at capturing State power did attract support from more 'proletarian' sectors of the labour force which had been relatively quiescent in 1848–51. In 1870–1, for the first time, the (ageing) community of Croix-Rousse skilled silk-weavers were not in the vanguard of Lyons militancy (Sheridan, 1981).

One criticism of E.P. Thompson's classic study is that while it evokes brilliantly a lost world of popular protest its true theme is not 'the making of the English working class' but the artisanate's last stand. The lull in class conflict in mid-Victorian Britain may suggest that class identity among the new proletariat of mill, mine and iron-works remained to be created (Thompson, 1968). French labour history faces a comparable problem. The post-1830 decades witnessed sustained protest spearheaded by 'artisanal' workers against a bourgeoisie which maintained a precarious hegemony through denial of trade union rights, screwing-down of wage levels to maintain international competitiveness and by resort to authoritarian Bonapartism to resist workers' political demands. Yet if the language of 'socialism' and 'working-class solidarity' emerged, one question remains. Did the experiences, struggles and co-operative ideologies of threatened craftsmen offer a model for the new proletariat of the Second Industrial Revolution? Or did the 'working class' need to be 're-made'? Was there a long forward march of labour — or were there brutal discontinuities? (One could argue that there is nothing here unique to the French experience, that every 'working class' is always in 'process of formation'.) Surviving Democratic-Socialists from 1848 were manifestly ill at ease in the proletarianised world of Third Republic labour politics. The Commune's defeat decimated the artisan vanguard. The shift of population towards new industries in new regions and the rapid expansion of a new working class of miners, railmen and metal workers, heralded a shift in the balance away from the world of the artisan. In a new national economy workers needed wider solidarities, new forms of organisation, fresh attitudes to the role of the State.

Industrial unrest and a tactical alliance between some workers' leaders and Gambetta's bourgeois Republicans combined to desta-bilise the Bonapartist regime. However as the Commune, which briefly united artisan 'Proudhonists' and 'political' militants, made brutally clear, most Republicans did not share workers' aspirations for a 'social Republic'. The bloody repression of the Commune confirmed and strengthened an underlying consensus among all streams of the labour movement — a consensus forged by political experiences since 1830 — that State power was always likely to be controlled by capitalists and exerted against workers. If 1871 weakened hopes of an insurrectionary path to power for workers, it equally made future worker accommodation with the Third Re-public more difficult — despite the long pro-Republican tradition in French popular consciousness. Possibly the French labour move-ment's 'peculiar' character grew out of its historic experience of State repression between 1830 and 1871. By the time the 'democra-tic' Third Republic at last provided an opportunity for reformism this had, as Judt[3] notes, only a tenuous hold on the imagination of militant workers who saw the State as the tool of capitalists, parliamentary government as a sham facade and seizure of the State and 'direct democracy' as prerequisites for an egalitarian society.

With workers apparently cowed after the Commune's repression the young Republic rested on an alliance between 'progressive' bourgeois (lawyers, academics, some sectors of industry) with petty bourgeois and peasant electors. Republicans viewed Bonapartism's erratic foreign policy, free trade economics, clerical education and repressive labour laws as threats to long-term sociopolitical stabil-ity. They now posed as the true conservatives, offering wider educational opportunities, local railways for peasant farmers and protectionist tariffs for threatened businessmen. While workers' interests were not given major priority, it was hoped that workers would welcome anti-clerical and education reforms and liberalised assembly laws (Elwitt, 1975).

There remained a real threat to the Republic from the political right. Legitimist aristocrats retained influence over the peasantry (at least in the West and the Massif Central), and power within the army. The clergy and the Catholic provincial bourgeoisie loathed Ferry's education laws. Major industrialists such as de Solages

3. Ibid.

(coal), d'Azy (iron) or Motte (textiles) retained royalist sympathies. And when royalism waned anti-Republicans learned to manipulate the economic grievances of peasants, small-businessmen, even workers, through populist-nationalist, xenophobic or anti-Semitic rhetoric.

The Third Republic and the workers

The Republican myth retained a potent appeal for many workers. Gambettists emphasised that workers were now free, equal citizens of a democratic Republic representing 'progress' and 'the people' against parasitic, clerical/royalist feudalism. Universal suffrage offered workers the essential prerequisite for peaceful advance. As the young Republic faced the threat of monarchical restoration in 1876–7 most workers hoped for its survival. The sudden upsurge in strike militancy in 1879–80 emerged from the workers' belief that they would receive sympathetic treatment from Republican prefects in struggles against large, often royalist, employers. Studies of the culture of Nord industrial workers chart the emergence in these years of political *patois* songs voicing optimistic faith in the Republic.[4] Two decades later the entry of the reformist-socialist Millerand into Waldeck-Rousseau's cabinet during the Dreyfus crisis engendered a comparable strike wave, with Dion-Bouton car workers justifying their strike by arguing that their employer was a prominent right-wing anti-Dreyfusard (Berlanstein, 1984). In company-towns the first, halting protests against authoritarian management taken by miners were encouraged by Republic municipalities (Reid 1985c).

Industrial and social reforms were introduced to consolidate this working-class Republicanism. Trade union legalisation (1884) was an attempt to 'normalise' industrial relations and ease class tensions by encouraging 'moderate' British-style unionism. The first Bourses du Travail (BT) (headquarters for co-ordinating local union activities) were established with financial subsidies from Republican municipalities, with the implicit corollary that funding would cease if 'extremists' took control. Two distinct but related ideologies — 'Solidarism' and 'Interventionism' — emerged, arguing for social

4. See L. Marty, *Chanter pour survivre: Culture ouvrière, travail et techniques dans la textile Roubaux 1850–1914* (Paris, 1982).

insurance, factory legislation and state-sponsored arbitration machinery to wean workers from atavistic revolutionary yearnings.
'Solidarists' saw poverty as a denial of Republican ideals of the free,
independent citizen. *Laissez-faire* dogmas required adjustment to
realities of industrial society which was an organic whole, not a
collection of atomised individuals. 'Social diseases' required positive
intervention by reformist 'social physicians' — 'experts' who could
offer 'scientific' remedies. Once paid the 'social debt' owed to them
workers could negotiate on equal terms with employers. Justice *and*
enlightened self-interest should persuade the bourgeoisie to espouse
'Solidarism', whose target was 'abuses of capitalism . . . not capitalism itself'. There was 'only one genuinely conservative politics. . . . , [that] of justice and solidarity, since it alone creates social
peace' (Stone, 1985).

Such rhetorical clichés dominated Radical Party congresses,
alongside those of 'Interventionists' who advocated a slightly greater
degree of state initiative. The latter, mainly university professors
(Paul Pic, C.Rist), argued that traditional paternalism and workers'
self-help — eulogised by business *notables* of the *Musée Social*
group — was inadequate (Elwitt, 1986). With the evil of class
conflict manifest, social peace required legislation. Businessmen
need not tremble, for legislative limitation of factory hours could
make industry *more* competitive by encouraging labour-saving
machinery. State-backed industrial arbitration would eradicate the
'French disease', wildcat strikes. As Commerce Minister after 1899
Millerand attempted this strategy, arguing that 'the best means to
attach, to return if there is . . . need to do so, [workers] to the
Republic is to show . . . by *deeds* that the Republic government is
above all the government of the small and weak'.[5] Already hours
limitation for female and child workers (1892) and compensation
rights for victims of industrial accidents (1898) had been introduced.
Millerand introduced a Ten-Hour Act which applied to some adult
male workers and sought to encourage a larger, 'moderate' trade
union movement by establishing a tripartite forum where representatives of unions, management and the State could settle industrial
problems via discussion. Since voluntary conciliation/arbitration
procedures established in 1892 had been invoked in only 20% of
strikes, Millerand attempted, abortively, to introduce compulsory
arbitration linked to secret strike ballots. Radical governments also

5. Quoted in J. Stone, *The Search for Social Peace* (Albany, NY, 1985).

introduced weekly rest-days for workers (1906) and involved trade unions in running of State naval dockyards (Reid, 1985b). 'In what other epoch . . . has government demonstrated so much . . . devotion to workers?' asked a Republican deputy, P. Deschanel, with apparent sincerity.

The Republic's appeal was also cultural and ideological. Anticlericalism and educational reform touched responsive chords among workers. Catholicism remained influential over many women and among workers in Flanders or some Midi towns. Elsewhere Catholic clergy were widely hated for their support of authoritarian Bonapartism and their royalist sympathies. They preached the divine origins of social inequalities and that élite charity was the only remedy for poverty. In Lyons male silk-weavers loathed the nun-supervised 'convent-workshop', where ill-paid young female workers undercut local wage rates. In company-towns (Carmaux, Montceau-les-Mines) clergy ran company-schools, and supplied mass-attendance certificates for promotion or employment. Many workers had bitter memories of the paupers' benches of Catholic schools, where they had learned to recite Catechism and accept the social hierarchy. Ferry's education reforms, providing free secular primary education, won genuine worker approval since educational qualifications implied wider career prospects and possible social promotion. *Laicité* (secularism) was an ideology shared by bourgeois Republicans and labour militants. Carmaux miners viewed struggles for the *laic* (secular) school, in alliance with Republican doctors and shopkeepers, as major steps towards social emancipation. Worker militants had joined Macé's bourgeois-led, secularist Ligue de l'Enseignement. In the Nord and the Midi many joined Libre-Pensée (Free Thought) societies. Renewed Republic–Church confrontation during the Dreyfus crisis accelerated workers' 'dechristianisation'. In Limoges the percentage of unbaptised infants rose from 2.5 to 19.2% between 1899 and 1904, civil marriages from 14 to 32.8%. The city's socialist municipality pursued anti-clerical policies — banning church processions, 'de-baptising' streets, demolishing crucifixes — with Combes-like zeal.

Ironically Ferry was a social conservative, maintaining a bourgeois monopoly of secondary and higher education. His primary schools taught patriotism and acceptance of conscription. By 1890 thousands of Nord primary pupils belonged to *bataillons scolaires*, school cadet corps. School textbooks portrayed the Third Republic as the culmination of the democratic promises of 1789; run by benevolent 'experts', devotees of science and progress, it rendered further social change unnecessary.

As architect of the 'New Imperialism' Ferry had a further role in strengthening bourgeois hegemony. Traditionally this is interpreted as related to revival of national prestige after 1870–1, as of minimal economic importance and as the object of apathy rather than enthusiasm. However, Lyons relied increasingly on raw silk imports from Indo-China. Marseilles' shipping and industries depended on colonial trade. 'Social Imperialism' became a major preoccupation of Republicans faced with depression, unemployment and social unrest in the 1880s. Popular newspapers 'sold' Imperialism to their petty bourgeois and working-class readership essentially on economic grounds. A *Petit Journal* editorial (April 1881) proclaimed, in lurid social-darwinist phraseology: 'Aged Europe can no longer feed its inhabitants. It must find other feeding grounds. Mechanisation and cut-throat competition in manufacture have transformed . . . conditions so completely that the struggle for life among the human species will soon be more terrible than among animal species. If this vicious circles continues we will arrive at periodic revolutions'. Growing trade deficits meant 'we *must* have colonies'. Justifying war in Sudan *Petit Parisien* (1891) emphasised: 'Each gunshot opens another outlet for French industry. More than one worker [weaving] cloth in some obscure factory only has work . . . because our victory has pacified an entire country, allowing thousands to become part of our markets'.

Such newspapers with their illustrated weekly supplements fed the appetite of a newly literate readership for adventure and exotica — even if pictures of snake-worship or jungle warfare contrasted strangely with images of a fertile Africa ripe for economic penetration. Both visions of Empire co-existed in the colonial exhibitions which featured prominently in urban culture in the 1890s. Some 2.7 million visited the West Africa exposition (1893). Exhibitions in the Paris Jardin d'Acclimation degenerated into circuses featuring native dances, mock tribal wars, baggage races between African porters and Marseilles dockers. Conversely the Marseilles Colonial Exhibition (1906), organised by shipping magnate Charles-Roux, portrayed Empire 'not only in its picturesque but in its utilitarian side . . . to convince the country that . . . sacrifices have not been in vain'.[6]

6. Quoted in W. Schneider, *An Empire for the Masses* (Westport, Conn., 1982).

Workers were exposed to a barrage of propaganda re-enforcing the mythology of France's 'civilising mission', glamorising colonial warfare, asserting the necessity of colonial markets. This had domestic political implications. In 1880s Marseilles, socialists denounced colonialism for squandering resources better invested at home and for subjugating colonial peoples for businessmen's profits; but by 1906, as crowds flocked to Marseilles' colonial exhibition, local belief that jobs of seamen, dockers and industrial workers depended on colonies muted socialist anti-colonialism (Schneider, 1982).

The emergence of a united labour movement was hindered not only by the appeal of the Republic to workers but also by rising living standards, sectionalism within the working class, and by the survival of paternalism and deference.

1. Living standards: most studies suggest a modest rise in average real wages in the decades after 1870. Though the working day remained very long the norm did shorten — from fourteen to eleven hours in the Lyonnais. Unemployment, high in the 1880s, and remaining above contemporary British levels, fell after 1896. Improved rail transport and the Atlantic shipping revolution eliminated subsistence crises. Workers now ate white bread, more varied vegetables, more dairy produce. Child-care clinics reduced Paris infant mortality by 46% between 1881–5 and 1901–5. Conscript records suggest health improvements as a result of cumulative dietary and medical improvements. In 1869 one-sixth of Parisian conscripts were below 1.6 metres in height; by 1903, one in thirty (Berlanstein, 1984). Clothes became cheaper, more varied. Workers in 1870s group photos appear in *blouses* and caps; Le Creusot strikers photographed in *Vie Illustrée* in 1899 are wearing suits and bowler hats! Department stores permitted some worker-families to buy furniture on credit.

2. The composition of the working class: while the 'artisanate' had by no means disappeared its relative weight within the labour force was in sharp decline. Silk, badly hit by the Great Depression, ceased to be the key to the Lyonnais economy — and the role of artisan *canuts* in Lyons shrank as coarser silk weaving shifted to the mechanised mills of the city's hinterland. In Paris craftsmen still dominated quality furniture and jewellery production, but increasing numbers of workers in such trades were reduced to simple, repetitive, subdivided tasks, working for expanding petty bourgeois markets. The growth sectors of Parisian economy lay in *banlieue* (industrial suburbs) mass production (chemicals, rubber, automobiles) and in tertiary and service sectors (banks, offices, department stores) (Berlanstein, 1984).

Changes accelerated *within* factories. Where once skilled workers in St Etienne engineering plants, in glassworks or Limoges porcelain enjoyed much independence and job control, passing on skills, and know-how to apprentices, technological innovation and new management disciplinary strategies eroded these. The advent of new gas ovens in glass-making rapidly undercut the status of skilled glassblowers, enabling management to introduce quickly trained, cheaper and less independent-minded semi-skilled *ouvriers specialisés* (OS). The rise of the OS worker, often a first-generation proletarian fresh from the depression-hit countryside, characterised these decades. The sad lament of old craft-militants or would-be union organisers was that OS workers lacked traditions of skill, class-consciousness or political awareness, and far from resenting monotonous machine-minding they perceived in regular employment an advance on the harsh uncertainties of farm labour. After skilled puddlers were sacked for striking in 1883 at the huge Compagnie des Aciéries de la Marne plant in St Chamond (Loire) the OS work-force, subject to tight factory-floor supervision, 'bowed their heads' in 'shameful apathy' according to trade union organisers. When price inflation prompted them into a request for a pay-rise, this came as an obsequious petition: 'If we have asked . . . for a wage-rise it is in a spirit of confidence in the success of our demands. There is no question of a strike or any conflict which might stop production'.[7]

Bretons recruited into rubber and cable plants in Bézons (N.W.Paris) came from conservative, Catholic backgrounds, and remained isolated by distance and poor *banlieue* transport from contact with radical Parisian artisans. They rarely joined unions, and voted for their employers' candidates. A similar mentality persisted among chemical and leather workers in the northern *faubourg* of St Denis. Exasperated socialists lamented the 'monstrous indifference of the exploited'; Breton priests were imported to run missions, organise lodgings and direct Breton voters to the right. Employment agencies imported docile rural or Spanish ado-

7. Quoted in M. Hanagan, *The Logic of Solidarity* (Urbana, Ill., 1980).

lescents to break strikes. In 1912, fifteen workers in one glass factory were below the legal minimum age; they lodged in slum dormitories and fed on scraps from cafés (Berlanstein, 1984).

3. *Sexual tensions*: conflicts between threatened craftsmen and OS workers were compounded by sexual divisions. Women, nearly 40% of the labour force by 1900, were frequently introduced — in silk, tailoring, shoemaking, porcelain and printing — to undercut wage levels and dilute skills of male craftsmen, thereby rekindling the Proudhonist male chauvinism of skilled workers who viewed women workers as capitalism's Trojan horse. As late as 1898 national trade union conferences demanded elimination of women from industrial employment, for their exposure to factory exploitation, excessive toil and sexual molestation by foremen were portrayed as capitalism's greatest crimes. Stillborn babies and stunted, malformed children of working mothers were the casualties of crude employer strategies to 'bastardise' the proletarian 'race'. Male unionists used 'equal pay for women' demands as a cynical device to persuade employers that it was no longer profitable to employ women. One effect of the 1892 Law, which aimed to control hours and conditions for women factory workers, was to increase the numbers of 'sweated' female domestic outworkers, particularly seamstresses and artificial flower makers. Many strikes involved attempts to get women sacked. Such disputes culminated in the Couriau affair (1913) when the printers' union, bastion of atavistic 'Proudhonism', expelled a printer who had secured a job for his wife (at union rates). The union still resented events at Nancy, a decade earlier, when women blacklegs, encouraged by bourgeois feminists, had broken a strike.

Female workers faced accusations of undermining strikes by their 'natural docility'. Certainly they were less strike-prone than their male counterparts, and under 10% of unionised workers were female. However, recent studies of Nord textile workers question the neo-Proudhonist stereotype of female passivity and religiosity. Women earned wages 40% below comparable male workers, making independence, payment of trade union dues or spending evenings in cafés — focal points of union 'sociability' — difficult. Female workers started mill-work younger, were less literate and suffered more serious illnesses at an earlier age. Paradoxically the 1892 Eleven-Hour Act 'protecting' female workers obliged them to increase work speed in order to maintain piece-rate wage levels — thereby forcing women to undercut male resistance to management speed-ups. Most women faced the double burden of factory work and domestic obligations. Above all, in mill-towns dominated by paternalist Catholic employers women were subject to social control from clergy who ran factory chapel groups, spied on women's social and sexual activities and wielded the weapon of control over charity and welfare to which most working-class families needed to have frequent recourse. Women needed, therefore, to 'keep in' with clergy, attend Mass, for their family's sake. They faced specific pressures, at work and in their social lives, which made participation in a (male-dominated) labour movement which showed insufficient sensitivity to their problems, difficult (Hilden, 1986; Sowerwine, 1982). Women also lacked the vote. During the 1880s the emerging Marxist *Parti Ouvrier Français* (POF) won some support from women textile workers in the Nord. However, the party's emphasis on women's issues faded as its electoral prospects improved — largely, Hilden suggests,[8] because of fears of alienating male voters. Unsurprisingly, women workers felt betrayed and lost interest in the POF.

4. *Racial tensions*: the presence of one million immigrant workers accentuated divisions within the working class, fuelled xenophobia and weakened unionism. Employment agencies recruited labour from Poland, Portugal and North Africa. Some employers faced labour supply difficulties. Rural exodus was gradual rather than rapid. French workers increasingly practiced birth control, in part to give their fewer offspring a better chance in life, in part because compulsory schooling limited child-employment opportunities. Catholic employers campaigned to outlaw contraception — but foreign labour recruitment offered a quicker short-term remedy. 'Without foreign assistance it would have been necessary to pay workers exorbitant wages [raising] even further the costs to hard-pressed enterprises' (thus Leroy-Beaulieu in 1888). Both older low productivity sectors (e.g. construction) and expanding new sectors (chemicals, iron-mining) relied on low-paid immigrants for unpleasant jobs shunned by the surrounding peasantry. Some French workers were thus permitted 'promotion' into tertiary-sector employment.

Nevertheless, racial tension was endemic. Xenophobia fed Boulangism's populist-nationalist appeal to French workers in the late

8. P. Hilden, *Working Women and Socialist Politics in France 1880–1914* (Oxford, 1986).

1880s. Belgian workers, one-third of the textile work-force, created headaches for the Roubaix labour movement. Flemish-speaking and strongly Catholic, they remained culturally distinct from French workers and lived in ghetto areas. Employers appreciated their docile acceptance of low wages. Although socialists, aided by *laic* schools which narrowed the linguistic and religious gulf between immigrant and native workers, recruited some Belgians, their continued use as blacklegs confirmed the anti-immigrant sentiments of many French workers. A Parliamentary enquiry confessed that employers imported them to 'modify working-conditions, [and] discourage collective resistance' of other workers 'to mechanisation'. Unionised glassworkers' anti-immigrant arguments exhibited a confusing mixture of xenophobia (with Italians portrayed as greasy, knife-wielding) with 'left-wing' denunciation of Catholic-clerical blacklegs undercutting skilled worker resistance to technological change. Lorraine iron magnate Cavillier openly declared his preference for 'Italians, Germans or Belgians rather than workers from central regions of France where strikes are endemic'.

Gradually unions did make efforts to overcome both their own prejudices and cultural barriers to mobilise immigrants. However, immigrants, lacking civil and legal rights, were easily intimidated by deportation threats. Cavallazzi, an Italian socialist organiser, was deported when iron masters complained of his role in the 1905 Lorraine strikes. Dark ironies multiplied. Immigrants, imported by employers, undercut French wage levels. Yet when French unions responded by organising immigrants they were confronted by 'yellow' unions, often secretly funded by employers, which denounced 'red' unions for being unpatriotic, soft on foreigners, and contemptuous of the interests of native workers! (Cross, 1983; Reardon, 1981)

5. *The web of paternalism*: the tightly controlled environment of company-towns in which many workers lived constituted a further obstacle to the embryonic labour movement (Reid 1985a, 1985c). In Le Creusot or Decazeville employers provided schools, crèches, houses, company stores, pension funds, clinics. To strike, even to vote, against employers was to risk loss of home or pension contribution. Critics spoke, plausibly, of 'industrial feudalism'. At Le Creusot Schneider was deputy, lived in a chateau, and had his statue in the town square; his valet brought wedding gifts to loyal employees. Job security, housing and medical provision was often superior to that available to other French workers — though the eulogistic

health report of the company doctor of Japy, noting that happy, healthy, loyal workers happened to have green hair after exposure to copper, inspires little confidence! The belated emergence of the labour movement in Belfort-Montbéliard has been attributed to the paternalism of local employers — Peugeot, Vieillard-Migeon and Japy. The latter made its paternalism explicit: 'Certainly [the workers] are big children who ask only for protection and think of revolt only when they feel that protection is being denied them' (1901). Such attitudes were most common in provincial, single industry, towns. Yet even in northern Paris the Christofle firm provided hospital beds, gold medals, old people's homes. 'Thus there are still workers and bosses who love and esteem one another' crowed *Le Figaro* (1907).[9]

Labour militants thus faced formidable problems. Workers' alienation frequently found individualistic, chaotic outlet — in absenteeism, job turnover, alcoholism or petty crime. The spate of muggings by teenagers which captured public attention in the 1900s was symptomatic of a crisis of generational conflict within the working-class family as adolescents were forced to stay on at school, then emerge into a world where apprenticeship schemes were collapsing. Yet response to this crime wave was manipulated by the mass press whose demands for draconian penal sentences attracted some support from older, settled working-class readers alarmed at the breakdown of law and order (Nye, 1985).

The image of a sectionally fragmented working class increasingly seduced by Republican social-imperialism is not easy to reconcile with periods of bourgeois panic (1893; 1906) at the prospect of cataclysmic social upheaval. Nye[10] has portrayed the *belle époque* élites not as secure and confident but as plagued by visions of national decline and social disintegration. Fears of Germany, French demographic stagnation, rampant alcoholism and venereal disease mingled with images of anarchist bombers and syndicalist strikers. Industrial relations in Paris suggest not gradual 'integration' of the 'alienated' working-class of the Commune but a trajectory in which an uneasy period of management/worker

9. Quoted in L. Berlanstein, *The Working People of Paris 1871–1914* (Baltimore and London, 1984).

10. R. Nye, *Crime, Madness and Politics in Modern France* (Princeton, 1985).

accommodation was shattered by a 'revolt against industrial discipline' after *c*.1890 (Berlanstein, 1984). Unskilled and OS workers, rural migrants, women workers, immigrants and tertiary sector workers all displayed some capacity for mobilisation. Chemical workers in Pantin-Aubervilliers (northern Paris) struck to demand banning of noxious white phospherous. Lorraine ironmasters facing Italian strikers in Briey began to specify that they wanted workers from Piedmont not from a Romagna already 'corrupted' by socialism. Spectacular strikes at Decazeville and Carmaux suggested that company paternalism was coming to appear an intolerable infringement of mine-workers' dignity. Strikes by silk, tobacco and vineyard workers signalled an unprecedented growth of female militancy. Threatened skilled workers sought to unionise the unskilled in their industries or localities, while militancy among shop, food and postal workers hinted that expansion of tertiary and service sector employment was not necessarily a recipe for petty bourgeois values.

Does such militancy suggest that working-class faith in the Republic was wearing a little thin by the 1890s? Whereas Nord *patois* songs of the 1870s expressed confidence in the new regime, those of the 1890s often denounced the inadequacy of social reform.[11] While Millerand's ministerial promotion aroused a fresh wave of working-class optimism, the actual social reform achievements of Radical-led governments proved deeply disappointing. Republican small businessmen resisted the financial costs of reform while large industrialists, jealous of their authority within the factory, proved intransigent opponents of factory legislation and of Millerand's efforts to 'modernise' industrial relations. All industrialists rejected the reformers' thesis that shorter-hours legislation would push French industry into rationalisation, hence to efficiency not to higher costs. Businessmen claimed that French industry was too diverse to be 'imprisoned in the vice of uniform, immutable legislative texts' (R.Pinot). With 600,000 workers covered by company pension schemes, why introduce state pensions? Business lobbying swayed Radical governments, whose grass-roots peasant and petty bourgeois electorate were reluctant to bear the taxes required for social reform. Repeatedly the Senate, voice of rural and small-town France and bastion of '*a priori* assertions of orthodox political economy' (P.Pic), blocked reforms which squeezed through the lower house, such as the 1896 income tax bill — despite a protest

11. Marty, *Chanter pour survivre.*

demonstration of 10,000 Parisian workers. During the 1900s would-be reformers — liberal academics and bureaucrats seeking to stabilise capitalism by purchasing workers' acceptance of the system — faced cruel dilemmas as fellow liberals stressed the need for repression of 'anarchistic' syndicalist strikes, and assertion of government's duty to govern (Stone, 1985).

The appointment of Millerand was a tactical ploy to ensure worker support for the Republic during the Dreyfus crisis. Waldeck-Rousseau confessed privately 'we had to make concessions of principle while . . . endeavouring to avoid their realisation'. A decade later Herriot, Radical mayor of Lyons, denounced his party's 'idle declarations' on social reforms. Housing debates in the 1890s foreshadowed subsequent half-hearted legislation. In Paris, whose population doubled to nearly four million, the expanding *banlieue* labour force lacked adequate sewage, transport and accommodation. Businessman-politician J. Siegfried perceived housing as both danger and opportunity for the Republic. 'Do you wish simultaneously to create contented men who are true conservatives? Do you wish to combat misery *and* socialist errors? Do you want to increase guarantees of order and morality, of political and social moderation? Then let us create working-class housing.'[12] Already housing was an election issue; anarchist newspapers ran articles denouncing evil landlords. A popular song began 'If you want to be happy — hang your landlord!' Yet Siegfried's anaemic 1894 Bill merely offered tax concessions to firms building cheap housing. City land prices and rents rose rapidly. Republicans confessed their dilemma. A housing crisis existed, but given *laissez-faire* principles this was insoluble — hence workers should not be deluded with futile hopes! When old-age pensions — denounced by conservatives as Bismarckean, therefore un-French — were finally introduced (1910) the age qualification, 65, made them 'pensions for the dead'. The 1898 Industrial Accident Compensation Act failed to provide for state or employer insurance schemes and referred disputes to ordinary courts where judges usually set compensation rates at minimum levels. French welfare systems, dominated by a patchwork of private, Catholic hospices and under-funded municipal Bureaux de Bienfaisance, lagged behind those of her neighbours — provisions for the indigent and sick reached only 20% of contemporary British levels (Shapiro, 1985; Weiss, 1983).

12. Quoted in A. Shapiro, *Housing the Poor of Paris* (Madison, Wis., 1985).

In 1900 Dr Emile Rey warned fellow Republicans, 'we must not fool ourselves: the poor classes are becoming impatient with the Republic which, after 29 years, has not brought . . . appreciable relief for their sad situation. It would be *dangerous* . . . to continue to deny them legitimate satisfaction.'[13] Heightened yet unfulfilled expectations generated anger. Provision of slum clinics halved *infant* mortality in the Paris *banlieue*; with workers' fatalism thus broken, anger was that much greater when workers' *children* continued to die in enormous numbers because Republican municipalities made inadequate provision for sewage and water. Many workers drank recycled sewage from bourgeois Paris upstream. Socialists won municipal elections in the 1890s with the slogan that a Republican vote was a vote for polluted water. 'The class struggle in Paris had hydrological dimensions.'[14]

Glaring social inequalities persisted. In Lille income distribution remained unchanged from 1850 to 1914, with 90% of wealth controlled by under 10% of the population, and two-thirds of inhabitants dying almost destitute. In Paris one 1890s survey of 800 families found that on average 80% of expenditure went on food and rent. In 1899 in 13th Arrondissement 41% of families earned below the official medical poverty line figure of one franc per day per capita. Average unemployment levels may have been as high as 8% in 1895–1908, while many trades suffered heavy seasonal lay-offs. Doubtless strike propensity tended to decline in years of high unemployment (1883–7, 1900, 1902, 1908), when fear of sackings 'makes us swallow our bitterness and put up with humiliation', as Parisian shoeworker R. Michaud confessed in his autobiography.[15] Yet high unemployment also fuelled union short-hours crusades. The years 1909–14 witnessed price inflation, falling real wages and food riots and demonstrations, in 1911, of a type unknown for several decades.

Industrial conflict grew rather than declined. Militants feared that Millerand's policies were Machiavellian attempts to appeal to the silent majority of 'moderate' workers, to 'kill the legitimate spirit of rebellion'. The effectiveness of his strategy remained untested since employers sabotaged it in both 1900 and 1906. Marseilles dock-owner Savon voiced support for Millerand. 'We must recognise that the age of employer's arbitrary rule is over — unfortunately. A tide

13. Quoted in Stone, *Search for Social Peace*.
14. Berlanstein, *Working People*.
15. R. Michaud, *J'avais vingt ans: Un jeune ouvrier au debut de siecle* (Paris, 1967).

threatens to drown us — to stop it is impossible. Let us channel it . . .'
Most employers, however, echoed Schneider's response. 'I accept the
intervention of *no-one* from outside the factory in contacts I have with
my workers.'[16] Negotiation with unions remained anathema. Barely
1% of strikes between 1898 and 1914 were settled by employer –
union negotiation; the 1892 Act authorising intercession of JPs as
conciliators was invoked in 22% of strikes between 1893 and 1902,
in a mere 17% in 1910–13 (Tilly and Shorter, 1974).

Management became increasingly intransigent and heavy-handed.
The Great Depression pushed employers to emphasise efficiency.
'Progressive' engineering manufacturers flirted with Taylorism.
Many firms imposed stricter discipline, tighter foreman supervision,
speed-ups and undermined the remaining job-autonomy of skilled
workers in a conscious strategy to destroy workers' collective
practices and assert management hegemony. Until the 1890s pottery
workers rejected piece-work systems as 'trials of strength' which
'inevitably produce the departure of the weak and aged'. Bottlemak-
ers established their own daily targets, smashing 'surplus' bottles to
avoid overproduction. Systematic, direct, management control was
facilitated in engineering by universal machine-tools which permitted standardised production and required merely semi-skilled oper-
ators. Piece-rates and bonus incentives were introduced to increase
work-speed (Perrot, 1979).

In Paris new management strategies provoked a 'crisis of discipline'. In 'artisanal' sectors, where hitherto foremen had included
ex-skilled workers sympathetic to craft culture, the tone of workshop relations was soured as foreign import penetration and market
trends away from 'quality' products caused jewellery, furniture and
ceramics employers to cut costs. Wages of furniture craftsmen fell
by 25% in 1880–93. 'Specialised' shoe-stitchers and finishers were
'sweated' as they sought to compete with mechanised *banlieue*
factories. A new breed of foremen, ex-NCOs, aroused hatred,
provoking thirteen strikes in 1910 alone in the Parisian craft sector.
Whereas earlier Parisian strikes had been wage-orientated, one-
third in 1898–1902 were over work organisation. Auto and engineering plants were worst hit — there was a machine-smashing riot
at one Boulogne-Billancourt engineering works after an 'arrogant'
foreman drew a revolver. But shoe, printing, match and distillery
works were involved, with OS workers drawn into protests against

16. Quoted in Stone, *Search for Social Peace*.

piece-work, speed-ups and crude foremen who insulted their 'dignity'. Wider political implications remain unclear. Barely 3% of such strikers were unionised, their rhetoric denounced evil foremen rather than management authority *per se* and the strikes do not correlate in any clear way with socialist electoral gains. Yet at the very least questions about the degree of 'integration' of Parisian workers were unavoidable (Berlanstein, 1984). Similar 'indiscipline' among Limoges porcelain workers under threat from larger mechanised factories, 'dilution' and foreman control suggests that unrest was by no means confined to the capital (Merriman, 1985).

Employers organised effective counter-offensives against this strike wave. Employers' Associations financed 'yellow' unions, imported blacklegs and hired gunmen to intimidate pickets (Stearns, 1971). Behind them stood the Republican state machine with its courts, police, troops. Beneath the Republic velvet glove lay an iron fist. Workers' faith in Millerandism received a blow when troops shot strikers in Chalon-sur-Saône. The ferocity of post-1906 strike repression was doubly shocking to workers since it was authorised by Radicals who had once resolutely denounced such 'reactionary' policies. Clemenceau, *briseur des grèves* — 'France's Top Cop' — took perverse delight in his new role. He swamped mining villages with 95,000 troops during the strike which followed the Courrières pit disaster, then arrested trade union leaders in the May 1906 general strike. He rejected his own back-benchers' protests when police shot into the strike headquarters of the quarrymen's union during the Draveil strike, and when charging cavalrymen killed four and wounded sixty-seven during the subsequent protest march at Villeneuve-St-George. The tone of a letter sent to a Lorraine newspaper after cavalry charged a peaceful march of iron-miners (1905) captures the shocked incredulity of many workers.

I saw the war of 1870. Well, Monsieur, if officers had then exhibited as much courage as they did yesterday against strikers, certainly [France] would not have lost. But their courage is only revealed in face of unarmed Frenchmen. The ignoble conduct of some officers has done more than five years of antimilitarist propaganda. I myself, an old woman of 66 . . . filled my apron . . . with stones to hurl at them! What brutes . . . They have killed forever in Pont-à-Mousson — which, however, is so nationalistic — all idea of *Patrie*.[17]

17. Quoted in S. Bonnet, *La ligne rouge des hauts-fourneaux* (Metz-Serpenoise, 1981).

Police personnel and tactics changed little in the transition from 'authoritarian' Bonapartism to 'liberal' Republic. A 'slush fund', outside Parliamentary control, was used to pay agents to infiltrate unions, *agents provocateurs* to foment strikes, even plant bombs. The 'anarchist' whose shot provoked the Villeneuve-St-George cavalry charge was a police agent! Annual ritual clashes between working-class demonstrators and police during processions to the Communards' cemetery at Père-Lachaise helped maintain socialism's 'revolutionary' image.

The 1910 rail strike was the classic confrontation between rising worker frustration, employer intransigence and State repression. Employers refused negotiation on union pay and pension claims, provoking a strike which was ruthlessly crushed by troops and by call-up of strikers into the armed forces. Three thousand strikers were subsequently sacked. Yet railmen had been quintessential 'moderates'. Rail companies' elaborate, quasi-military hierarchy had encountered little strike disruption. Footplatemen were tenured, skilled, well-paid, eligible for company pensions. They took pride in 'their' locomotives. Their craft union remained aloof from the *Syndicat National* of humbler rail employees. It disavowed strikes, looked to Parliamentary protection from Republican deputies who sponsored legislation on hours and conditions on the railways. Yet in 1910 drivers led the strike. In part the new militancy of a once moderate craft union derived from deteriorating work conditions — stagnating wages, more tiring schedules due to large, faster locomotives. Yet a reductionism which explains all worker protest as a pragmatic response to work experience and technological change is unconvincing. Drivers abandoned the rhetoric of craft-particularism for that of 'class solidarity'. Politics and ideology played a role in this change. Initially Republicans had wooed railmen with promises of legislative reform; by 1910 the inadequacy of such reforms was apparent. Employers responded to shorter-hours legislation by squeezing wages, tightening discipline and increasing fines. During the 1900s Radical governments failed to protect railmen. Drivers came to rely not on the goodwill of Republican politicians but on an alliance with the wider labour movement. Revolutionary syndicalist militants had some influence in the 1910 strike; in 1912 the drivers' trade union joined the Confédération Générale du Travail. The strikers' discourse was revealing. One denounced the 'Opportuno-Radical Party — worse than the monarchists'. Another condemned arbitrary company policies as 'a state of affairs that should not exist in a Republic'. A third contrasted his own militancy with the mentality of his railman father: 'There are two generations, with very different perspectives. Our generation was beginning to be more interested in politics. You see, politics is the link which holds unionism together. I never heard my father discuss politics or union, only work. . . .'[18]

The growth of the socialist labour movement.

Channelling of workers' grievances into effective action required ideological and organisational guidance from unions and parties. In the 1880s' Depression, with the labour movement still embryonic, workers' frustrations erupted all too easily into anti-immigrant xenophobia or 'anti-capitalist' anti-Semitism — from which elements of the left were not immune (Hutton, 1981). The danger of internecine sectionalism in a heterogeneous working class was acute.

How successfully did the labour movement overcome these dangers? Frequently ideological or organisational squabbles between rival socialist groups, between socialist parties and unions or within the unions mirrored, even exacerbated, sectionalism. After the nadir of the post-Commune repression socialist groups resurfaced in the late 1870s. Vigorous missionary work in the following decade led to the capture of some municipal seats. By 1893 there were fifty assorted socialist deputies, by 1898 some 750,000 socialist voters (some 8% of electorate). Yet until 1905 socialism remained hopelessly fragmented into feuding sects — socialist or anarchist; reformist or revolutionary; heirs of French traditions of Blanqui, Proudhon and Blanc or apostles of new imported Marxism. Brousse's Possibilists championed a gradual, electoralist path to socialism, with priority given to 'municipal socialism'. Guesde's Parti Ouvrier Français (POF) preached a simplified Marxism targeted at factory proletarians. After 1891 the Parti Ouvrier Socialiste Révolutionnaire (Revolutionary Socialist Workers' Party, POSR), led by printer Allemane, broke from Possibilist reformism, emphasising a revolutionary, 'workerist' ideology, suspicious of electoralism and sympathetic to industrial militancy. The Comité Central

18. Quoted in M. Stein, 'The Meaning of Skill: The Case of French Engine Drivers 1837–1917', *Politics and Society* (1978) 8, 3–4, pp.339–428.

Révolutionnaire (Central Revolutionary Committee, CRC) was closest to the POSR in ideology and style, though less hostile to Parliamentary politics. Its leader, Vaillant, proved a key figure in eventual socialist unification. His grasp of Marxist theory was subtler than Guesde's, his blend of reformism and revolution, of Marxism and historic French socialism, potentially fruitful. His earlier political career was linked, misleadingly, with the neo-Blanquists whose blend of Jacobin patriotism, élite vanguardism and *putschism* survived into the 1880s. However, their relevance to labour politics diminished amidst bizarre rituals and questionable strategies. In St Denis they won municipal power only to alienate working-class voters by ignoring social issues and wasting energy on symbolic provocation of clergy and police. Others developed Blanqui's Jacobin-nationalism, cult of virile action and anti-capitalist anti-Semitism into proto-fascism, flirting with Boulangism, and contrasting their 'French' socialism with that of 'German-Jew' Marx (Hutton, 1981).

Radical politics was further complicated by anarchist groups whose influence on the *tone* of the left was out of proportion to their numerical strength of perhaps 5,000 militants. Anarchist papers (e.g. *Père Peinard*), written in argot and tapping popular grievances and prejudices, had a sizeable audience. Anarchists were active in unemployment demonstrations and attacks on landlords. Their flirtation with terrorist bombings ('propaganda of the deed') finally provoked a police backlash and repressive legislation (1893) passed in an atmosphere of bourgeois panic. While expressing sympathy with such violence as expressions of genuine rage at real injustices socialists condemned such tactics as bankrupt. 'Our entire socialist politics has as its object to substitute for vain individual action the collective . . . action of the working-class' (Vaillant).[19]

Prospects for socialist unity improved briefly in the 1890s as electoral successes increased. Socialist capture of 150 municipalities persuaded even Guesdists, hitherto sceptical about Possibilist enthusiasm for 'socialism in one city', that the experience of municipal socialism might give workers self-confidence and practical administrative skills and, by ameliorating local conditions, provide an advertisement for the benefits of a future socialist society. The net results proved disappointing. Limoges workers greeted their socialist council (1895) with euphoria and mass rallies. The Bourses du

19. Quoted in J. Howarth, *E. Vaillant* (Paris, 1982).

Travail (BTs) received subsidies, new unions multiplied and urban renewal projects brought amenities to the city's slums. Elsewhere socialist councils subsidised school meals, crèches, clinics. The crunch came when prefects and judges vetoed schemes for council housing, municipal gas and transport, and local tax reform as excessive burdens on local taxpayers, infringements of private property rights or as beyond the legal competence of councils, whose scope for action proved much narrower than that of Chamberlain's Birmingham. Possibly such blatant obstruction of sensible projects desired by working-class voters may have radicalised workers' consciousness, while socialist mayors' support for local strikers against police and troops could symbolise popular resentment at the alliance between capitalists and central Government (Scott, 1981).

Sadly, internecine feuding persisted even during the honeymoon period of the mid-1890s. Conservatives won an 1893 Paris by-election when the local POF (ignoring Guesde's advice) split the working-class vote by fielding a candidate against the CRC. Protracted friction occurred between the ideologically similar POSR and the CRC, culminating in four POSR deputies joining the CRC because of exasperation with the former's indifference to electoral politics. The Dreyfus crisis engendered a new schism as reformists and POSR (soon to form the Parti Socialiste Français: French Socialist Party, PSF) defended the 'threatened' Republic, while the POF and CRC (who merged to form the Parti Socialiste de France, PS de F) refused support for 'bourgeois' governments. The disastrous consequences may be illustrated in Bourges I constituency (Cher). In 1898 the CRC almost captured the seat, with 38% of the vote. By 1902 rival PSF and PS de F candidates paid for two years of fratricidal insults by polling only 18% between them.

By 1904–5, with the Republic 'safe', reformist socialists were tempted out of support for the Radical-dominated Bloc whose social programme had been disappointing. The united Section Française de l'Internationale Ouvrière (SFIO, i.e. the French Section of the Workers' International) (1905) combined a quasi-Marxist revolutionary perspective with short-term reformism and electoralism. Some 'independent' reformists remained outside the SFIO which was a broad church, holding together an uneasy alliance of reformists (A.Thomas), Republican-Marxists (Jaurès), Marxist-Republicans (Vaillant), Guesdists, quasi-syndicalists (Lagardelle), and anti-militarists (Hervé). By 1914 it had secured modest gains, increasing its vote to 1.4 million, securing 100 parliamentary seats. Yet since it secured votes from peasantry and petty bourgeoisie it clearly failed to capture much of the working class electorate.

In France bitter demarcation disputes between 'political' and 'industrial' wings of the labour movement made parties and unions appear as rivals more than as partners. Since trade unions remained illegal until 1884, radical popular politics preceded effective union organisation by well over half a century. Guesdism allocated a subordinate role to neophyte unionism, adopting an 'iron law of wages' analysis which insisted that union activity was reformist and futile and should be under party control. Brousse's Possibilists emphasised electoralism and undervalued industrial militancy. The smaller POSR and CRC adopted a more sympathetic stance. Vaillant preached 'total action'. Unions and strikes were as important as political parties in raising workers' consciousness and giving experience of organisation for class struggle. Trade unions and socialist parties should evolve at their own pace towards alliance; any assertions of party supremacy would be counter-productive.

In 1894 the Nantes trade union conference voted against POF control of unions. This assertion of union autonomy was achieved by a heterogeneous coalition of pragmatic, reformist unionists, of POSR and CRC militants, and of anarchists and syndicalists championing a socialism of worker *autogestion* rather than of State nationalisations, achievable via industrial militancy *not* through 'politics'. The latter current was strengthened after 1900 by renewed socialist in-fighting and by the shooting of strikers by troops (1900) commanded by a government in which the socialist Millerand was a minister. 'If the Empire shot down workers at La Ricamarie [1869] [the Republican] Constans did the same at Fourmies [1891], and Millerand did the same at Chalons. . . . How can we rely even on a socialist government to satisfy our demands?' asked a delegate at a 1903 trade union conference.

However, the strength and unity of this autonomous trade union movement remained in doubt. True BTs, established in major towns, provided a focal point for local union activity. The Confédération Générale du Travail (CGT), established in 1895, aspired to function as a central organising institution for all unions, championing local union federations and the replacement of particularist craft unions by broad industrial unions (e.g. the construction workers' Fédération du Batiment, FB). By 1902 the CGT and the federation of BTs united, adopting a syndicalist ideology. Yet unionism appeared weak and fragmented. Membership grew only gradually to around one million. Of these under one half were affiliated to the CGT, while *within* the CGT syndicalist domination remained challenged by an apolitical reformist current. Unionisation remained low in new, expanding industries; membership turnover was high as strikers flooded into unions only to surge out with equal rapidity, as in the Lorraine iron strikes of 1905 (Lorwin, 1954).

A major problem for socialism was inability to achieve consensus on the historical nature and tactical utility of Republican institutions. French socialism was weak on theory, and unresolved debates persisted. Were 'formal' Republican liberties an asset, or a trap? How would the 'social' Republic differ from the 'bourgeois' Republic — and was a 'revolutionary rupture' necessary to achieve it? Socialists groped towards appropriate attitudes and strategies to adopt towards the State, reform and elections within the unprecedented context of a liberal parliamentary system. As Howarth insists it is misleading to imagine unbridgeable ideological gulfs between consistent philosophies.[20] Initially few rejected *all* reforms, few excluded totally the revolutionary option.

Three main approaches emerged. For Guesdists the Republic remained a capitalist regime within which no meaningful reform was possible. At most, socialists should press for reforms in order to expose to workers how the system refused them. Republican liberties were a snare, Republican bourgeois were as much the enemy as royalists or authoritarian-nationalists. Guesde's response to the Dreyfus crisis was 'a plague on all their houses'. Waldeck-Rousseau was a business lawyer implicated in aiding a Catholic textile employer to unseat Guesde at Roubaix in 1898. Guesdism's emphasis on a revolutionary overthrow of the capitalist State had merits of clarity; but it had the danger of paralysing 'immobilism', since any action short of revolution appeared futile. And it flew in the face of a century of popular struggle to establish a Republic. Faced with Catholic-royalist employers even Nord Guesdists championed *laic* education.

20. J. Howarth, 'From the Bourgeois Republic to the Social Republic', in S. Williams (ed.), *Socialism in France from Jaurès to Mitterand* (Paris, 1983).

Reformists viewed the Republic as a stage in 'linear' progress, offering freedoms which allowed workers to construct socialism gradually, reform by reform. To 'save' the Republic from right-wing threats, or to achieve reforms, socialists could ally with 'progressive' left-Republicans. Although Millerand was expelled as a renegade in 1904, his entry into Waldeck-Rousseau's cabinet aroused genuine grass-roots enthusiasm. Thousands cheered him as 'the first minister to love the proletariat' when he visited militant Limoges in 1899. Jaurès, who voted for the Bloc des Gauches (1899–1905) without entering government, argued that the State had ceased to be entirely 'bourgeois'. Workers had now 'penetrated' it, were *sharing* state power, even though the balance within the State still favoured the bourgeoisie. Whether working-class pupils in state schools or bourgeois socialist deputies in Parliament proved his case remined questionable (Goldberg, 1964).

Vaillant's synthesis fused Marxism with the French historic experience. Vaillant denied that the Republican State was benevolent or a neutral arbiter, above class forces. Its 'democracy' was distorted by the repressive role of army, police and judiciary. Economic and educational inequalities permitted the bourgeoisie to 'govern by the vote as it rules by religion and . . . the gun'. An ex-Communard, Vaillant denounced Millerand for sitting in a cabinet alongside General Gallifet, the 'butcher' of 1871. If, in the last resort, the Republic needed defence, socialist workers should defend it themselves. The Republic was 'an indispensable framework' for worker emancipation because it permitted priority for capital versus labour class conflicts — whereas a monarchy, restoring alliance between workers and 'progressive' bourgeois, would obscure the real conflict. Republican 'liberties' were not 'bourgeois' but rights, won by popular struggles, for workers to mobilise. Reforms under capitalism were obviously inadequate. Yet an exhausted, overworked proletariat was unlikely to fight for socialism. Reforms achieved by struggle raised consciousness.

Vaillant hoped to build socialist unity around his 'revolutionary evolutionism'. He experienced the 1899–1905 schism, in which latent differences became explicit, as a tragic nightmare. Vaillant's atheism and pro-*laic* sympathies put him closer to Jaurès than to Guesde, who dismissed anti-clericalism as a red herring. Yet he refused to approve Jaurès' support for the Bloc. Workers' defence of the Republic should be 'in full proletarian and socialist independence'.

Eventually lack of effective reform eroded workers' sympathy for the Bloc even within the PSF. Jaurès was forced to reconsider his strategy. While his own charisma dominated the post-1905 SF10, the party ideology owed more to Vaillant, for electoralism and pursuit of reforms were fused with a 'revolutionary' perspective and rejection of electoral alliances.

One-third of POF voters, half of its members, were in the Nord textile towns. Marxist emphasis on the factory proletariat as *the* vanguard class appeared relevant in a region with weak artisanal traditions, relatively untouched by earlier socialist traditions and, thus, offering virgin soil for quasi-messianic Marxist preaching promising imminent victory and a new Eden.

Nord workers exhibited little obvious political or industrial militancy before 1880. Slum squalor has been seen as engendering despair and apathy, not protest. Unskilled factory workers, including female and child labourers working exhausting hours, may have been difficult to organise, Catholic migrants possibly susceptible to the *patronat's* religious paternalism. Reddy has questioned these stereotypes, arguing that factory workers had textile-outwork experience before entering mills, that low strike incidence reflects survival of patterns of independent work within early mills, and that portraits of immiserated, hapless, alcoholic, incestuous slum-dwelling dregs are caricatures drawn from Villermé's 1830s surveys and their successors.[21] One analysis of popular culture suggests that though songs of the 1860s reflect workers' awareness of their inability, faced with Bonapartist authoritarianism, to change society they also reflect a sense of irony, stoicism, quixotic pride in dirty old towns and celebration of the warmth of communal culture.[22] Cafés, street festivals, puppet-theatres suggest a *sociabilité* as developed as that of Provençal peasants, even if the sun shone only *inside* Roubaix cabarets! Mockery and practical jokes were used frequently against employers.

After 1870 textiles became increasingly strike-prone. Guesdists exploited deteriorating industrial relations, emphasising the need for organisation to push class war to a victorious conclusion. The 'typical' Guesdist leader was a blacklisted, ex-textile worker who

21. W. Reddy, *The Rise of Market Culture* (Cambridge, 1984).
22. Marty, *Chanter pour survivre*.

became a café-owner and then municipal councillor. Municipal councils offered Guesdists a power base to counter-balance the shop-floor weakness of textile trade unions faced with uncompromising employers — a weakness 'justifying' POF emphasis on subordination of unions to party. Nevertheless, periodic quasi-millenial strikes suggest that Guesdism was never totally in tune with textile workers' aspirations. The POF sought to channel protest into *votes*, and disliked wildcats. However, workers' grievances — over work processes, fines for breakages, authoritarian management — exploded (as in May 1890) into sudden strikes marked by violence, arson threats and symbolic protests. In face of these the POF would plead for a return to work, 'rational' wage bargaining — the response of the French Communist Party in 1936! (Reddy, 1984)

After 1893 the POF made electoral gains, winning parliamentary seats in Lille and Roubaix. As the Nord vote doubled to 82,000, Guesde developed electoralist illusions. 'The Revolution is near. It will mean neither piles of cobblestones — nor dead bodies', simply 'the peaceful seizure of power.' In eager quest for votes the POF contemplated 'deals' with Radicals, flirted with 'municipal socialism', and supported the Tsarist alliance — the historic mission of the French proletariat necessitated a strong France! Guesde's 1898 electoral defeat terminated this electorialist aberration. Thereafter Guesdism resembled a miniature SPD. 'Revolutionary' rejection of Millerandism lost them over one-third of their 300,000 votes between 1898 and 1902. Yet they lacked both revolutionary strategy, the ideological subtlety or intellectual capacity for creative Marxist analysis of specific French conditions. Their 'intellectual', Lafargue, understood Enlightenment rationalism better than the 'algebra' of *Das Kapital* Vol. II. 'Just as two and two make four, so socialist truths never alter' affirmed the mayor of Roubaix, typical of Guedism's self-educated local militants. After 1900 Guesdism's poll share in Nord towns levelled off, at between 35 and 45%, or declined as textiles stagnated and workers in expanding metal or mining sectors turned to syndicalism or reformism. Despite their ideological suspicions about co-operatives they ran a flourishing consumer co-operative movement and used songs, poetry and theatre to tap northern communal sociability and to combat Catholic cultural influences which, particularly in Tourcoing, remained strong. Though the Nord remained a socialist bastion, with 15% of SFIO members, Guesdists were uneasy within the united party, resenting the SFIO tolerance towards reformist and quasi-syndicalist ideas. Grown 'solitary, sulky and ageing', Guesdists resented Jaurès' charisma (Baker, 1967).

By 1914 coal-mining areas were electing reformist socialist deputies. Two explanations for miners' reformism are plausible. Geographical concentration allowed miners to dominate individual constituencies and elect parliamentary spokesmen. And mineral rights were leased out by the State, whose mining engineers exercised safety controls in privately operated pits. Hence miners turned 'naturally' to parliament for safety legislation. The 1890 law, authorising miners to elect safety delegates, provided one justification of miners' faith in reformism.

Until c.1880 mining strikes had been relatively infrequent and miners appeared geographically and culturally segregated from artisan-based socialism. Low wages and poor conditions were often tolerated because pit-work remained frequently a mere supplement to incomes from peasant farming. Three factors influenced miners' metamorphosis into the archetypal proletarians immortalised in Zola's *Germinal*. Management's efforts to increase productivity by regular attendance and timekeeping 'proletarianised' peasant miners. As urban consumers, miners were now vulnerable to wage cuts during the Great Depression. Consequently, miners turned to new Republican authorities for support against authoritarian employers.

Trajectories of socialist penetration varied between coalfields. Classic labourism typified the fast-expanding Pas-de-Calais/Nord coalfield, where strike defeats (e.g. 1884) taught union leader Basly the futility of industrial militancy. Rejecting syndicalism, he utilised the trade union machine to elect pro-miner deputies. He admired British 'Lib–Labism' and Ruhr 'business unionism'. In return for the withdrawal of pro-employer election candidates Basly made concessions to employer's demands in collective contract negotiations and supported employers' lobbying for Protectionist coal tariffs. To spare Millerand embarrassment he moderated wage demands. When grass-roots militancy built up he detonated strikes prematurely (1902) to ensure their failure. He refused to join the CGT Eight-Hour campaign. His local union secretaries, café-owners whose role was to 'deliver' the vote, showed little concern with pit-face grievances (e.g. piece-rate systems); their role was to *prevent* strikes. Eventually such cynical pragmatism provoked a syndicalist breakaway *'Jeune Syndicat'* which denounced Basly as a bosses' man, a parliamentary gossip. By 1907 this had recruited 20% of unionised northern miners, but its support subsequently declined.

Except around St Etienne miners' politics in the south evolved towards reformism much more gradually. In 1914 Gard coal-owner/deputy de Ramel was finally unseated by an SFIO reformist. However, during the 1880s the struggles of 14,000 miners against the 'capitalist theocracies' of Catholic employers were characterised by a repudiation of Basly — a 'sound potato' made rotten by the corruption of a bourgeois parliament. In quasi-syndicalist strikes against wage cuts company stores were attacked, engineers' homes and pit-shafts dynamited. When troops were brought in, militants took refuge in the hills, their millenial rhetoric evoking the distant religious wars of their Camisard forefathers. However, since it lacked a broader strategic vision strike militancy foundered in the face of continued economic recession. Electoral politics, encouraged by the example of local winegrowers, offered an alternative tactic.

At Decazeville, too, labour tactics oscillated wildly. The 1886 strike against company stores and management surveillance of miners' voting culminated in the violent death of hated company-engineer Watrin, hurled from the upper windows of the company offices. During the 1890s reliance on municipal socialism proved excessively optimistic in the face of tighter management controls at the pit face. During the ensuing syndicalist phase union leader Mazars expressed scepticism about electoralism and even about state nationalisation. Haunted by premonitions of a future Gallic Monsieur MacGregor he asked: 'Who says that the future State boss will be less of a skunk than the shareholder?' The election (1914) of a reformist SFIO deputy expressed a belated awareness of union weakness in face of the growing influx of immigrant miners. Carmaux made this transition to reformism more smoothly. By 1890 the embryonic miners' union was growing disillusioned with the anti-clerical Republicans to whom they had turned for support against Catholic-royalist employer de Solages. 'Reforms which your party programmes promise — none have been implemented. Since the bourgeoisie to whom we give our votes, have failed to understand our needs, we can count only on ourselves.' Jaurès was elected (1893) in the aftermath of a strike provoked by the sacking of a miners' leader who had the effrontery to be elected mayor. Briefly a quasi-revolutionary tone surfaced in Carmaux socialist discourse in reaction against the unholy alliance of Republican prefects and Catholic-royalist mine-owners which unseated Jaurès in 1898. Yet while repudiating Basly's 'repugnant egoism' the local union, faced by a rival 'yellow' union which cut its membership to 15% of the coalfields (4,000 miners), rejected syndicalism. Essentially they shared Jaurès' own ambivalence towards a Republic which they denounced as a tool of capitalist oppression yet to which they looked as arbiter and legislative ally (Reid, 1985c).

In several regions miners' conversion to socialism was aided by contact with skilled metal or glass workers, migrants from outside the coalfields with broader intellectual horizons. Carmaux socialism rested on a miner–glassworker alliance. Carmaux glassworkers had been geographically mobile, coming from other towns and leaving after a few years. Glassblowing required dexterity and experience in regulating heat and knowing when to turn bottles. They passed skills onto their sons and formed a highly paid labour aristocracy. They inhabited their own *quartier*, did not speak local *patois*, and had few contacts with miners. Continuous-flow gas-ovens and mechanised turning then threatened their skills. A national union, the Fédération National du Verre (National Glassworkers Federation), FNV co-ordinated resistance to the undermining of wage levels. Faced with declining national job opportunities, glassworkers had to stay and fight. An alliance with the miners to win municipal and Parliamentary elections in order to mobilise support was now essential. The rhetoric of class unity ('we proletarians . . . ') replaced that of craft-exclusiveness — helped by the presence of coal-owner de Solages on the board of the glassworks! The defeat of glassworker strikes and the rapid decline of the FNV, which lost two-thirds of its 7,000 members in 1894–7, exposed the fragility of glassworker resistance. Skilled glassblowers were sacked. Many left Carmaux to form a co-operative in Albi — an exodus which weakened the left and cost Jaurès his seat in 1898. The new OS work-force came from rural backgrounds, lacked experience of union organisation and remained unorganised into the inter-war period. Carmaux illustrates in microcosm the difficulties faced by the French labour movement. Technological change could fuel militancy—but also undermine it. Defeats and sharp discontinuities meant that the labour movement had to be continually reconstituted rather than built steadily from past foundations (Scott, 1974).

Nevertheless, fruitful interaction of skilled and OS workers was possible in certain circumstances. As Judt argues, it is implausible to suggest an occupational determinism which 'explains' workers' political opinions by the type of tools they wield.[23] Some community of ideas, ideals and loyalties frequently cause 'artisans' to appear in the vanguard of proletarian movements. The workshop is not the *only* place where opinions may be acquired and not all worker politics derives from work-related attitudes. In the 'red city' of Limoges the 'dilution' of skills of porcelain and shoemaker artisans by mechanisation and factory production in 1880–1905 failed to prevent the emergence of a militant unionism backed by a socialist municipality as older skilled workers in the popular *faubourgs* passed on local traditions of protest to younger migrants recruited from the radicalised, dechristianised Limousin countryside (Merriman, 1985). In Rive-de-Gier (Loire) threatened glassworkers encouraged unionisation of OS workers in heavy-metal plants whose capacity for collective action was limited by tight managerial supervision and residential dispersal. While the strikes of 1893–4 were defeated, the glassworker–metalworker coalition elected a reformist socialist lawyer (1893). In nearby Chambon-Feugerolles, the gradualness of technological change permitted skilled file-cutters to resist 'dilution' by unionising less skilled local metalwokers to prevent an influx of locally recruited blacklegs (Hanagan, 1980). In contrast to Victorian Britain, where craft-unionism took root *within* modern industry, French skilled workers had little chance, because of belated trade union legalisation, to construct national craft unions before being confronted by rapid technological change. Instead they improvised hasty alliances with the unskilled, to win electoral allies to vote for socialist deputies who could defend them in parliament. Many French strikes aimed at pressuring the State into intervention (Tilly and Shorter, 1974).

While socialism remained weak in several industrial regions (e.g. Lorraine) eight of the twelve departments where its vote exceeded 20% in 1914 were semi-rural regions of the Centre and South — in part a legacy of Democratic-Socialist penetration during the Second Republic. As the Depression confronted agricultural labourers with wage cuts and small peasants with the spectre of indebtedness and expropriation, socialists awoke belatedly to the opportunity of tapping resultant grievances, with the POF jettisoning land-

23. Judt, *Marxism and the French Left.*

collectivisation dogmas in favour of pragmatic promises of cheap credit, improved share-cropper lease terms and support for co-operatives.

Formulation of coherent rural strategies was complicated by the diversity of a potential audience comprising small-owners, tenants, share-croppers, labourers and non-farming groups such as lumber-men. Lumbermen's strikes were important to the revival of rural socialism in the Centre. Vaillant's CRC was active in supporting lumber unions in its Cher bastion, where left's base was typically heterogeneous, and its ideological divisions typically complex. Mili-tant lumbermen, porcelain and metalworkers oscillated between the CRC and syndicalism. *Vignerons* (small) winegrowers and Bourges arsenal workers, pensioned state employees, favoured reformism.

Share-croppers' class position remained ambiguous, since many farmed sizeable holdings employing wage labour. Their traditional deference was, however, shaken as greater involvement in market agriculture increased vulnerability to price fluctuations and as land-owners responded to the Depression by shortening lease terms. A share-cropper's union, Fédération des Travailleurs de la Terre (FTT), in the Allier campaigned for improving leasing contracts and compensation for farm improvements. Habits of deference died hard, fear of eviction persisted, strikes were double-edged weapons which threatened share-croppers' own crops. Yet, though by 1912 the FTT had declined from a membership peak of 2,000, its legacy included election of reformist SFIO deputies to champion their cause, for Republican politicians had proved to be hand-in-glove with the big landowners.

In Provence small-owners embraced POF collectivism because the collapse of cork, olive and shoe production had reduced villages to dependence on wine monoculture in decades marked first by phylloxera, which destroyed 60% of vines, then by wine price collapse. Since strikes were an inappropriate weapon a *vigneron* protest was inevitably 'political'. Individualistic Radical remedies appeared inadequate to the severity of the region's economic crisis, whereas State regulation of wine markets and collectivisation of big wine estates, held responsible for over production, appeared sen-sible. Communal solidarities in single-class peasant villages nur-tured a collectivist consciousness, which supported thirty-five co-operatives which stored wine to avoid rapid sale to wine mer-chants on depressed post-harvest markets. By 1914 the Var boasted four SFIO deputies (Judt, 1979).

In Lower Languedoc small-owners co-existed alongside big vine-yards employing a sizeable proletariat. A powerful resident Catholic royalist élite made right-wing threats to the Republic appear, still, to be a real possibility. Hence 80% of Herault socialist members in 1899 favoured the Bloc. To defend *vignerons* struggling in unequal competition with heavily capitalised coastal estates socialists demanded taxation of big landowners, encouraged co-operative cellars and marketing, but played down collectivism. During the 'Revolt of the Midi' (1905–7) triggered by catastrophic price collapse, the local SFIO co-operated with capitalist winegrow-ers in the wine-defence lobby, the Confédération Generale des Vignerons du Midi (CGVM), blaming overproduction on fraudu-lent 'northern' sugaring of wine and advocating a 'fraternal' alliance of capital and labour 'among children of the Midi'. The local SFIO's corporatist/regionalist 'pro wine' rhetoric exluded class analysis, refused to blame large landowners for overproduction and ignored the grievances of vineyard labourers — many marginal peasants bankrupted and proletarianised by phylloxera. The heavy capital outlay of vineyard replanting favoured 'industrial' vine estates, where work discipline became harsher and wage levels fell. Strikes, led by the syndicalist-dominated Fédération des Travailleurs Agri-cole du Midi (Federation of Southern Agricultural Labourers, FTAM), exploded in 1904–5 and 1911–13. Army protection of blacklegs nurtured anti-militarism. The FTAM experienced volatile fluctuations in membership, peaking at 15,000 in 1905, collapsing, then reviving. Yet it expressed workers' resentment at SFIO re-formism and grievances of skilled pruners and grafters, with their collective work practices and village solidarities, over erosion of wage levels and of job controls and of the 'independence' which ownership of small plots had once provided. While socialist voting rose steadily (e.g. 16,000 to 27,000 in Hérault in 1900–14), the SFIO did *least* well in the Aude where the FTAM was strongest. FTAM propaganda denounced socialist class collaboration, urged electoral abstention (nearly 50% in some wine villages) and criticised 'social-ist' *vignerons* for exploiting their hired hands. The largest and most active BTs (e.g. Béziers) were syndicalist-led, and their strikes drew in non-unionised labour, women and immigrants ignored by SFIO electoralism (Frader, 1981).

As Rébérioux remarks, SFIO history in the period 1905–14 remains an under-researched subject.[24] Socialist unity brought no sudden upsurge in party dynamism — indeed the buoyant optimism which had characterised 'red' bastions like Limoges in the 1890's had waned (Merriman, 1985). Growth was gradual, patchy — a 60% vote increase to 1.4 million, a doubling of membership to 90,000. Despite the occasional rhetorical flourish, insurrectionist strategy had been abandoned. 'New' areas of party growth — Auvergne, Belfort-Montbéliard, Brittany — were solidly 'reformist'. Yet since the left rejected electoral deals immediate prospects of power were minimal. Education and propaganda activity to prepare socialist voters for distant power took priority. Yet the scope and success of this propaganda was modest, party publications were few, and key industrial areas (e.g. St Etienne) lacked effective socialist newspapers.

Despite the party's quasi-Marxist ideology elections had priority. Lagardelle and others who questioned this were marginalised. An organisational structure based on departmental federations not factory-cells or collective trade union membership made it a 'citizen' rather than a 'proletarian' party. Electoralist concerns caused a neglect of non-voters, a preoccupation with adult French males. Catholics and Nationalists were more successful at founding sport and youth clubs. Under 3% of members were women, most of these wives and daughters of male members. There was an abject failure to mobilise female support or participation. Jaurès, whose own household was traditionalist *vieille France*, totally failed to keep promises to feminist delegations to give priority to women's rights, to which socialists paid lip-service. Guesde was openly hostile to neo-Proudhonist male chauvinism. Yet while the POF used women orators (P. Mink, A. Valette) it emphasised *economic* issues, refused to back 'illegal' female election candidates, denounced 'bourgeois' feminism for splitting the working class and postponed sexual equality until 'after the Revolution'. Socialists feared that espousal of feminism would alienate male workers, and that female 'clericalism' would make women reactionary voters if enfranchised. Women who tried to combine socialism and feminism, to criticise party inertia on women's rights and the ignorant prejudices of many 'socialist' male workers were marginalised. Dr Madelaine Pelletier was successively Guesdist, Hervé-ist and anarchist before aban-

24. M. Rébérioux, 'Party Practice and the Jaurèsian Vision: the SFIO 1905–14', in S. Williams (ed.), *Socialism in France*.

doning organised left-wing politics in despair at the empty pious platitudes of party congresses. Conversely Louise Saumoneau, who remained a party activist, denounced 'bourgeois' feminism, asserted the class unity of male and female workers and remained insensitive to specifically female problems (Boxer, 1978; Sowerwine, 1982).

Although Guesdism's Nord bastion made it the largest organised group Jaurès clearly emerged as the SFIO's charismatic figure. He edited *L'Humanité*. He gave persuasive voice to feelings that socialism was the true heir to Enlightenment culture. His intellectual openness allowed him to *learn*. In the 1880s he had been a Republican, keen on Imperialism's civilising mission. By 1914, though over-optimistic about peaceful settlement of colonial disputes, he questioned France's imperial role, condemned imperialist exploitation, valued non-European cultures. He read *Das Kapital* and tried to synthesise his French humanism with Marx's insights into class struggle and the proletariat's vanguard role. He had broad cultural concerns — admiration for Occitan culture, distaste for excessive bourgeois individualism. He was aware that the French proletariat's minority position made class alliances necessary. As a product of Occitan rural society with experience of the academic world and a passion for *laic* education he was uniquely equipped to woo peasants, students and teachers to socialism. His solidarity with Carmaux strikers in the 1890s made him an admired workers' tribune. Briefly seduced by Millerand's vision of modernised industrial relations he came to share Vaillant's sympathy towards syndicalism as an authentic proletarian socialism — though also urging the CGT to build more effective union organisation, to eliminate suicidal strikes and to construct closer links with the SFIO (Goldberg, 1964).

Despite this, SFIO–CGT hostilies continued to plague the labour movement. Guesdists and reformists never subscribed to Jaurès sympathy for the CGT. Jaurès himself became preoccupied with threats to peace, giving low priority to workers' struggles against Taylorism. Conversely hard-line syndicalists (e.g. Monatte) continued to denounce 'Professor' Jaurès as a seductive bourgeois intellectual reformist — a real competitor for the CGT's working-class audience. Formal and personal 'contacts' between the SFIO and the trade union movement remained rare and strained.

Revolutionary syndicalism and French labour

Some historians view 'revolutionary syndicalism' as capturing the quintessential mentality of the French working class, expressing the aspirations of a work-force imbued with the psychology of workshop not factory, inheritor of a 'revolutionary tradition' suspicious of bourgeois policies. Artisanal job control, producer co-operatives, selective borrowings from Proudhon all nurtured a 'socialism' favouring worker control at the point of production, a federalism of independent producers (Moss, 1976). 'Electoralism' was suspect because it accepted reform 'from above'. Workers divided by religious and political beliefs could be united only by work experience. Industrial militancy alone could bring worker self-emancipation.

In reality socialism and syndicalism obviously overlapped. One study of 126 syndicalist militants found that one-third were at some stage socialist party members. Nevertheless syndicalism had its own identity — finding ideologists in Pelloutier and Pouget, charismatic strike leaders in Griffuelhes and Yvetot, organisational expression in the alliance of CGT and Fédération des Bourses du Travail (FBT). Scorning sectarian, reformist and impotent socialist parties, it pursued strike agitation to raise class consciousness for a future revolutionary General Strike. Its ultimate failure may be attributed to the swamping of craft traditions by accelerated mass-production compounded by the apostasy of leaders who sought to utilise the CGT's role in the war economy to win unions a place alongside industrialists and bureaucrats in a tripartite corporatist system. Despite its ignominious fate syndicalism could be regarded as the authentic voice of pre-1914 French workers.

Yet even in 1907 C. Bouglé questioned this thesis, dubbing the CGT a 'general staff without an army'. Stearns insists that most workers came to accept the capitalist system, that syndicalism ignored this silent majority's real aspirations.[25] Strike waves, economic responses to temporary real wage stagnation, implied no fundamental rejection of the system. Learning the 'rules of the game', pragmatic workers sought a larger share of the capitalist cake. Barely 10% of workers were unionised, and syndicalists were an unrepresentative minority within that minority. Bigger unions (miners, railmen, textile workers) scorned syndicalist tactics. Syndi-

25. P. Stearns, *Revolutionary Syndicalism and French Labor* (New Brunswick, NJ, 1971).

calist control of the CGT reflected merely the absence of proportional representation which permitted 2,000 'radical' barbers an equal voice with 20,000 moderate textile workers. Syndicalist 'leaders' proved incapable of mobilising mass support for their strategic goals. Their utopian apoliticism was ill-suited to the world of universal suffrage. Eulogies of warrior-like 'active minorities' reflected frustration at inability to rouse an inert rank and file. Refusal of realistic industrial bargaining left the 'poor bloody infantry' of strikers' families, subsisting on soup-kitchens, to pay the price for syndicalists' fantasies (Stearns, 1971).

While Stearns' approach has value in forcing historians to move beyond leaders' ideologies and congress resolutions to study rank and file attitudes, emphasis on the chasm dividing militants from 'real' workers may reflect modern scepticism about the possibility of worker radicalism; mere positivistic quantification of strikes, correlating their frequency with cost-of-living indices, unemployment etc. tends to reduce workers' behaviour to statistical probabilities — thereby ignoring craft traditions, doctrines, lived frustrations and aspirations (Tilly and Shorter, 1974).

Undeniably syndicalism lost momentum after 1908. Undoubtedly many workers *were* reformist, conservative, deferential, apathetic. Diehard syndicalists admitted that many 'strikers' spent May Day playing *boules*! However, neo-Perlmanite assumptions that 'real' workers are, by definition, pragmatists, indifferent to radical ideas, are an inverted American bourgeois version of Leninism. Stearns assumes an implausibly high degree of worker 'integration'. His reading of the 1900s strikes as purely economistic is unconvincing, for Parisian industrial unrest was *less* wage-orientated than in the 1880s (Berlanstein, 1984).

Provincial France, from Nantes to the Lyonnais, experienced a mood of quasi-millenarian revolt in 1905–6. Even Basly's union machine faced a syndicalist rival. Limoges porcelain and shoe workers raised barricades and clashed with troops. Clemenceau mobilised 60,000 troops to contain potential disorder during CGT's (1906) 1 May strike campaign, while the mass press demanded tough law and order policies to contain syndicalist violence (Merriman, 1985; Nye, 1985). Cavalier dismissal of syndicalism is, thus, unpersuasive. Nor can it be characterised merely as a movement of threatened organised craftsmen. Syndicalist-led strikes involved non-unionised and semi-skilled workers in vineyards and autoplants, and among navvies, dockers, quarrymen and lumbermen. Railmen and miners were not immune. The CGT explicitly rejected craft unionism, sponsoring industrial federations among builders, metal and food workers.

During the post-Commune repression only ostentatiously moderate artisanal *chambres syndicales*, patronised by Republicans and rejecting strikes, enjoyed a semi-legal existence. Even after 1884 employer intransigence and high employment hindered rapid union growth. Divisions emerged between moderates, encouraged by Radical and Possibilist politicians, who favoured petitioning of Parliament, and anarchist-influenced militants urging direct action. Most strikes were 'defensive' attempts to resist lay-offs or wage-cuts. Most failed. In 1890 trade union membership was only 139,000.

Union co-ordination improved in the 1890s as the BT network spread to fifty-one towns. Initially many BTs had been sponsored by Republican municipalities eager to encourage and 'co-opt' reformist unionism; but by 1895 many had fallen under syndicalist control. Pelloutier, syndicalism's major strategist, championed BTs as cultural centres to educate a worker élite 'capable of governing'. Syndicalism was a moral crusade, for in a corrupt capitalist world only workers proud of their skills, devoted to their families, retained the potential for virtue. Capitalist brewers were denounced for encouraging workers' drinking to weaken the 'proletarian race'. Speakers at BT conferences observed that among colonial peoples Arabs, who drank no alcohol, exhibited the healthiest rebelliousness. Whereas nationalism encouraged sport to produce healthy army conscripts, syndicalists had the class war in view ('Let us work to develop our biceps . . . and you women, breast feed your kids to produce men: we will need them in the next Revolution'). Birth control was championed to reduce that reserve army of labour which depressed wages — although a minority argued that prolific proletarian breeding was needed to prevent 'swamping' by immigrants and to produce troops for the class war.

Belatedly syndicalist rhetoric shifted from 'Proudhonist' sexual prejudices to a reluctant acceptance that unions had to come to terms with the reality of women workers, that low levels of female unionisation stemmed, in part, from male unionists' attitudes. Proudhon's views were denounced as 'reactionary' and 'Christian'. The printers' antediluvian prejudices expressed in the Couriau affair attracted CGT condemnation. Union propaganda for the 'English

Week' targeted working mothers, offering alluring visions of 'free' Saturday afternoons in which women could cook and clean while dad fished with the kids!

'Direct action' won syndicalism its notoriety. Despite Pelloutier's initial lukewarm attitude toward strikes, support for General Strike doctrine grew. 'A strike', claimed CGT leader Griffuelhes, 'is worth more than all the contents of libraries.' It tapped latent energies and raised consciousness by exposing the alliance between capitalists and the State. Even strike defeats were 'deposits in the workers' memory bank', stimulating 'desires for revenge' (Pouget). Endorsement of 'sabotage' implied more than cutting telegraph wires. It could mean quality workmanship when employers wanted shoddy goods, or chefs doling out larger portions than restaurant owners prescribed! Syndicalists never posed reform and revolution as *alternatives* — since reforms which were defended by direct action offered a revolutionary challenge. Furthermore 'the miserable slave . . . is incapable of desiring liberty, with an empty stomach . . . it is impossible to make an effort'.[26] An *à la carte* menu of flexible tactics was offered, from which a heterogeneous working class could choose those suited to local requirements. Lacking centralised bureaucracy, syndicalism made a virtue of local autonomy.

Syndicalism's brief apogee lay in the strike waves of 1900–8 when economic upturn produced a climate conducive to militancy. Pelloutier's assumption that partial strikes were doomed to fail became questionable as failure rates fell from 46% (1890–99) to 33% (1904). Rapid disillusionment with Millerandism influenced the strikers' mood — some reformist socialist deputies actually voted against a public enquiry when troops shot strikers at Chalons. Did the coincidence of strike militancy with syndicalist leadership of the CGT and of major unions (building, metal) make these strikes 'syndicalist' or were they, as Stearns argues, wage-orientated? In 1906 more than one-third of the (record) 1,306 strikes involved hours issues. Building and metalworkers spearheaded the strike of over 200,000 in May for the eight-hour day, pressuring parliament into rushing through an Act introducing a weekly rest-day. Syndicalist propaganda argued that shorter hours would force industrialists to employ more workers and would provide leisure for cultural and family life. Such demands were *not* occurring within a context

26. Quoted in B. Mitchell (1983), *French Revolutionary Syndicalism: A study in pragmatic revolt*. PhD thesis, University of California.

where management envisaged a trade-off between more intense/less autonomous work and shorter hours/higher wages in order to create a consumerism where leisured affluent workers could expand internal consumer demand — for such 'Americanism' was alien to the *patronat* of the 1920s, let alone that of the 1900s. Hours disputes involved bitter conflict on issues on which, historically, French employers gave ground only in moments of quasi-revolutionary crisis (1848; 1919; 1936) (Cross, 1984).

Two contrasting trades offer insights into grass-roots syndicalism. Building workers were a vanguard group. Their trade was highly stratified, ranging from skilled masons and wood-workers with craft traditions to unorganised navvies. Opportunities for ascension into the *patronat* receded as large contractors monopolised public works projects. Joiners and carpenters faced threats from the use of concrete, metal and power-saws. Real wages stagnated. Eventually craftsmen, overcoming their exclusiveness, organised labourers in the Fédération du Bâtiment (FB). In 1907 Paris experienced forty-seven construction strikes, including one of eleven months on the Métro where serious accidents were frequent. However, after police and troops shot strikers and demonstrators in the 1908 Draveil strike, government repression and employer counter-offensives (lock-outs, armed strike-breakers, company unions) checked the FB's momentum. Strike failures increased, craft divisions resurfaced, syndicalist leaders like Péricat faced challenges from reformist rivals.

More surprising was the syndicalism of the Fédération de l'Alimentation (FA) which mobilised a fragmented work-force with little history of militancy. Pastry cooks served apprenticeships only to find jobs which prostituted their skills. Chefs, suffering long hours and female competition, aspired to restore cuisine 'to its rightful place among the liberal arts'. Bakers, working nightshifts in overheated conditions, saw chances of establishing their own shops eroded by industrial bakeries. At the bottom of the food trades were waiters, grocery assistants in chain stores, factory sugar and cake-workers. The FA sought to unify this diverse work-force — heavily female, migrant, foreign — to secure shorter hours in order to reduce unemployment, and to abolish hated private job agencies. In 1903 'direct action', used as a conscious strategy to offset low unionisation levels, led to 500 arrests in clashes with police but succeeded in prompting legislation against job agencies. In 1907 the FA mixed street demonstrations (168 arrests) with peaceful propaganda to enforce implementation of the weekly rest-day legislation. Subsequent FA evolution mirrored that of other syndicalist unions. After strike defeats pragmatic new leaders urged caution. Bakers' strikes (1913) exhibited stricter organisation, narrower wage demands and avoidance of the volatile spontaneity of 1903–7.

'Proletarian' bakers, not craft-conscious pastry cooks, spearheaded FA syndicalism — a salutary warning against rigid correlation of syndicalism with threatened artisans. Similarly unskilled Limoges porcelain workers shared the syndicalism of skilled painters-on-porcelain (Merriman, 1985). 'Dilution' *was* an issue in metalworker syndicalism, but by no means the only one. The Fédération des Métaux (FM), uniting craftsmen and OS workers in an expanding sector, was a syndicalist bastion, its secretary Merrheim among the CGT's most thoughtful leaders. In 1905–6 as roving strike organiser in Lorraine, Brittany and points in between he urged largely non-unionised strikers to learn from army repression that 'the Republic is no better than any other regime'. However, his experiences led him to question syndicalist strategies. Unorganised workers *were* capable of sudden outbursts of militancy. Isolated, ill-planned, these proved easy targets for employer counter-offensives. After strike defeat (1905) Lorraine metal unionism collapsed. Technological change made defence of craft skills increasingly futile (Papayanis, 1985). In 1912–13 strikes erupted at Renault over time-and-motion studies. Syndicalists denounced Taylorism as a cynical de-skilling strategy designed to destroy workers' solidarity and to use speed-ups to drive workers to an early grave in an enlarged Boulogne-Billancourt cemetery. Capitalism's 'contempt for the working class' was compounded by Renault's decision to lock out his workers, holiday on the Riviera, then sack 400 craftsmen. By 1914 the CGT had fifty members in Renault's 4,000-strong workforce.

The FM proved a colossus with feet of clay, organising barely 25,000 (3%) of 800,000 metal/engineering workers. Berliet Autos (Lyons: 2,000 workers) had not a single union member — and shop-floor delegates sent to protest at time-and-motion studies were sacked before reaching the manager's office! In 1913 there were 137 metalworker strikes, many against management innovations. Strikers were frequently syndicalist-led but non-unionised — one-third of all days lost in metal strikes in 1913–14 were in Marseilles, where only 3% of 15,000 metalworkers were unionised. Two-thirds of metal strikes in 1913–14 failed. As one syndicalist lamented: 'spontaneous anger drove them from the factory, but lacking organisation they returned more submissive.'

Syndicalist leaders from skilled backgrounds lamented the demise of craft culture and lacked empathy with 'ignorant masses' of OS workers in large, mechanised factories — perceived as deficient in professional pride, concerned only with wages. Capitalism had 'corrupted the working-class conscience'. During the Arbel strike (Nord) Merrheim claimed to hear 'not a single word about working class dignity. Not one! Nothing but fear — of factory informers, of workers for one another.'[27] However, Merrheim argued not for last-ditch defence of craft skills but for adjustment to unavoidable mass production. Large, well-organised unions could impose some measure of worker influence on the use of new technologies. 'Taylorism . . . *will* be introduced more and more. Worker's interests are to supervise this process, favour [it] to the extent [it does] not harm their moral, economic or physical interests.' His strategy stood no chance of immediate implementation. Some skilled workers retreated into craft-corporatism to resist 'dilution', while small, vociferous syndicalist groups urged mass strikes — even expelling Merrheim from the Seine FM for his heresies, only themselves to be expelled from the national Federation.

Merrheim found supporters within the CGT, where some criticised the *patronat* not for introducing new technologies but for failure to emulate American entrepreneurial dynamism which brought US workers higher pay! Also, the advent of industrial technologies might create a more homogeneous proletariat by eroding skill divisions. Jouhaux, Griffuelhes' heir, saw atavistic hostility to bureaucratised unions as outmoded. The CGT was in obvious disarray, its membership stagnant since 1908. Strike levels remained high, but failures rose alarmingly to 48% by 1912–14. Weak union footholds in expanding sectors (chemicals, electrics) facilitated employer intransigence. Strikes were no proxy for union strength. Ex-syndicalist Latapie, of the FM, disavowed further rash militancy: 'I, for one, refuse henceforth to lead workers to the slaughter house.'

As an ex-anarchist Jouhaux remained instinctively hostile to arbitration schemes, collective contracts and strike ballots. Yet behind his syndicalist rhetoric his attitudes changed. Impressed,

27. Quoted in N. Papayanis, *Alphonse Merrheim: The Emergence of Reformism in Revolutionary Syndicalism* (The Hague, 1985).

despite himself, by German union size, he urged French unionists to 'regularise fleeting ideas, substitute continuous, co-ordinated action for (short-lived) bouts of nervous energy'. The CGT needed centralised bureaucracy, reliable data, without which its leaders 'groped blindly in the dark', and strikers fell into enemy traps. Tactical retreat was necessary. Syndicalism was fighting on terrain where it could not win. 'We are *for* active minorities — only these grow weary if their efforts remain fruitless. We must encourage them by making their actions *effective*, to allow them to drag along in their wake the unorganised masses' (Jouhaux). Clear, attainable goals (e.g. defence of real wages) should be set. Syndicalist anti-militarists should avoid quixotic confrontations with State power.

French labour, anti-militarism and the approach of war

In August 1914 French workers mobilised to fight in the war without bellicose enthusiasm but with a reluctant sense of their duty to defend the Republican *patrie* against Kaiserist aggression. Dozens of minor incidents occurred as militants sang the *Internationale* or urged conscripts to return home. Yet despite Government fears under 2% failed to report for the colours. Fearing that arrests would provoke more unrest than they stifled, the Interior Minister decided not to round up the 2,000 militants on the specially prepared list of 'subversives', the *Carnet B* — largely local syndicalist militants who had talked of resisting war mobilisation but had made few plans to do so.

Leftist rhetoric contained two contradictory discourses. Jacobin patriotism portrayed France as the Motherland of Revolution whose defence (1793, 1871) served the cause of social liberation. Patriotism and socialist convictions could, thus, be reconciled. In 1870–1, J.B. Dumay led the workers' revolt at Le Creusot, proclaimed a miniature Commune, and organised a militia to resist the Prussian advance. In August 1914, after decades of faithful militancy as a socialist deputy and syndicalist official, he roamed the eastern Paris *banlieue*, pistols in belt, to establish a militia to fight the Germans. The less attractive side of this neo-Jacobinism, illustrated by the role of some Blanquists in the Boulangist movement, was its potential xenophobia and contempt for foreign workers (Cahm and Fisera, 1979).

The second discourse claimed that the proletariat had no *patrie*.

At Amiens (1906) the CGTs call for intensified anti-militarist and anti-patriotic propaganda emphasised that workers were victims of wars fought for the 'parasitic employer class'. Confusion arose because of the common assumption that anti-militarism, undoubtedly widespread, was synonymous with anti-patriotism. Hostility to the army had specific causes relating to the role of the Catholic-royalist officers in the Dreyfus affair and to army strike-breaking. The POF electoral breakthrough in Lille followed local outrage at the Fourmies massacre of unarmed working-class demonstrators (1891). Allemanists accused barracks of 'bastardising' the proletarian race by corrupting conscripts with brothels and VD; syndicalists' *Sou du Soldat* (Soldier's or Conscript's Penny) campaign attempted to keep conscripts in touch with trade unions, urging them not to fire on fellow workers.

Syndicalists sought to tap this fund of popular anti-militarism to promote 'anti-patriotism'. Bellicose imperialism would produce a senseless war, butchering proletarian conscripts for capitalist profits. A General Strike to prevent war mobilisation was the only sane response. However, the audience for this campaign proved limited, even in the Midi convulsed by regionalist revolt. Efforts to liaise with the German left were a fiasco. German unions were allied to the SPD which had helped expel the 'anarchist' CGT from the Second International and had no sympathy with general strikes, whether as revolutionary weapons or as tactics against war. The 1910 visit of CGT leaders to Germany proved a tragic farce. Snubbed by Legien, narrowly avoiding arrest before fleeing across the frontier, Yvetot's first words on regaining French territory ('Expelled from Germany, here I am in France. Salut à "Ma patrie"!') sound strange emerging from the lips of syndicalism's leading anti-patriotic orator. Syndicalists suddenly discovered unsuspected virtues in 'bourgeois' Republican liberties. They were trapped in a hopeless dilemma. How could one wage a fervent anti-militant crusade when German labour leaders appeared increasingly cautious and patriotic? (Howarth, 1985).

Syndicalist anti-militarists faced increasing repression. African penal battalions were established (March 1912) for propagandists who subverted conscripts. Lukewarm response to an anti-war strike (December 1912) convinced an increasingly pessimistic Jouhaux that collaboration with the socialists was essential. Inevitably the SFIO itself was divided. Guesdists argued that capitalism made war probable but that an anti-war strike was naïve romanticism, and the

Guesdist Nord witnessed minimal anti-militarist propaganda. Conversely Hervé's *Guerre Sociale* (circulation 60,000) won support for anti-militarism in central France where socialist peasants resented conscription which deprived small farms of family labour. Yet *Guerre Sociale* lacked any clear ideological position, even arguing sometimes that Germany should be conceded colonies to avoid war; and Hervé, disillusioned by SPD patriotism, came to question the wisdom of unilateral French anti-war activities. Jaurès and Vaillant sought to synthesise conflicting attitudes. Both were sympathetic to German culture, and active in the internationalist projects of the Second International. Both flirted with the idea of multilateral General Strikes. Yet in the last resort, both remained Jacobin-patriots. 'We too', claimed Jaurès, 'seek to defend national independence from foreign aggression. We know that in the present state of the world nations are preconditions for ... freedom ... and progress.' The more workers united to form a class 'the more they have a country' — to be defended, preferably, by a citizens' militia.

In 1913 a bill establishing extended, three-year military service was passed by Parliament in the face of strong united SFIO/CGT opposition. Its real purpose was to provide additional trained troops for a secret *offensive* strategy (Plan XVIII) and to reassure the Tsarist government of France's commitment to the alliance. However, alarmed at leftist denunciation of such bellicose plans, the bill was portrayed by the government as a *defensive* measure against an imminent German invasion. Unconvinced of the evidence for such a threat the left organised a protest campaign which won support from some Radicals, alarmed by the hostility of their peasant electors to conscription. Government newpapers wooed back some Radical waverers by portraying localised mutinies by conscripts against a third year in barracks as a subversive 'anarchist' plot — although the only evidence of treasonable activity produced by the Rouen public prosecutor after police raids on the local BT was packets of contraceptives!

The conscription issue helped the SFIO make twenty-seven gains in the 1914 election from which a centre–left government under 'independent socialist' Viviani eventually emerged. SFIO propaganda highlighted the reactionary drift of recent French politics, the onerous burden which an unjust taxation system placed on workers as the costs of the arms race escalated, and the hypocrisy of capitalist 'patriots' whose business lobbies obstructed tax reform on the ground that this would cripple industry at a time of national peril. Paradoxically, the election result may have weakened the labour movement's anti-war protests during the July Crisis. Since the real purpose of the Three-Year Act remained secret the left remained oblivious to its real implications. SFIO leaders retained naïve illusions that Republican foreign policies were *ipso facto* less bellicose than those of undemocratic monarchies. However Poincaré, the conservative-nationalist president, worried that Viviani might capitulate to socialist pressure, repeal the Act and thus weaken the army, may have felt that the war — which he saw as inevitable — should begin as soon as possible. Poincaré thus secretly encouraged Russian firmness. Ensuing German mobilisation was then interpreted by the SFIO as evidence that France faced a war of self-defence. Already dubious about the will and ability of the German left to resist war mobilisation the French labour movement made only token resistance against the slide into war (Krumeich, 1984). Since 1912–13 CGT leaders had abandoned 'direct action' tactics advocated by militants like Péricat. A few mass peace rallies were held in July, but Jouhaux's funeral oration for the assassinated Jaurès implied that martyred tribune would have rallied to national defence. When war came ex-Communard Vaillant shook hands with the social-Catholic de Mun, who as a young officer had suppressed the Commune. Guesde metamorphosed not into a Lenin but into a Minister in a government of national unity. Jouhaux was drawn into collaboration with planning the economic war effort.

Was the '*Union Sacrée*' conclusive proof of the reality of working class integration? Laic school textbooks had spoken of a single class of French citizens, never of antagonistic classes. Workers' children had been drilled in *bataillons scolaires*, and chanted patriotic songs. 'If the schoolboy does not became a soldier who loves his gun, the teacher will have wasted his time' proclaimed the doyen of *laic* education, Lavisse. For years syndicalists such as Delasalle had viewed the consequences of such indoctrination with prophetic disquiet.

And yet . . . The bitterness of labour unrest in the *belle époque* suggests that workers' support for the *patrie* in its hour of apparent need may not necessarily imply fundamental satisfaction with the status quo (Geary, 1981). The strike waves of 1917–18 suggested that the *Union Sacrée* consensus soon wore thin. The quasi-insurrectionary strikes of 1919–20 which preceded the foundation of the Communist Party must obviously be interpreted in part as the outcome of wartime hardships blended with the euphoric optimism generated by the Bolshevik Revolution. However, it would surely be rash to attribute the militancy of, say, the rail strikes of 1920 simply to wartime radicalisation and to deny any connection with the bitter memories bequeathed by the savage repression of the rail strike of 1910?

BIBLIOGRAPHY

D. Baker (1967), 'Socialism in the Nord 1880–1914', *International Review of Social History* 12, pp.357–389

L. Berlanstein (1984), *The Working People of Paris 1871–1914* (Baltimore and London)

R. Bezucha (1974), *The Lyon Uprising of 1834* (Cambridge, Mass.)

M. Boxer (1978), 'Socialism faces feminism: the failure of the synthesis in France 1879–1914', in M. Boxer and J. Quartaert (eds), *Socialist Women* (New York)

E. Cahm and V. Fisera (eds) (1979), *Socialism and Nationalism* (vol. 2; Nottingham)

G. Cross (1983) *Immigrant Workers in Industrial France: The Making of a New Laboring Class* (Philadelphia)

——— (1984), 'The quest for leisure: reassessing the eight-hour day in France', *Journal of Social History*

G. Eley (1984), 'Combining Two Histories: the S.P.D. and the German Working-class before 1914', *Radical History Review* 28–30, pp.13–44

S. Elwitt (1975), *The Making of the Third Republic: 1868–1882* (Baton Rouge, La.)

——— (1986), *The Third Republic Defended: Bourgeois Reform in France 1880–1914* (Baton Rouge, La.)

L. Frader (1981), 'The Grapes of Wrath: Vineyard Workers, labour unions and strikes in the Aude 1860–1913', in C. Tilly and L. Tilly (eds), *Class Conflict and Collective Action* (London and Beverly Hills)

D. Geary (1981), *European Labour Protest 1848–1939* (New York)

H. Goldberg (1964), *The Life of Jean Jaurès* (Madison, Wis.)

M. Hanagan (1980), *The Logic of Solidarity: Artisans and Workers in Three Industrial Towns* (Urbana, Ill.)

P. Hilden (1986), *Working Women and Socialist Politics in France 1880–1914: A Regional Study* (Oxford)

J. Howarth (1982), *Edouard Vaillant* (Paris)

—— (1985), 'French Workers and German Workers: the Impossibility of Internationalism 1900–1914', *European History Quarterly* 15, 1, pp.71–98

P. Hutton (1981), *The Cult of Revolutionary Tradition: The Blanquists in French Politics* (Berkeley, Calif.)

T. Judt (1979), *Socialism in Provence* (Cambridge)

—— (1986), *Marxism and the French Left* (Oxford)

G. Krumeich (1984), *Armaments and Politics in France on the Eve of the First World War* (Oxford)

V. Lorwin (1954), *The French Labor Movement* (Cambridge, Mass.)

J. Merriman (1985), *The Red City: Limoges and the French Nineteenth Century* (Oxford)

B. Moss (1976), *The Origins of the French Labour Movement: The Socialism of Skilled Workers* (Berkeley, Calif.)

R. Nye (1985), *Crime, Madness and Politics in Modern France: The Medical Concept of National Decline* (Princeton)

N. Papayanis (1985) *Alphonse Merrheim: The Emergence of Reformism in Revolutionary Syndicalism* (The Hague)

M. Perrot (1979), 'The Three Ages of Industrial Discipline', in J. Merriman (ed.) *Consciousness and Class Experience* (New York)

—— (1987), *Workers on Strike: France 1871–90* (Leamington Spa)

J. Reardon (1981), 'Belgian and French Workers in nineteenth-century Roubaix', in C. Tilly and L. Tilly (eds), *Class Conflict and Collective Action* (London and Beverly Hills)

M. Rébérioux (1983), 'Party Practice and the Jaurèsian Vision: The S.F.I.O. 1905–14', in S. Williams (ed.), *Socialism in France from Jaurès to Mitterrand* (Paris)

W. Reddy (1984), *The Rise of Market Culture: The Textile Trade and French Society 1750–1900* (Cambridge)

D. Reid (1985a), 'Industrial Paternalism: Discourse and Practice in French Mining and Metallurgy', *Comparative Studies in Society and History* (1985)

—— (1985b), 'The Third Republic as Manager 1892–1920: Labour Policy in the Naval Dockyards', *International Review of Social History* 30, pp.183–206

—— (1985c), *The Miners of Decazeville* (Cambridge, Mass.)

W. Schneider (1982), *An Empire for the Masses* (Westport, Conn.)

J. Scott (1974), *The Glassmakers of Carmaux* (Cambridge, Mass.)

—— (1981), 'Socialist Municipalities confront the French State', in J. Merriman (ed.), *French Cities in the Nineteenth Century* (New York)

W. Sewell (1980), *Work and Revolution: The Language of Labour from Ancien Regime to Revolution* (Cambridge)

A. Shapiro (1985), *Housing the Poor of Paris* (Madison, Wis.)

G. Sheridan (1981), *The Social and Economic Foundations of Associationism among Silk Weavers in Lyon 1852–70* (New York)

C. Sowerwine (1982), *Sisters or Citizens? Women and Socialism in France since 1876* (Cambridge)

P. Stearns (1971), *Revolutionary Syndicalism and French Labor* (New Brunswick, NJ)

P. Stearns and H. Mitchell (1971), *Workers and Protest 1890–1914* (Ithaca, NY)

M. Stein (1978), 'The Meaning of Skill: The Case of French Engine Drivers 1837–1917', *Politics and Society* 8, 3–4, pp.399–428

J. Stone (1985), *The Search for Social Peace: Reform Legislation in France 1890–1914* (Albany, NY)

E.P Thompson (1968), *The Making of the English Working Class* (London)

C. Tilly and E. Shorter (1974) *Strikes in France 1830–1968* (Cambridge)

J. Weiss (1983), 'The Origin of the French Welfare State', *French Historical Studies* 13, pp.47–78

3

SOCIALISM AND THE GERMAN LABOUR MOVEMENT BEFORE 1914

Dick Geary

Introduction

By 1914 Germany possessed the largest socialist party in the world and more workers there voted socialist than in any other country. On the eve of the First World War the German Social Democratic Party (SPD) could count over one million individual fee-paying members and had successfully mobilised more than four million voters (about one-third of the popular vote) in the Reichstag elections of 1912. This party was far more than just an impressive electoral machine, however, for it brought into existence or adopted a plethora of ancillary organisations which reached into the daily life and leisure of a significant section of the German working class. In 1914, for example, the *Arbeitersängerbund* (The Federation of Socialist Choral Societies) could boast of almost 200,000 members; *Solidarität* (Solidarity), the social-democratic cycling club, embraced more than 130,000 workers; and the popular *Arbeiter Turn–und Sportbund* (Workers' Gymnastics and Sports Federation) saw its membership climb to just under 190,000. There were in addition SPD chess, ramblers', theatrical and educational societies; and even smoking clubs, which on occasion organised 'smoking competitions'!

No less impressive was the growth of a trade union movement closely associated with German Social Democracy. These so-called Free Trade Unions were in their infancy as late as 1872, with a mere

Table 3.1 Number of employees per firm in Germany in 1882 and 1907
(as a percentage of total)

| | Size of firm (no. of employees) | | | | | |
	1–5	6–10	11–50	51–200	201–1,000	Over 1,000
	%	%	%	%	%	%
1882	59.8	4.4	13.0	11.8	9.1	1.9
1907	31.2	7.0	19.4	20.8	16.7	4.9

Source: G. Hohorst, J. Kocka and G. A. Ritter, *Sozialgeschichtliches Arbeitsbuch II* (Munich, 1978), p. 75. These figures are for employees in industry and manufacture. Levels of concentration were much higher in mining, with 58.2% of the labour force employed in pits of over 1,000 men in 1907.

19,000 members, and suffered serious setbacks under the persecution of the anti-socialist laws of 1878 to 1890. By 1914, however, the Free Trade Unions could claim a membership of 2,600,000, one of the largest figures in Europe. At the same time a further 342,000 workers, mainly Catholics, belonged to the predominantly Christian Trade Unions, 107,000 to the liberal Hirsch-Duncker Unions and another 279,000 to company ('yellow') unions.

It is obvious that the growth of labour organisation over the long term was a product of the industrialisation of Germany. Whereas industry was responsible for approximately 26% of the value of the national product in 1870, when approximately one half of the active population was still employed in agriculture, its share had increased to 41% in 1913, when less than one-third of the labour force found employment in the agrarian sector. At the same time there was a significant increase in the number of Germans employed in 'industry and manufacture', rising from 6,396,000 in 1882 to 11,256,000 in 1907, the year of the last pre-war occupational census. There was also a significant and increasingly rapid increase in the size of the tertiary sector, with trade and transport employing 1,570,000 workers in 1882 and almost 3,500,000 twenty-five years later. The percentage of wage earners, as distinct from the self-employed, within the industrial sector also grew from 56.7% in 1875 to over 76% in 1907, whilst an increasing number of these employees worked in firms of some size, as Table 3.1 demonstrates.

Germany was transformed from a predominantly agrarian society in 1860 to Europe's leading industrial nation by 1914. Although her overall wealth and national product did not match those of Great

Britain on account of the latter's massive financial and commercial empires, the Second Reich lagged behind only the United States of America as a manufacturing country. The Ruhr region, until the middle of the century almost untouched by urban and industrial life, became the centre of a huge, concentrated and integrated coal, iron and steel industry, typified by the Krupp works in Essen. Dynamic and highly skilled engineering companies established themselves in various parts of Germany: Augsburg, Nuremberg, Stuttgart, Düsseldorf, some of the Saxon industrial towns and the capital, Berlin, where the clothing and textile industry also flourished, as it did in Aachen, Barmen, Elberfeld, Bielefeld and large parts of Saxony and Silesia. Gigantic firms such as Siemens and AEG came to dominate the electrical industry, which with that sector in the USA was a world leader. Many of the chemical companies, which remain household names to this day (BASF, Bayer, Höechst), were established in this period; and by 1914 Germany controlled no less than 90% of the world's trade in chemical dyestuffs. Hamburg, the nation's second city, not only remained a successful commercial and trading port, but also became the centre of a thriving shipbuilding industry, stimulated both by the creation of the Imperial navy and by Germany's emergence—from more or less nothing—as a major mercantile power.

This process of industrialisation, was, of course, accompanied by an equally rapid and spectacular transition from rural to urban society. Between 1875 and 1914 the coal, steel and brewing town of Dortmund increase its population from 57,742 to 214,226 inhabitants. Chemnitz, a centre of the Saxon textile and engineering industries, grew from a town of just over 78,000 citizens to one of slightly less than 290,00 in the same thirty-five years. Duisburg, inland port, gateway to the Ruhr and home to many of the giant firms of heavy industry, increased in size, from 37,380 to almost 230,000 inhabitants at the same time, a population increase of almost 514%! In part such growth was a consequence of natural population increase; but it was most famously the result of a massive transfer of population, especially from the east, to the burgeoning industrial towns that were crying out for labour. This population transfer had a number of important consequences for the history of German labour, as we will see. In the first place it meant that as late as 1914 approximately half of Germany's industrial labour force were first-generation factory or mine workers. Secondly, it often meant that the newly formed work-force consisted of people from a multiplicity of backgrounds, in terms of region, race, religion and occupation. Rapidly growing industrial towns, especially those in the Ruhr, had to cope with a massive influx of rural immigrants, many of whom were Poles and Masurians and who often spoke little or no German. In the Ruhr mining town of Herne, for example, roughly one-quarter of the inhabitants on the eve of the First World War were Polish. The existence of ethnic and confessional divisions within a single area or even firm was a major factor which served to fragment the German working class and make collective action difficult.

Most obviously such a rapid and massive transfer of population placed a huge burden on the housing market. One solution to this problem in areas not already densely populated and where land prices were relatively low, such as the Ruhr, at least initially, was the provision of company housing, which had the additional advantage for the employer of enabling him to control his workers with the threat of eviction. By 1889 the Bochumer Verein, one of the largest Ruhr steel firms, owned over 1,000 dwellings. In 1906 the Krupp business could count 6,000 company dwellings; whilst a whole district of Berlin (Siemensstadt) had been built by one of the electrical giants. Such company housing tended to be more spacious than dwellings occupied by workers in the private sector (municipal housing only came into its own in Germany between the wars) and rents were, in general, more reasonable. But even in the Ruhr such housing provision did not prevent a degree of overcrowding which would these days be regarded as intolerable and which led contemporary bourgeois commentators to fear for the morality of the working class. In areas like the Ruhr, with the population expanding so rapidly and thus with a permanent housing problem and where there were few opportunities for female employment outside the home, the taking in of lodgers became essential to make ends meet for many working-class families. In Essen in 1900, 11% of all households took in six lodgers or more, 15% three and 26% two. In the Ruhr as a whole over half of all dwellings took in some lodgers; and 70% of all such households had at least one child of their own. Yet the situation was even worse in the older and already overcrowded cities such as Berlin and Hamburg, where land prices and rents were so much higher and where cramped and unhygienic living conditions were the rule. Here there arose the so-called 'rental barracks' (*Mietskasernen*), the huge and drab tenement blocks that one can still see today in the — predominantly Turkish — Kreuzberg district of Berlin, where individual families often occupied a single room and where young, single workers would often use the same bed on a shift basis.

The consequences of such appalling housing conditions for German labour can scarcely be underestimated. They rendered a satisfactory family and home life almost impossible, as was reflected in a famous survey of Berlin metalworkers shortly before the First World War: when asked what gave them satisfaction, only 7% of those surveyed mentioned the family or home. As a result male social life took place outside the home, often in the pub, which, as Karl Kautsky commented at the time, often served as the focal point of social-democratic cultural and leisure activities. The greater appeal of the SPD's ancillary organisations than of any equivalent in pre-war Britain can be explained not least by the inability of German workers to enjoy that 'modest domesticity', of which skilled British workers in single-family terraced housing could take advantage. The fact that a process of residential segregation within the working class, which creamed off the better-paid from the inner cities, was at most in its infancy in Germany before 1914, may have helped to generate a degree of class solidarity absent in the 'sectionalism' of the British working class. The relationship between older workers and newcomers may also have been cemented, at least in mining communities, by the practice of lodging, in which the lodger often became part of the 'half-open family'.

The massive growth of labour organisations in Germany after 1890 clearly correlates with the processes of industrialisation and urbanisation described above: the German Social Democratic Party was indubitably a party of manual industrial workers (to the tune of approximately 90% in 1914) in the large industrial towns of Protestant Germany, whilst both the party and the trade unions were usually disproportionately weak in small provincial towns and industrial villages. Thus it is tempting to explain trade union growth and socialist political mobilisation as a direct consequence of the infamous hardships generated by industrialisation, especially in its early stages. The horrendously cramped housing conditions have already been described; but life and work in the factory were scarcely pleasant for many. Industrial accidents, which actually increased in the period before the First World War, and industrial diseases were far from uncommon; and for the unskilled especially, long hours (thirteen a day in some textile mills in the 1890s) were rewarded with very low wages, in turn often reduced by employer fines for various forms of undisciplined behaviour. It took many a good deal of time to get used to the time-discipline of factory work; and the controls of foreman and employer generated a great deal of resentment, as did attempts to prevent the consumption of alcohol on the job. The new urban environment was equally alien to many rural immigrants, with its overcrowding and persistent disease, which almost invariably hit the proletarian quarters of the large towns hardest, as during the infamous outbreaks of cholera. Now it is certainly true that labour organisations were formed to combat these evils, to improve wages and living conditions — or at least to prevent any further deterioration; and that the socialist ideal sought to offer a qualitatitively different life to an exploited working class. But the connection between the less salutary aspects of industriali-sation on the one hand and the growth of collective working-class action and organisation on the other is far less clear or immediate than one might imagine.

The origins of collective action and organisation

In the first place the roots of trade union and socialist organisation pre-dated the dominance of large-scale factory industry in Ger-many, just as it had done in France and Britain. It is true that strike action, the formation of trade unions, co-operatives, Friendly So-cieties and educational associations on the part of German workers took on a significant size and new importance at a time of rapid economic expansion in the period between 1860 and 1873, sometimes on the initiative of workers themselves, at other times at the instigation of the middle-class liberals desirous of mobilising their support. It was also at this time that two independent working-class political parties (Ferdinand Lassalle's General Union of German Workers, and the so-called Eisenach Party of August Bebel and Wilhelm Liebknecht) came into existence. However, many of the new trade unions, especially those of the printers, skilled building workers and engineers and the tobacco workers, had roots which reached back to the craft associations of the 1840s and flourished during the temporary liberalisation of the 1848 revolutions. In Hamburg a workers' educational association could trace a continu-ous existence from the 1840s to the 1860s, despite certain changes in outlook; whilst the re-emergence of labour organisation in Berlin in 1863 and Lassalle's success there were regarded by some contemporaries as a 'rebirth' of the Brotherhood of German Workers, an organisation of artisan journeymen that had achieved some degree of prominence in that city during the events of 1848. In fact there are many cases of personal continuity between the artisan activists of 1848 and some of the later labour leaders. What is more, the trade union organisations of the 1860s and early 1870s were not created by the most impoverished groups of workers, nor did their membership comprise the unskilled working long hours in large factories or big concerns. The first sections of the German labour force to engage in trade union activity were relatively well-paid, by the admittedly low standards of the manual working class, they were skilled men and they had served apprenticeships, which not only taught them a wide variety of skills and made them difficult to replace but also initiated them into a set of attitudes concerning the dignity and importance of their trade. The organisations which such workers created were almost as often concerned to defend their skills and status against their less skilled countrymen (and foreign competition) as to combat the employer. In the 1860s and early 1870s it was just these skilled groups of workers who benefited from the economic boom, rising living standards and full employment; and to a large extent their ability to organise stemmed from this situation which enhanced their bargaining power and from the liberalisation of previously repressive laws of association in most German states. Where these men concerned themselves with politics, which the élite group of printers specifically refused to do, it was at this stage more often the politics of liberalism rather than socialism, as in the case of Berlin engineering workers.

Even those working men who did turn to the emergent German socialist movement of the 1860s, however, were not in any meaningful sense an unskilled factory proletariat. The Hamburg branch of Lassalle's General Union of German Workers, for example, was dominated by artisans or craft workers in 1868: seven out of every nine members were cigar-makers, cobblers, joiners or tailors. In Saxony in the elections to the North German Confederation's parliament in the late 1860s August Bebel won votes not in Chemnitz, the German 'Manchester' and seat of a factory textile industry, but in semi-rural areas dominated by domestic textile manufacture. Skilled workers in buoyant industries with some degree of power in the labour market stuck to their unions (e.g. printers and engineers) at this point in time, whilst political action was more the preserve of the 'degraded' artisan trades, such as cobbling and tailoring, as well as some branches of woodwork. In these trades workers with some degree of craft skill, who had served apprenticeships, had enjoyed a certain independence and known better days, found themselves threatened not so much — except in some specific trades such as nail-making and cotton-spinning — by factory competition and mechanised production as by the growth of *merchant* capitalism. Their trades were characterised by overmanning, competition from sweated labour and from off-the-peg (standardised and less skilled, albeit non-mechanised) production (*Konfektion*), most notably in tailoring. Textile workers, some cobblers and woodworkers also found themselves becoming increasingly dependent upon merchants, even where they were nominally still small 'masters'. These merchants provided the raw materials, and bought and distributed the finished product, often in markets of some scale and distance. It was also they who loaned credit in difficult times, thus tightening the bonds of artisan dependence. This explains how an ideology of 'labour' came to characterise the early socialism of both the 1840s and the 1860s: for unlike the older artisan master who had at least served an apprenticeship himself, possessed the skills of the trade and 'laboured' with his hands, the power of the merchant (some of whom had emerged from the group of larger and more successful master craftsmen) resided primarily and in some cases exclusively in his possession of capital. Hence the critique of 'parasites' and the fact that early socialism has been seen as containing 'pre-industrial' elements, especially in its concern with small-scale craft co-operative production. It was rooted in social relations which were precisely not those of mechanised factory production.

It was the case after the 1870s that both the German trade unions and the Social Democratic Party became organisations of more 'modern' factory labour. Yet once again it was not the most poorly paid or unskilled who formed the backbone of these movements. By 1914 there existed in the Second Reich thirty-nine craft and seven 'industrial' Free Trade Unions, the latter each seeking to recruit from all skill levels in one particular industry (as in the cases of construction and metalwork). Even in the industrial unions, however, it was the skilled workers who predominated: on the eve of the First World War only 18% of the German Metalworkers Union (DMV), the largest trade union in the world and one which was explicitly committed to 'industrial' rather than 'craft' principles, were semi- or unskilled labourers. Equally the SPD's *membership* was dominated by skilled men, though the electoral appeal of the party must have been much broader within the German working class, given the sheer size of its vote in national elections. In 1904 the SPD branch organisation in Leipzig was composed in the following way: 138 recruits from the lower middle class, 200 unskilled workers, but over 1,300 plumbers, painters, bricklayers, printers and other skilled men. In Baden skilled engineering workers, woodworkers and printers were prominent in social-democratic organisations, whilst the Hamburg party branch was similarly the preserve of skilled building and woodworkers as well as printers. This suggests that grievance and poverty alone were not sufficient to generate collective industrial or political organisation on the part of wage earners (though it is true that certain groups of less skilled men and women with relatively low levels of organisation could and did engage to an increasing and sometimes successful extent in strike action, as in the case of textile workers and dockers). Rather it was those in a position to defend themselves or even make gains, those with a certain level of expectations, traditions of organisation and bargaining strength in the labour market, who were the first to form stable organisations.

That low wages, appalling factory conditions and poor housing do not suffice to explain the emergence of collective labour protest is further demonstrated by the *timing* of trade union organisation, strike action and political mobilisation. Strikes and especially strike waves (clusters of more or less simultaneous strikes embracing more than one industry), as well as to an even greater degree trade union formation, tended to occur not in times of economic depression and unemployment (the late 1870s and early 1880s), but at upturns in the trade cycle, as in the massive boom of the 1869–73 period or between 1905 and 1907. In such economic conjunctures workers often had to do overtime to fulfil expanding order books and experienced an increased pace of work. Such times also tended to be ones of marked price inflation, which eroded wage gains in real terms. These then were the stimuli to action. But crucially these periods increased the *ability* of workers, especially the skilled, to take action: economic boom meant a tight labour market, full employment and often in key sectors an actual shortage of labour, which granted the work-force a bargaining strength *vis-à-vis* its employers which did not exist at times of recession, when unemployment robbed labour of its industrial muscle and meant that militant workers were relatively easy to replace. The bargaining power of skilled workers who had served lengthy apprenticeships further explains why it was they who mounted the most successful strikes, some of which were of an 'offensive' nature, in so far as they aimed not just to defend existing living standards but to *improve* them. Their weaker and less skilled colleagues were more likely to engage in 'defensive' strikes to preserve existing rates of pay and work processes. Significantly such defensive strikes were less likely to correlate with upturns in the business cycle; and not least for this reason they were more likely to be unsuccessful.

As we have already seen, the period between 1890 and 1914 witnessed an unprecedented and massive expansion of the membership of both the trade union movement and the German Social Democratic party. There also took place a marked escalation of industrial conflict at the same time, in terms of both the number of strikes and the number of strikers: 321,000 German workers came out in 1,468 strikes in 1900; 681,000 in 3,228 in 1910 (the peak year in number of *strikes* before the First World War); and over 1,000,000 workers in 2,834 strikes in 1912 (the peak year for the number of *strikers*). An increasing percentage of these strikes were 'organised', in the sense that they saw some degree of trade union involvement. Others, however, were more 'spontaneous', were the acts of the less well organised; and some were undertaken by trade unionists but in defiance of the official trade union leadership. In connection with this last point, one commentator spoke of a 'syndicalist undercurrent' in the German labour movement in the years immediately before the outbreak of war. From 1905 in the German building industry, down the mines and amongst skilled metalworkers there occurred a significant number of strikes which led to overt conflict between the local rank and file of the unions and the official and extremely cautious national leadership, as in the Hamburg dock strike of 1913. Whatever the origin or nature of these strikes, however, one thing is quite clear: the escalation of industrial conflict in Wilhelmine Germany did *not* occur at a time of declining living standards, but rather the reverse.

There was a more or less continuous rise in German real wages from 1880 to 1900; and although historians differ as to whether real wages continue to rise significantly or whether they stagnated between 1900 and 1914, no one argues that they actually fell or that there was a decline in living standards. The length of the working day also declined significantly in the last two decades before the First World War. In the case of Silesian coalminers, for example, 45% still worked a twelve-hour day in 1891. By 1910 only 9.4% of these miners had to work so many hours, and for 70% of them the ten-hour day had become the norm. That the German economy was in a state of more or less continual boom between 1896 and 1914 (with only minor hiccups in 1903–4 and 1907–9) meant the insecurity bred of widespread unemployment was almost absent. At the same time the welfare measures of Bismarckian and later governments, which saw the introduction of old-age pensions and sickness benefits, albeit on a relatively slight scale, certainly did nothing to worsen the lot of the German working class. Thus increased strike activity, trade union mobilisation and the rise of the SPD to a mass party in no sense correlate with increased poverty.

This is not meant to suggest that the Wilhelmine working class was not confronted with any degree of economic hardship; and the concept of an 'affluent' working class before 1914 is simply ludicrous. Although wages did rise significantly before 1900, the increase in the value of real wages between then and 1914 was much less marked on account of price inflation. At the same time the increased strength and organisation of German employers, to which we will return, enabled them to counter strikes with increasingly effective lock-outs. This was precisely why the national leadership of trade unions became increasingly cautious in this period; which further explains the tension between it and a rank and file faced with inflation. Some workers still had to suffer joblessness on a seasonal basis (building workers and those in the garment industry), whilst others lost jobs in downturns of the trade cycle (as in 1907–9). It is in any case obviously difficult to generalise about the 'living standards' of *the* working class. Differentials between regions, between different trades, above all between the skilled and the unskilled and between male and female labour remained large, and in the last case massive. Size of family, whether husband and wife were both wage earners, even different styles of expenditure, all affected the degree of comfort of working-class existence. Ill-health and increasing age also produced poverty and insecurity on no small scale. The modern welfare state was a long way away; and even if the real wages of the German working class did increase in the pre-war period, they increased nothing like as rapidly as profits and dividends. Furthermore, the working class of Imperial Germany not only experienced many of the traditional hardships associated with manual labour. New threats were also emerging. Certain technological innovations seemed to strike at the status, skills and security of the craftsman. The use of concrete, iron and steel, and of prefabricated wooden

units altered labour processes in the building industry. Glass-
bottling plants reduced the demand for the skilled blower. More
specialised and in some cases automatic lathes, combined with new
drilling and grinding machines disposed of some of the traditional
skills in engineering and led to the increased employment of semi-
skilled labour. Petrol engines and the increased application of
electric power even threatened the lot of the unskilled in lifting and
hauling occupations.

Yet it would be wrong to stress the de-skilling of craftsmen in the
period before 1914. In the German engineering industry, for example, the systematic introduction of American lathes and the employment of female rather than male labour was very definitely the
exception rather than the rule, even in the largest factories. Before
1914, technological innovation rarely meant the advent of intercon-
nected processes run from a single power source, but rather the
introduction of single machines, whose repair and maintenance still
demanded high levels of skill from the labour force. Where there
was fully mechanised mass production, as in some branches of the
textile and chemical industries, jobs were filled not by dequalified
formerly skilled men but by unskilled workers, often from rural
backgrounds. Having said this, all sections of the German labour
force were subjected to increased demands on the factory floor,
sometimes as a result of newer and faster machinery and processes
of production, but primarily as a result of the intensification of
labour. Hours at work may have been reduced, but productivity
during those hours increased dramatically as a result of an increased
division of labour, new systems of payment and employer supervision. Under these circumstances some German metalworkers actually complained of nervous exhaustion. It was such factors, together
with inflationary pressures, which stimulated large-scale industrial
unrest between 1910 and 1912 in particular.

To return to the main argument: the lot of the German working
class before the First World War Varied enormously from time
to time, region to region, trade to trade, sex to sex, but it certainly
was not worsening at the time when trade unions and the SPD
experienced unprecedented growth. Furthermore it was relatively
well-off men (by working-class standards) who formed the rank and
file of these movements. The absence of less skilled workers from
trade unions or German Social Democracy should not surprise us.
The unskilled lacked the traditions of organisation which in the case
of some craft workers went back to the days of the guild. This is one

of the reasons why both the unions and the SPD were stronger in the older industrial towns, such as Leipzig, Hamburg and Berlin, than in the newer and rapidly expanding towns of the Ruhr. The fact that the unskilled entered the world of industrial labour with relatively low expectations, that many came from rural backgrounds, from different kinds of family backgrounds and occupations, sometimes speaking different languages, all militated against *collective* action and organisation. New networks of communication had to be built between such disparate individuals or groups of workers, both through common experience at work (though work experience could often set older and younger workers against one another where group piece-rates were paid, as in the mines, or skilled workers on piece-rates against the unskilled on hourly wages) and in the residential community. Indeed it was if anything more in the neighbourhood, through shared accommodation and common leisure pursuits, often in the public house, that unity was forged; and the overcoming of fragmentation and sectionalism within the working class required the active intervention of party and union. In this sense class solidarity was as much *created* as a natural consequence of industrialisation. It has also been argued by some German historians that solidarity can only really come about with the creation of a 'hereditary proletariat', i.e. when the workers of different backgrounds intermarry and produce, as it were, a second generation of factory workers. As a result there was often a 'time-lag' (Eric Hobsbawm) between the formation of an industrial labour force and its subsequent participation in the organisations of the labour movement. This implies that the 'uprooting' associated with migration and the transition from rural to industrial society constituted a barrier rather than a help to successful organisation in the short term: it was the settled, resident craftsmen who first organised, not the immigrants.

This is not to say that these newcomers to urban and industrial Germany were in any sense 'contented', whatever that might mean; and their dissatisfaction was expressed in a variety of what might be described as individualistic responses—absenteeism ('Blue Monday') was rife in the pits, whilst job changing (from firm to firm or even from one occupation to another) was common, with labour turnover approaching 150% per annum in the Ruhr mines shortly before the outbreak of war. Once again, however, such individualistic actions, though common to large numbers of men, were scarcely conducive to *collective* protest or organisation; and whether they can be legitimately interpreted as 'protest' is a matter of some debate. Absenteeism, for example, might be regarded as some form of protest against the employer, but could as easily be seen (and has been) as a continuation of pre-industrial forms of behaviour, when men were not subjected to the labour discipline of an industrial age. At the most banal level absenteeism might stem from nothing more than a hangover!

The economic situation of the unskilled was the most basic factor which made their participation in industrial or political organisations unlikely. By definition the unskilled lacked bargaining power in the labour market and were easily replaced, especially at times of recession. Thus strike action or overt participation in socialist politics was at best risky, and could lead to dismissal and bring about financial disaster in the days before the welfare state. It was, furthermore, precisely the unskilled who in most situations worked the longest hours for the lowest wages. As a result they simply had neither the time, the resources, nor the energy to sustain successful organisation, though they were capable of quite elemental and violent forms of protest when traditional authority broke down, as in Germany at the end of the First World War, when many of the previously unorganised, especially in the Ruhr, became involved in syndicalist and left-communist movements. It is also the case that less skilled workers did sometimes join trade unions, especially during strike waves and in especially favourable upturns in the trade cycle; but the trade union mobilisation of the unskilled itself tended to be cyclical and was often rapidly quashed by downturns in the economy or by a counter-offensive on the part of the employers.

The weakness of German labour, especially of the less skilled, in the face of their employers is a crucial factor which distinguished the German situation from that in Britain. In part this was a function of the high levels of concentration in German heavy industry, chemicals and electro-technology. This made it easier for employers to organise and embark upon common strategies to counter labour organisation. That industrialisation in Imperial Germany was less labour-intensive than in Victorian Britain, as a result of the introduction of more modern technology, also left German firms less vulnerable to the withdrawal of skilled labour. The protection of German industry's prices through protective tariffs (after 1879) and cartels meant that the employers could sit out industrial disputes more comfortably than their British counterparts, who were vulnerable to domestic and overseas competition in a non-protected market. In this situation German industry was able to adopt a series of strategies to tie workers to their employers and make successful industrial action and trade union organisation difficult.

The renowned 'paternalism' of German employers was no simple consequence of religious or ethical values, or a bad conscience. In part it was intended to attract and keep a labour force in circumstances of high labour turnover and sometimes labour shortage; but the provision of company houses, schools and clinics, the introduction of pension and sickness insurance schemes, most notably by the industrial giants of coal, iron and steel (Krupp in Essen, Stumm-Halberg in the Saarland), but also in the newer sectors of electro-technology (Siemens) and chemicals (BASF), could be manipulated to guarantee quiescence on the part of employees: for the company house had to be vacated and company welfare benefits were often forfeited if a worker fell foul of his employer by participating in industrial unrest or joining the SPD. Some Ruhr industrialists paid bonuses to workers who informed on those of their colleagues who joined trade unions. Many employers agreed upon 'blacklists' of union and political 'agitators'; and some tried to control the hiring of labour by the development of employer labour exchanges, which was especially effective in the days before a national and state-funded system of labour exchanges. Increasingly, especially after the industrial militancy of 1903–5, German firms resorted to a relatively successful strategy of lock-outs to defeat strike action; whilst many companies created 'yellow' (i.e. company) trade unions, financed by the bosses and dedicated to co-operation and industrial peace. By 1914 the yellow unions had a nationwide membership of 279,000 workers and were larger in the iron and steel plants of the Ruhr than was the Metalworkers' Union (DMV). In the BASF chemical plant at Ludwigshafen over 50% of the work-force had joined the company union by 1914; 82% of the Berlin labour force of Siemens had done the same! Under these circumstances the apparent quiescence of many workers, but especially of the unskilled, is scarcely surprising, though it should not be construed as 'satisfaction' with the status quo. We know that even some yellow union members of BASF in Ludwigshafen voted for the SPD in the Reichstag elections, which were conducted by secret ballot; and that, as already mentioned, workers organised and protested *where able*. Thus when employer controls over labour crumbled in the revolutionary upheavals at the end of the First World War, between 1918 and 1923, many of the previously unorganised workers in the giant plants of the Thyssen concern in Mühlheim (Ruhr) and Gelsenkirchen turned to anarcho-syndicalism and a left-wing variant of communism. There is even evidence that some of the most radical workers in the civil war which engulfed the Ruhr in 1920 had been members of company unions and thus defenders of industrial peace before 1914!

The archetype of the unskilled worker and of the unorganised was female. This is not to say that no women organised: in fact the SPD's women's organisation recruited around 200,000 members by 1914, making it probably the largest women's organisation in the world at that time. It was also true that the continued growth in the membership of the German Social Democratic Party after 1908 was due to this influx of female members, for the male membership had begun to stagnate. Significantly, however, most of these women socialists were not factory workers but 'housewives': in the main they were married to craftsmen, themselves already SPD members, and rarely worked outside the home. This suggests that their mobilisation took place primarily through the home and family environment, at least in the first instance. In any case women remained grossly under-represented in a party of over one million members. The same applied to the membership of the trade unions in Wilhelmine Germany. In 1912 only 4.5% of the liberal Hirsch-Duncker trade unionists were female. The figures for the Christian and the Socialist Free Trade Unions were 7.9% and 8.7% respectively. Female participation in strikes was somewhat more common; and some of the greatest disputes in the Saxon textile industry after the turn of the century, such as those in Chemnitz and Crimmitschau, were primarily the actions of women. Women also played a major role in helping to sustain the strikes and picketing of their menfolk. Yet it remains the case that female workers proved much more difficult to organise on a permanent basis than males.

This can be explained in the first instance in terms that are not gender-specific but which relate to the nature of women's work. Women workers were disproportionately concentrated in sectors in which men too scarcely organised: agriculture, domestic service, cottage industry, unskilled textile manufacture. As a result they often worked in trades that were geographically dispersed and in which communication was difficult. They were poorly paid and had to endure some of the longest working days. Thus their difficulties were precisely those of their unskilled male colleagues: they had little bargaining power, were easily replaced and did not possess the resources to sustain successful organisation. However, these difficulties of organisation were compounded by additional and more sexually specific factors. Their working hours tended to be even more numerous than those of their male colleagues, especially where — as was usually the case — they had to perform household chores in addition to factory labour; and they were paid even lower wages (often half to a third of the going male rate for the same job). Of considerable significance is the fact that the overwhelming majority of women in factory employment were single and aged between 16 and 21 years. In 1907 only 26% of female factory workers were married, and the vast majority of these came from families with very low incomes, whilst 40% were widowed. The conclusion is inescapable: most women who worked outside the home did so because they *had to*. For most, factory work was but a transitional stage in life before marriage. (Given the low wages and often appalling factory conditions this can hardly surprise.) This factor compounded the difficulty of those organisations which sought to recruit female members on a permanent basis.

These arguments apply to both the industrial and the political mobilisation of women; but additional factors intrude to explain the distance between the SPD and most of German womanhood. Apart from the fact that the law forbade women to join political parties or attend their meetings in many parts of Germany, most notably in Prussia, before 1908, when a new Imperial Law of Association was introduced, and the fact that women simply did not have the vote before 1914, the different relationship that existed between the churches and the two sexes cannot be discounted. As we will see, German Social Democracy enjoyed its greatest successes in those parts of the Reich that were Protestant but in which religious observance was already weak. It was far less successful in Catholic areas and in areas in which the process of secularisation was less advanced. In this context the fact that women continued to attend the churches in much greater numbers than men is of some importance. In Berlin in the 1890s the majority of Protestant communicants were female, whilst 62% of those who had left the Evangelical church of that city by 1913 were male. Now although the SPD proclaimed religion to be a 'private matter', precisely so as not to alienate potential support from church-goers, its official ideology was atheistic; and so it was perceived as a materialistic and godless

movement, not least because many of its members revealed an open
hostility, contempt and scorn for both the church and church-goers
in their daily behaviour. To the many women, for whom the church
played an important role in their lives (perhaps the only important
one outside family and home), the SPD may thus have appeared
alien and godless. (Significantly, when women were enfranchised in
1919 they were more likely to vote for the parties most closely
associated with the churches (Centre Party if Catholic, German
National People's Party if Evangelical) than for any of the left-wing
organisations.) It is also probable that some women were put off by
the admittedly unofficial but nonetheless rampant sexism of male
trade unionists and party members. The former continued to blame
women for 'stealing' male jobs at times of economic recession;
whilst even the world of organised Social Democracy was one of
pubs, clubs, and masculinity.

So far we have seen that the emergence of collective working-
class organisations in Germany before the First World War was
no immediate or simple consequence of the problems and hardships spawned by industrialisation, and that such organisations
were usually the preserve of skilled males. In this respect the
experience of Imperial Germany differed little from that of other
industrial nations. The development of trade unions and working
class associational life also bore a striking resemblance to developments elsewhere, at least as far as industrial matters were
concerned. Where Germany was somewhat unique was firstly in
the rapidity with which certain sections of the working class
adopted *independent* and radical politics (namely in the 1860s),
and secondly in the scale of support given thereafter to the
socialist movement, as indicated by the figures at the start of this
chapter.

The politicisation of German labour

In the 1860s German workers emulated their British, Belgian and
French counterparts in forming Friendly Societies, co-operative
organisations, educational associations and trade unions, sometimes
— except in the last case — in alliance with progressive liberals,
sometimes on their own initiative. Some of these workers, however,
also became involved in the activities of two political parties, which
by the end of the 1860s had adopted expressly socialist prog-

rammes, albeit in both cases of a very eclectic nature, and which specifically addressed their message at and claimed to represent *workers*. These parties were: the General Union of German Workers, founded by Ferdinand Lassalle in 1863 and recruiting workers primarily from Prussia and Northern Germany, and a party based primarily in Saxony, led by Wilhelm Liebknecht and August Bebel and which came to be known as the Eisenach Party in 1869. Partly as a result of pressure from the rank-and-file membership of both organisations, experiencing common struggles against employers and government, but above all as a result of persecution at the hands of the newly founded Imperial state (especially in Prussia, where the new chief prosecutor, Hermann Tessendorf, was successful in bringing to trial a number of trade unionists and radical politicians), these two parties came together at a conference in Gotha in 1875 to form what subsequently became known as the German Social Democratic Party (*Sozialdemokratische Partei Deutschlands*). After two unsuccessful attempts on the life of the Kaiser in no way connected with the social-democratic movement, Bismarck was none the less able to steer through the Reichstag an 'exceptional' law against socialists, under which between 1878 and 1890, when the legislation was not renewed, the SPD and all other organisations suspected of socialist sympathies were closed down by the authorities, many socialists were arrested or deported to other parts of Germany deemed to be less dangerous than the centres of socialist agitation, 150 periodicals and 1,500 books were banned, and even trade union activity became more or less impossible. The SPD survived this onslaught and in fact increased its support in these years of persecution, which came to be seen as the 'heroic years' by the party faithful; and in fact the persecution not only failed to destroy the party but radicalised its membership, and led to a process of theoretical clarification which culminated in the adoption at the Erfurt party congress of 1891 of a programme written by Karl Kautsky that was avowedly Marxist: it proclaimed the inevitability of class conflict and economic crisis, and saw the only solution to the exploitation of the proletariat as residing in the socialisation of the means of production. With the ending of the anti-socialist laws in 1890, the SPD was able to enjoy what might best be described as a 'semi-legal' existence, for reasons that will become clear later, and achieved unparalleled success in mobilising a veritable army of supporters. By 1914 the SPD was Germany's largest political party and, despite extremely unfair electoral boundaries, which grossly under-represented urban areas and thus socialist voters, held no fewer than 110 seats in the Reichstag.

As we have already seen, this striking success is not easily ascribed to poverty or declining living standards, given what was happening to real wages and the kind of workers who joined the party. We therefore have to look elsewhere for the roots of radical politics amongst the German working class, especially as the industrial proletariat of certain other countries, such as the United States and Britain, rarely found the socialist message appealing at any stage before the First World War. It is a matter of some debate about the extent to which official party ideology or the work of political theorists explains the mobilisation of 'ordinary' workers behind the banner of socialism, though in the persons of Karl Kautsky, Rosa Luxemburg, Parvus (Israel Helphand) and other Marxist intellectuals the SPD had more than its fair share of such theorists. We know that even amongst organised workers only a small minority availed themselves of the library facilities provided by party and trade unions: in Hamburg the overall figure was 3%! We also know that those workers who did use these libraries rarely read the Marxist classics (with the singular exceptions of Bebel's *Woman and Socialism* and Kautsky's *Economic Doctrines of Karl Marx*) but preferred vocational textbooks which improved their skills, works of evolutionary biology and above all historical fiction, with the writings of Alexander Dumas being especially popular! In any case, even if political theory did have a meaning for the SPD's rank and file, we still need to explain what made a radical message more appealing than the more cautious but less taxing politics of reformism; for just to be a Social Democrat was to risk the ire of employer and policeman in Imperial Germany. Both the politicisation and radicalisation of working-class attitudes in Imperial Germany after 1860 were related to, if not directly caused by, a set of interacting factors: the role and attitude of the German bourgeoisie, the policies adopted by German employers towards their labour force, and above all the nature of the Imperial *state* before 1914. These factors were then reinforced by certain residential factors described earlier.

The nineteenth century saw a rapid expansion not only of a new industrial working class but also of an industrial, commercial and professional middle class, stemming from the growth of trade and industry, the role of the modern state and its servants, and the servicing of civil needs by an army of lawyers, doctors, engineers, journalists and so on. Many expected this growing middle class to be the bearer of liberal values, to challenge autocracy and to bring about a 'bourgeois revolution', which would introduce democratic reform and civil liberties. This, after all, was what had appeared to happen in the USA, France and nineteenth-century Britain; or so some people thought. In Germany a liberal movement did exist and experienced significant growth in the 1830s and 1840s. But it found its hopes cruelly dashed in the repression that followed the revolutions of 1848–9, not least because of its own internal divisions and inconstancy. Such a movement re-emerged in the early 1860s and in Prussia challenged the power of the monarch in the constitutional crisis of 1861–3. Once again, however, it was the King and in particular his chief minister, Otto von Bismarck, who emerged victorious. Thereafter the liberal movement split and declined in strength, whilst a significant section of the German middle class came to support semi-authoritarian government against the forces of change. The abolition of restrictions on trade and industry in the 1860s, national unification and the fear of an emergent socialist movement served to increase middle-class identification with the Imperial state, even if it was one in which democratic institutions were not sovereign. Intermarriage with the aristocratic families of the agrarian élite, the purchase of East Elbian noble estates (*Rittergüter*) on the part of wealthy merchants and businessmen, the ennoblement of bourgeois entrepreneurs all helped in the process that was characterised then, as now, as the 'feudalisation' of the German middle class, many of whose members prided themselves on their position of Reserve Officer in the Prussian army. Tariffs won over heavy industry, whilst jingoistic foreign policy evinced middle-class enthusiam. Indeed navalism and *Weltpolitik* were more keenly supported in bourgeois than in aristocratic circles.

Although the German middle class was divided over the issue of protectionism and the extent of further constitutional reform, the 'red peril', exploited effectively by governmental propaganda, led many to prefer the political present rather than the dangers which might unfold with a democratisation of the Reich, a process that could only increase the power and influence of the ever-growing but as yet politically impotent and ostracised social-democratic movement. 'Lib–Lab' politics, characterised by co-operation and alliance between middle-class liberals and a working-class constituency (which remained so much the order of the day in Britain before the First World War and which had seen some temporary success in Germany in the 1860s, when a not inconsiderable number of craftsmen gave their support to the liberal movement) was mostly notable by its absence in Imperial Germany, except in some of the Southern states, most notably Baden, where a certain degree of co-operation in both associational life and high politics was noticeable between Social Democrats of reformist persuasion and local middle-class liberals. As the German bourgeoisie moved increasingly to the political right, with the National Liberals abandoning their call for reform of the discriminatory franchise in Prussia (of which more anon), so independent working-class politics became more rather than less likely; and this in turn fuelled middle-class neurosis in a kind of vicious circle. German liberalism collapsed in the face of mass politics: the mass politics of Social Democracy on the left, the mass politics of the agrarian right, exemplified most obviously by the *Bund der Landwirte* (Agrarian League), and the mass politics of German Catholicism, expressed not only in a political party (the Centre) and the Christian trade unions, but also in mass popular associations such as the People's Association for a Catholic Germany (*Volksverein für das katholische Deutschland*) and artisan and youth clubs. The *Mittelstand* (lower-middle class of small shopkeepers and businessmen, independent artisans) also mobilised and in 1913 joined with the Agrarian League and the Central Association of German Industrialists to form a reactionary anti-socialist alliance, the *Kartell der schaffenden Stände* (Cartel of Productive Estates), known to its social-democratic enemies as the Kartell der raffenden Hände ('cartel of grasping hands'). In Imperial Germany independent and radical working-class politics was very much the product of this isolation.

A second factor which led many workers to embrace radical and independent politics was the behaviour of Germany's employers before 1914. We have already seen that the adoption of various 'paternalistic' welfare measures on the part of large companies stemmed from a variety of motives, not least the desire to increase control over the labour force. Some employers placed greater emphasis on the loyalty of their workers than on formal qualifications or individual ability; and many refused to recognise trade unions or deal with workers' representatives, regarding this as an infringement of managerial prerogatives. This emerges clearly from the data concerning collective wage agreements in Germany before the First World War. By 1914 no more than approximately 16% of the

Table 3.2 Number of workers covered by collective wage agreements in certain industries in Britain and Germany

	Britain (1910)	Germany (1913)
Textiles	460 000	16 000
Metalwork	230 000	1 376
Mining	900 000	82 (!)

Source: Peter N. Stearns, *Lives of Labour* (London, 1975) p. 165 and p. 180.

German labour force was covered by such agreements. They were uncommon in the textile industry and almost completely absent in chemicals and heavy industry, as a comparison with contemporary British industry makes clear (see Table 3.2).

The few areas of industry in which German employers were prepared or forced to negotiate were printing, the skilled building trades, woodwork, and smaller-scale firms in light engineering. In 1913 two-thirds of all collective wage agreements in Germany were in firms employing fewer than twenty workers, whilst just over 30% were in firms of under five employees. In fact it was only in those sectors which depended upon a constant supply of highly skilled labour, where that labour was strongly unionised, and where employers were fragmented in a large number of relatively small concerns and thus weak in the labour market, that negotiation became the rule. The situation was completely different in coal, iron, steel, chemicals and the electrical industry, which in Germany were highly concentrated and cartellised and where employers were strongly organised. Conversely, the fact that labour was less skilled and less unionised in these sectors enabled the giant firms to refuse union recognition or negotiation. The high level of concentration and organisation also allowed employers to develop effective black-lists of agitators, to counter labour militancy by the development of 'yellow' unions and the use of the lock-out. In 1900 some 14,630 employees were locked out by their bosses in industrial disputes. Only five years later the figure was no fewer than 144,047 workers; whilst a single lock-out in the German building industry in 1910 laid idle 170,000 men.

The significant point in all this is that in industrial disputes German labour found itself confronted by a powerful adversary. In the period immediately before the outbreak of war lock-outs enjoyed a higher success rate than strikes; and the strikes of the

1910–13 period in Germany were far less successful than those taking place in Britain at the same time. Thus a large section of the German labour force could find little redress for its grievances through industrial struggle. This explains both the caution of trade union leaders and Rosa Luxemburg's famous dictum that trade union activity was a 'labour of Sisyphus'. It may also explain why more German workers turned to the political arena for a solution to their problems than did their considerably more successful counterparts in Britain, who enjoyed a relatively generous climate of industrial relations.

By far the most significant factor in the politicisation and radicalisation of German labour, however, was the role of the state. Firstly, even 'bread-and-butter' questions in Imperial Germany could not be disentangled from the issue of political power, unlike the situation in free-trading England. Food prices were determined not just by 'market forces' but by agricultural import duties imposed in 1879 and 1902 to protect German agriculture in general and aristocratic grain-producers in East Elbia in particular (the famous — or infamous — Junker) against cheaper foreign produce. Thus the SPD could and did make considerable electoral propaganda on consumerist issues, out of the fact that the state protected some, especially the agrarian élite (which still played such a prominent, though declining, role in government, the army and bureaucracy) at the expense of urban consumers, who found it impossible to buy foodstuffs as cheaply as their more fortunate British counterparts. A not dissimilar point could be and was made about the taxation system of Germany's Second Reich. The massive increase in government expenditure in the period before the First World War, partly as a result of welfare measures but primarily as a consequence of arms spending and the construction of the Kaiser's pet navy, was funded mostly by indirect taxation on articles of consumption rather than by progressive income taxation, thus hitting the poorer sections of the community disproportionately hard. At the same time, and incredibly, the state even gave a subsidy to large schnapps distillers (the so-called *Liebesgabe*), who were again normally large landowners. Conversely property taxes, and especially taxes on landed property, remained extremely low. In Imperial Germany you did not need to read Marx to know that the state benefited some at the expense of others.

Discrimination was even clearer in the constitutional systems of most of the states (Länder) which made up the federal Empire.

Some of these states, most significantly those with a large industrial working class (Prussia, Saxony, Hamburg) had adopted electoral systems which categorised low income earners as, at best, second-class citizens. Thus the infamous three-class franchise in Prussia divided the electorate into three classes according to income, with the result that a small number of wealthy electors in Class I had the same voting power as a larger number of middle incomes in Class II and an infinitely larger number of low income earners in Class III. In 1903 a contemporary Social Democrat, Paul Hirsch, claimed that 238,885 electors in Class I were matched by 856,914 voters in Class II but over 6 million voters in Class III. Such discrimination was reinforced by various underhand practices: during the 1903 Prussian Landtag elections, for example, polling stations opened only in the early afternoon in some places, thus making it difficult for many workers to cast their vote. If anything was likely to generate an awareness of class and discrimination this was surely it, as is testified by the massively popular campaigns and demonstrations against the three-class suffrage in Prussia between 1905 and 1914. On the basis of such suffrages the composition of the regional parliaments (Landtage) was determined; and these state bodies possessed considerable power. At first sight the system of national elections to the Reichstag was less unjust: all males aged twenty-five and over had a secret and equal vote. Yet this should not lead one to assume that the Second Reich was a democratic and parliamentary state. Essentially the Reichstag was not the centre of decision making, was not sovereign: the Chancellor and his ministers were responsible not to the elected representatives of the people in parliament but to the Kaiser, by whom they were appointed and dismissed, whilst certain areas of policy, in particular foreign policy, were the exclusive preserve of the monarch. Thus the SPD, easily the largest vote winner of all German political parties by the 1912 elections, was no nearer *power* and Eduard Bernstein's vision of a parliamentary road to socialism made little sense in Imperial Germany. A further form of discrimination resided in the fact that electoral boundaries were so drawn as to favour rural rather than urban voters, i.e. conservatives rather than Social Democrats; and this situation became worse with urbanisation, despite certain boundary revisions.

Obviously the national electoral system enabled workers to express their discontent through support for oppositional candidates; but the exclusion of their deputies from decision-making generated frustration rather than integration. The introduction of universal male suffrage, however, first to the North German Confederation (that area annexed by Prussia after her victory over Austria in 1866 and formed in 1867), and then to the newly created Reich in 1871, undoubtedly furthered the cause of socialism. At this time most German political parties had little or no formal structure, but were rather, as in the case of the liberals, controlled by cliques of *Honoratioren* (local notables). Thus, unlike the British case, where strong party machines were able to manage the gradual and never complete — even for men — expansion of the electorate before 1914, the sudden extension of the franchise in Germany opened up a political vacuum which could be and was exploited by new political parties speaking the language of *class*. Yet, as stated above, working-class political parties were excluded from the national polity before 1914. Furthermore, their members and supporters were subjected to a barrage of governmental hostility embodied in legislation of numerous kinds.

The most notorious example of state repression was, of course, the so-called 'exceptional' legislation against socialists, which was introduced after two attempts on the life of the Kaiser in 1878, and which remained in existence until 1890. Under this legislation the SPD was outlawed, many of its members arrested or deported to less sensitive areas of the Reich, and its literature banned. Significantly the police moved not just against the political organisations of labour in this period but also against strikers and the embryonic trade unions. It was this 'heroic' period of persecution which was crucial in turning so many workers towards socialism. For example, the unions of engineers and printers had remained hostile to social-democratic politics in the 1860s and had pursued élitist and section-alist policies of recruitment. By the end of the anti-socialist laws they found themselves in the socialist camp. Up until the 1880s the theory of the various socialist organisations had been eclectic in nature, not to say downright confused; and many looked to the state for a solution to their economic problems — hence the 'state-socialism' of Johann Rodbertus, Eugen Dühring and Ferdinand Lassalle. Persecution, on the other hand, coupled with the economic depression of 1878–96, seemed to demonstrate the validity both of the Marxian prognosis of capitalist crisis and of its insistence that the state was an instrument of class rule. The adoption of a Marxist programme at Erfurt in 1891 on the part of a radicalised SPD rank and file was scarcely surprising under these circumstances. Thus the social-democratic parliamentarian, Wilhelm Hasenclever, said to the Prussian Minister of the Interior, Puttkammer, in the Reichstag: 'your anti-socialist law has created another bond for us, the bond of all the persecuted — this bond unites us — Herr von Puttkammer, you have made us into a true party'.

It should be emphasised, nonetheless, that persecution did not cease with the demise of the 'exceptional law' in 1890. In Imperial Germany workers could be and were arrested for insulting the Kaiser, the Chancellor, the Bundesrat (a federal council which controlled Reichstag business) and even the Russian Tsar; and not a few socialist newspaper editors were imprisoned for contravention of these regulations. In Prussia the Law of Association forbade political involvement on the part of women and minors; and although replaced by a national law in 1908 which was somewhat more liberal, that new law was often harsher than what had hitherto been prevailing practice in many of the other German states. Police permission was required for public meetings, which were often dissolved by the ever-present policeman. In 1912 the local branches of the Free Trade Unions were declared to be 'political organisations', which brought them under the jurisdiction of the laws of association and further demonstrates that there was no unilinear process of liberalisation in the *Kaiserreich*. Furthermore, such laws were applied in a discriminatory fashion: they were rarely used against nationalist meetings or employers' organisations.

What needs to be stressed, as we have already seen of the period 1878 to 1890, is that the harassment of labour organisation was not restricted to the *political* sphere but was also extended to the world of industrial conflict. Various laws prevented the unionisation of rural labourers, domestic servants and railway workers in Prussia. Large strikes often saw the intervention of armed police and troops, as in the great miners' strikes of 1889 and 1912, leading to fatalities on both occasions. Moreover, whereas British and French workers could at least blame democratically elected governments for hostile policies and thus hope that a change in government would bring about a change in policy, German workers were faced with police action dictated by an essentially unelected state apparatus. (Again, the appeal of Marxism is scarcely surprising under these circumstances.) Significantly, the 1912 miners' strike saw more arrests for picketing than the whole of the previous ten years put together; once again indicating that the Second Reich was not becoming easier on its opponents. Of the 1,750 arrested and convicted after that strike no fewer than one-third had previous convictions, thus showing how difficult it was for German workers to keep out of the clutches of the law. This was so for another reason: the way in which the police authorities of the various German Länder interfered in everyday life. In many German states couples were not allowed to marry without police permission, whilst the authories in Brunswick sometimes forced cohabiting but unmarried couples to live apart and subsequently refused to give permission for marriage. Almost all forms of working-class leisure were subject to the control of suspicious policemen, including sports clubs and the miners' drinking establishments, the *Schnapskasinos*. A bemused American noted that the colour of cars and the length of hatpins were dictated by police regulation in the Berlin of 1914!

This picture of the Imperial state is somewhat one-sided, for it is true that the German Reich was not as repressive as its Tsarist counterpart. It was a state governed by law and a constitution. Citizens did have redress for false imprisonment in the courts, which did on occasion overturn sentences and criticise police excesses. There were labour courts in which arbitration could be sought in industrial disputes. In some German states, as in Baden, the franchise for the election of the local Landtag was not discriminatory. The implementation of the anti-socialist and other laws of association varied from time to time and from place to place, with Southern Germany, or at least the South-West, being predictably more liberal than the autocratic Prussian authorities. But at the end of the day it was Prussia, not Baden, which dominated the Reich. Discriminatory laws and franchises had still not been removed by 1914. The representatives of labour were still excluded from decision-making, both nationally and locally. It was this exclusion which generated a mass socialist movement demanding qualitative economic and social change, even if some of its members were none too sure about what this meant in concrete terms.

Radicalism or reformism

The extent to which German Social Democracy was or remained a 'radical' or 'revolutionary' movement has been a source of heated debate. From confused intellectual origins the party did come to adopt the Erfurt Programme in 1891. The first part of this programme was written by Karl Kautsky, the leading populariser of Marx in his day, and proclaimed the insolubility of labour's problems under capitalism, the need for the socialisation of the means of production and the inevitability both of class conflict and economic crisis. The second part of the programme, penned by Bernstein, who had still not forsaken Marxism at this stage, concentrated on short-term goals: democratic reform, improved working and living conditions. From this apparently radical high-point, conditioned by recession on the economic front and persecution on the political, the SPD is supposed to have become increasingly integrated into the political system of Wilhelmine Germany and to have lost its revolutionary fervour. There is not inconsiderable evidence to this effect. There developed a group of 'revisionist' intellectuals in the party around Bernstein, who questioned the central tenets of Marxism, advocated collaboration with progressive elements of the bourgeoisie and believed in the possibility of a gradualist solution to the plight of the working class, jettisoning any idea of 'revolution'. In South Germany, and especially in the state of Baden, there emerged a younger generation of reformist politicians, such as Ludwig Frank, who were prepared to defy national SPD policy and vote for the regional government budget, as well as to collaborate with liberals. The leadership of the Free Trade Unions, whose membership overtook that of the party in 1902, thus increasing their strength and influence, revealed a marked caution, preferring to concentrate on immediate bread-and-butter questions rather than on radical politics. It was they who led the SPD leadership to abandon discussion of the general strike as a potential weapon to win franchise reform, who saw to it that a radical youth movement was brought under central party control, and who were responsible for May Day no longer being strictly observed by strike action, which was replaced by Sunday meetings, demonstrations and festivals.

The cultural and leisure organisations of German Social Democracy could also scarcely be described as the bearers of a revolutionary counter-culture: at SPD concerts and festivals one heard the music of Léhar, Strauss and Wagner, as well as that of Beethoven. The workers' choral societies often sang traditional folk-songs, whilst the drama clubs performed the classical works of Goethe and Schiller. It is also extremely difficult to know what the official Marxism of the party meant to the ordinary member. We have already seen that historical fiction was more popular than the

Marxist classics. Paul Göhre, a clergyman who spent some time working in a factory, claimed that for most workers 'neither the official republicanism nor economic communism were really popular'; whilst Carl Severing, later to become a leading social-democratic Minister in Prussia after the war, believed that the majority of SPD members joined the party simply to improve their living conditions. What is indisputable is that as the years passed a new kind of leader emerged: the organiser or bureaucrat, typified by Friedrich Ebert. The contemporary sociologist Robert Michels argued that the emergence of a large bureaucracy to manage the affairs of the party produced petty-minded men of bureaucratic mentality, whose prime concern was the maintenance of party unity as an end in itself. Certainly men such as Ebert did reveal a marked caution in political affairs and refused to countenance the idea of a revolutionary general strike. The party leadership was criticised by both revisionists (Bernstein) and radicals (Rosa Luxemburg) for its *passivity* in the face of government harassment, as it was by the latter group for its failure to denounce imperialist adventures during the Moroccan crisis of 1911. In 1913 the SPD voted for the first time for a military budget, albeit on the grounds that the budget contained provisions for fairer, direct taxation. Above all, in August 1914, on the outbreak of the First World War, the SPD delegation in the Reichstag voted to support the government's war effort. The internationalism and commitment to class war of official programmes and conference declarations appeared to be a hollow sham. Patriotism appeared to have triumphed over radicalism.

None of the above can be denied; but it is only one side of the story. In fact the SPD was never monolithic in its views. Even during the persecution of 1878 to 1890 socialist deputies in the Reichstag had proved much more pragmatic and moderate than the local and illegal party branches, which were highly critical of the parliamentarians. After 1890 party branches tended to reformism in areas that were relatively liberal, but to be more radical in autocratic Prussia; and what needs to be remembered in this context is that, as August Bebel reminded the South Germans around the turn of the century, there were more Social Democrats in Berlin alone than in the whole of Germany south of the River Main. Local studies have revealed party organisations to the left of the national leadership, as in Brunswick, Göppingen, Stuttgart, Düsseldorf and Dortmund; and in some cases a radical continuity can be traced from pre-war times to the revolutionary upheavals at the end of the war. On the other hand, other local studies, such as one of the SPD in Göttingen, reinforce the impression of a predominantly reformist party. A lack of uniformity was again the order of the day.

Equally complex is the interpretation of the activities of the SPD's ancillary organisations, which, as we saw, often appeared simply to reproduce 'bourgeois' culture. The members of these clubs *were* Social Democrats; and the clubs proclaimed their class identity in their titles. Radical and revolutionary songs were performed as well as traditional works. Discussions in local party branches *were* given over to political issues. Membership of these bodies *reinforced* class identity in a society where even leisure organisations were class-specific, where workers and the middle class celebrated Schiller in *separate* festivals.

Even that great turning point, the SPD's vote for the war credits in August 1914, often regarded as a betrayal of revolutionary ideals, is less clear-cut in its significance than might be imagined. As much recent work has shown, the decision to vote for the war credits was no foregone conclusion. What ruled amongst party leaders in early August 1914 was, above all else, confusion. Reasons for supporting the war effort varied widely, with many making their support conditional upon the war being *defensive*. Indeed, the official statement of the SPD leadership in the Reichstag on 4 August made precisely this point. The fact that it was genuinely believed that Germany was about to be invaded by autocratic Russia was in this respect crucial. Only a small section on the right of the party actually welcomed the decision and saw it as a turning point; for most it was not taken with any long-term perspective in view. This was especially the case for Ebert, who was primarily concerned with the preservation of the party organisation. Thus August 1914 did *not* mark the integration of the German working class into the political nation, as subsequent upheavals proved only too clearly. The idea that popular enthusiasm for the war, recorded by many contemporaries, extended to the working classes has also been called into question recently, with evidence from Hamburg and Brunswick suggesting a much more nuanced and cautious reaction. In any case, the 'masses on the streets' could scarcely have been those condemned to factory labour; whilst the defence of the Fatherland was not necessarily incompatible with hostility to the prevailing political and social order.

The non-socialist working class

So far we have seen that there arose in Germany before the First
World War a socialist movement which generated mass support;
but secondly that such support was far from uniform in its aspirations. If the SPD was internally divided, between radicals and
reformists, Marxists and non-Marxists, the same is even more true
of the *whole* of the organised working class, not to mention the
large numbers of unorganised: for social-democratic bodies had no
monopoly of labour organisation in Imperial Germany. Support for
German Social Democracy was overwhelmingly concentrated in the
large towns of *Protestant* Germany: Berlin, Hamburg, Leipzig,
Dresden. In areas which were predominantly Catholic, even when
industrial, the SPD made little headway. This was true in Silesia, the
lower Rhineland (especially Aachen) and the Saarland. The steel
town of Essen remained dominated by the Centre Party until the
revolution of 1918; and as late as 1912 approximately 60% of the
Catholic electorate were still voting for the Centre Party. This is not
to say that Social Democracy made no inroads into the Catholic
working class before the First World War. In 1907 it took six of
twenty-eight constituencies that were Catholic *and* industrial, and
twelve of such constituencies in the elections of 1912. But the story
was far from one of unilinear success. Thus, although the SPD won
Köln-Stadt, Würzburg and Strassburg-Land from the Centre in
1912, it also lost Bochum and Bielefeld to that party in the same
election. Moreover, half of its victories then depended on electoral
alliances with local liberals. In fact, SPD electoral successes were
normally registered not in industrial areas that were overwhelmingly Catholic, such as Aachen and the Saarland, but in areas of
mixed confession, such as Dortmund, Bochum and Düsseldorf,
where one can assume that Catholics lived and worked cheek by
jowl with their Protestant colleagues.

The immunity of Catholics to socialist propaganda was in part
(and obviously) a consequence of religious belief, which regarded
the SPD as godless. But it was also sustained by other factors, above
all by the fact that German Catholicism adopted the politics of mass
mobilisation and interest-representation. Thus loyalty was fed by
numerous Catholic leisure and cultural associations, by the People's
Association for a Catholic Germany and by the Christian trade
unions. These unions, although believing *in principle* in class collaboration, increasingly came to function as militant representatives of

working-class interests and did not shun strike action, though there were important occasions when they refused to engage in joint action with the socialist unions, as in the Ruhr miners' strike of 1912.

Polish workers also formed their own, distinct economic and political organisations, whilst some employees joined the liberal Hirsch-Duncker unions. The 'yellow' unions, committed to industrial peace and support for the firm and employer, gained a foothold in the mines and foundries of the Ruhr, as well as in the electrical and chemical industries; whilst the largest union of white-collar workers in Germany before the First World War, the *Deutschnationale Handlungsgehilfenverband* (the German National Union of Commercial Employees), subscribed to a nationalist, racist and anti-socialist ideology. Enjoying closer contact with management, pension rights and holiday entitlement, different systems of remuneration by seniority — blue-collar workers had to watch their earnings decline with old age — and greater job security, the increasingly large white-collar salariat did not, at least at this point in time, identify with its 'inferior' manual colleagues, even where the wage differential between the two groups was not that large. This dividing line, the so-called 'collar line' (*Kragenlinie*), seems to have been especially pronounced in German society, not least because the state accorded white-collar employees in both the private (*Angestellte*) and the public sectors (*Beamte*) a different legal status from that of manual workers. Once again, therefore, fragmentation was the order of the day, even amongst the *organised* working class of Imperial Germany. Yet the majority of German workers belonged to neither the industrial nor the political organisations of the labour movement.

There is some evidence that the daily culture of trade union and social democratic organisations in Wilhelmine Germany expressed the attitudes and values of only certain sections of the working class, in particular those of the skilled, relatively well-paid and *respectable*. Alongside party and trade unions the leisure and cultural organisations of German Social Democracy saw themselves as the 'third pillar' of the labour movement, whose aim it was not just to instruct workers in the evils of capitalism but to 'educate' them more generally, to 'ennoble' their souls and to compensate for the disadvantages of daily working drudgery. Thus many SPD militants had little understanding of or sympathy for the less 'respectable' actions of a large section of the working class, for petty criminality and violence, which typified those enmeshed in a 'culture of poverty'. 'Rough' behaviour was castigated as the activity of the 'immature', the 'unschooled', the 'unorganised', the *'Lumpen'*. This self-definition of the party meant quite simply that it was not speaking the same language as many casual labourers and the frequently unemployed. For such groups of workers there was little point in developing a lifestyle geared to the future. There were also those who disliked formal organisation and wished to retain control over shop-floor decisions, not to surrender it to distant and cautious trade union leaders who thought in terms of a lengthy strategy. This was especially true amongst dockworkers and younger miners, mainly hauliers, in the pits of the Ruhr. Amongst many of the poorer workers there existed a tacit acceptance, even approval, of various kinds of 'self-help' of a very un-bourgeois kind, such as the rampant pilfering in the docks. Violence — against police, supervisors, blacklegs, other workers and even in the home — was far from unknown. Such rude manners were anathema to most spokesmen for organised labour; and their failure to identify with the daily practices of some 'rougher' workers of necessity limited their appeal.

The SPD and the Free Trade Unions also had enormous difficulties in mobilising the support of the unskilled, female labour, domestic servants and those in cottage industries, for reasons discussed above. They also remained organisations of the largest industrial towns of Protestant Germany and were disproportionately concentrated in places such as Berlin, Hamburg and Leipzig. The failure to win over those described as 'workers' in the small towns and villages of Germany was a failure of enormous significance: as late as 1925 approximately one half of all those categorised as 'workers' in the census of that year lived in small towns and villages of under 10,000 inhabitants. Equally serious was the failure to recruit from the countryside.

Amongst rural labourers German Social Democracy and the trade union movement had only limited success before 1914. In the East problems of recruitment were compounded by poor communications, by the fact that many of the labourers were migrants from Austrian and Russian territory, by linguistic difficulties, and by the tight hold that the large landowners could exercise over their workers, for whom they provided board and lodging. Only amongst rural labourers on relatively small farms did the labour movement make some headway, but then only rarely and only in the immediate vicinity of large industrial cities such as Hamburg and Königsberg. Sometimes rural craftsmen and occasionally commuters who lived in rural areas but worked in the urban factories, as in some communities around Mannheim, brought socialist ideas to the villages. But in rural areas labour organisation was normally lacking. Especially conspicuous was the SPD's inability to secure support from small peasant farmers, even from those with grievances against large landowners and who found themselves in serious economic difficulties. Peasant farmers had been given the land in various acts of emancipation between 1800 and the 1850s. They were landowning and felt threatened by the SPD's commitment to socialisation, even though the party was not in fact committed to the expropriation of small farms. Where farmers employed labourers they were hostile to union organisation. Furthermore, the SPD offered them little. Against the exhortations of revisionist intellectuals such as Eduard David and Bernstein, as well as the urging of Social Democrats from the peasant regions of Southern Germany, the party remained committed to the belief that the peasantry was doomed to extinction and that emancipation would be almost exclusively the act of the urban working class. The rejection of a specifically peasant programme on such grounds, argued most persuasively by Karl Kautsky, was not, however, simply a question of intractable Marxist theory. Above all one must remember that the SPD was a party of urban consumers to an overwhelming extent, and thus one that could not stomach any policy of peasant protection that implied higher food prices.

The lack of a socialist or union presence in rural Germany in the Imperial period had huge implications, for approximately one-third of the labour force earned its living through agriculture. This, together with the fragmentation of both organised and unorganised labour described above, not the somewhat fatalistic ideology of the SPD, is what explains the caution of both Social Democracy and the German trade unions before the First World War, in a world in which labour was isolated, divided and facing powerful enemies. However, the relative peace of 1913–14 was to prove deceptive; and many of the previously unorganised did enter the ranks of protest four years later.

BIBLIOGRAPHY

John Breuilly, 'Liberalism or Social Democracy', *European History Quarterly* (1985), 1, pp.3–42.

D. Crew, *Town in the Ruhr* (New York, 1979)

R.J. Evans (ed.), *Politics and Society in Wilhelmine Germany* (London, 1978)

—— (ed.), *The German Working Class* (London, 1982)

R. Fletcher, *Revisionism and Empire* (London, 1984)

—— (ed.), *From Bernstein to Brandt* (London, 1987)

D. Footman, *Lassalle* (New York, 1969)

P. Fröhlich, *Rosa Luxemburg* (London, 1940)

P. Gay, *The Dilemma of Democratic Socialism* (London, 1962)

D. Geary, 'The German Labour Movement', *European Studies Review* (1976) 6 no. 3, pp.297–330

—— *European Labour Protest* (London, 1981)

—— *Karl Kautsky* (Manchester, 1987)

N. Geras, *The Legacy of Rosa Luxemburg* (London, 1976)

H. Grebing, *History of the German Labour Movement* (London, 1969)

W. Guttsman, *The German Social Democratic Party* (London, 1981)

G. Haupt, *Socialism and the Great War* (Oxford, 1972)

S. Hickey, *Workers in Imperial Germany* (Oxford, 1985)

J. Joll, *The Second International* (London, 1955)

V.L. Lidtke, *The Outlawed Party* (Princeton, 1966)

—— *The Alternative Culture* (Oxford, 1985)

W.H. Maehl, *August Bebel* (Philadelphia, 1980)

H. Mitchell and P.N. Stearns, *Workers and Protest* (Ithaca, NY, 1971)

W.J. Mommsen and H.-G. Husung, *The Development of Trade Unionism in Britain and Germany* (London, 1986)

J. Moses, *Trade Unionism in Germany* (London, 1982)

J.P. Nettl, 'The Social Democratic Party as a Political Model', *Past and Present* (1965), 30

—— *Rosa Luxemburg* (Oxford, 1966)

M. Nolan, *Social Democracy and German Society* (Cambridge, 1981)

J. Quartaert, *Reluctant Feminists* (Princeton, 1979)

R.W. Reichard, *Crippled from Birth* (Ames, Ia., 1969)

G. Roth, *Social Democrats in Imperial Germany* (Totowa, NJ, 1963)

M. Salvadori, *Karl Kautsky* (London, 1979)

L. Schofer, *The Formation of a Modern Labour Force* (Berkeley, Calif., 1975)

C.E. Schorske, *German Social Democracy* (Cambridge, Mass, 1955)

P.N. Stearns, *Lives of Labour* (London, 1975)

G.P. Steenson, *Karl Kautsky* (Pittsburgh, 1978)

—— *'Not a Penny! Not a Man!'* (Pittsburgh, 1981)

H. Trotnow, *Karl Liebknecht* (New York, 1984)

4

LABOUR AND SOCIALISM IN TSARIST RUSSIA

Christopher Read

On 5 February 1880 the evening peace of St Petersburg was shattered by the sound of an explosion coming from the direction of the Winter Palace. It was the latest in a series of attempts on the life of Alexander II and, on this occasion as on all those preceding it, the Tsar survived. This was, however, the first time the revolutionary organisation behind the campaign of terror, the People's Will (*Narodnaia volia*), had penetrated the inner sanctum of a royal palace. They had been able to do this because the person who had planted the bomb, Stepan Khalturin, was a carpenter. The Tsarist police, expecting terror to emanate from the intelligentsia, had dropped its guard against workers and Khalturin had been able to enter employment in the palace and smuggle explosives into his quarters piece by piece and conceal them under his bed, the fumes supposedly giving him headaches, until he had accumulated sufficient to devastate the imperial reception room and kill eleven of those gathered in it awaiting a slightly delayed appearance by the Tsar. This delay postponed the moment of his assassination for another year. None the less, the incident testifies to the involvement of workers in the Russian revolutionary movement at a very early stage of the development of both that movement and the working class. It confirms that, on the face of it, the difference between the labour historian looking at Russia compared to his counterpart looking at Western Europe, is that the former sets out to explain why workers turned out to be revolutionary and the latter why they did not. The situation, needless to say, is not so straightforward. According to the expectations of radicals in Russia and Western Europe, the more highly developed and educated 'advanced' workers of the West should have been more consciously revolutionary than the barely emerging 'backward' working class of Russia. It was an axiom that Western workers would lead the revolution. And yet it was Russia alone that, in 1905 and 1917, underwent revolutions led by workers and their representatives.

Why was this so? Many theories existed. The populists had argued since the 1860s that the peasantry was potentially the most revolutionary class in society, and the very fact that capitalism had not developed in Russia meant that Russian society might proceed directly to socialism. They claimed that 1917 was a vindication of their views. Among the Bolsheviks, Bukharin believed that what had happened was that the chain of capitalism had broken at its weakest link; while Trotsky and, belatedly, Lenin had argued that world revolution was indivisible since capitalism was a world-wide structure and what was happening in Russia was only part of an international process. For Mensheviks, the revolution was essentially bourgeois rather than socialist and the prerequisites for genuine socialism were lacking. All these theories had been developed to justify particular courses of political action and to vindicate *a priori* dogmatic assumptions. All were based on at least partial misunderstandings of what was actually happening as opposed to what should have been happening according to the prescriptions of theory. For populists the revolutionary potential of the peasantry was an article of faith. For both Bolsheviks and Mensheviks it was the leading role of the workers, in particular the advanced workers, that was unquestionable. In practice, the actual revolution did not fully justify any of these presuppositions. The object of this current exercise is not to give an overall explanation of the roots of the Russian revolution but to look in particular at the relationship between labour, socialism and revolution in Russia. Naturally, this will go a long way to answering the larger question also. Before taking these issues up, however, it is necessary to look at the changing role of labour in the Russian economy in the last half century before the revolution.

Rural and urban labour in the late nineteenth century

The most prominent feature of Russian industrial labour between 1875 and 1917 is its rapid expansion, though it should be emphasised that this took place within the overall framework of an otherwise stagnant society and economy. The juxtaposition of the overwhelmingly large traditional society and the small, but highly important, industrial sector is the most important structural feature to be borne in mind. Many accounts of the internal features of the nascent Russian working class fail to give this aspect its due. This is all the more surprising in view of the fact that the interaction between the two sectors was, necessarily, very significant. In order to expand at the required rate the industrial work-force was being constantly replenished by rural recruits. Throughout the period the Russian working class remained overwhelmingly migrant. Even where one might expect to find the most developed, settled and urbanised work-force, in the armament factories of the capital, St Petersburg, the years immediately prior to the revolution were marked by yet another major wave of peasant recruitment as war production galloped ahead.

An examination of the figures for the growth of the industrial working class show the stages by which this process occurred. In 1885 there were 616,000 workers (around 0.7% of the population). Ten years later these figures had doubled. In 1904 there were 1.6 million workers in factories subject to the inspectorate of the Ministry of Finance. Textiles accounted for 600,000 of them, metal-working 235,000, minerals and mining 128,000, the sugar industry 118,000. In addition there were about 850,000 employed in transport, the vast majority of whom were workers. In 1902 more than half of the factory workers were employed in factories situated outside large cities.

Within the total population of Russia these figures represent a small minority. Around 1860 the total population of the Russian Empire was about 75 million. On the eve of the First World War this had risen to about 165 million. The 1897 census gives the most accurate breakdown of the social structure. The social 'pyramid' was extremely narrow at the top and very broad at the base. The élite comprised 1.2 million hereditary nobles, 0.6 million personal nobles and 0.35 million clergy. The urban upper class consisted of 0.35 million 'distinguished citizens' and 0.3 million merchants. An indication of the size of the very rich part of this population can be gauged from the fact that around 10,000 households each employed more than ten domestic servants while 112,000 employed from four to ten. An approximation of the size of the middle class can be obtained by adding together the figures for government employees and the professions. This gives a figure of slightly over 1.0 million. The rest of the urban population amounted to 13.3 million classified as *meshchane* which included shopkeepers, clerks, office workers, artisans and some urban workers. The bulk of the population, the peasants, consisted of 97 million persons, among whom the remainder of the workers were officially classified. In addition there were some 3 million Cossacks. It should be emphasised that most of these categories were very broad and contained wide differences of wealth and status. Even among hereditary nobles there was a sizeable minority who lived little differently from their peasants.

Industrial output had a much greater weight in the overall economy than the rather low proportion of workers would suggest. The most accurate recent estimates, by Paul Gregory, suggest that shortly before the First World War industry, construction, transport and communications accounted for about a third of Russian national income, agriculture for a half and trade and services for the remainder.

These raw figures, however, have to be refined by numerous other considerations before the overall picture can be clarified. First and foremost the geographical distribution of industry was anything but even. Most of this development was clustered in a small number of widely dispersed regions of European Russia: Moscow, St Petersburg, Warsaw, Riga, the Southern Urals, the Caspian, Odessa and the Ukraine. The growing division of labour left its imprint on this distribution. The extractive industries were concentrated in Poland, the Southern Urals and the Don basin, with the exceptions of Caspian oil and such widely scattered, usually small and, as is well known, often penal, mining enterprises as could make their way in the potentially rich but actually very inhospitable conditions of Asiatic Russia. The metal industries (largely synonymous with armaments) were concentrated in the Baltic region. Moscow was the centre of Russia's oldest and persistently traditional textile industry. In the Ukraine the processing of cash crops, notably sugar, was dominant. Given this wide dispersal and the almost total absence of surfaced roads the transport sector consisting of railways, internal waterways such as the Volga, and sea-going routes for foreign trade (mainly grain exports and machinery and coal imports) in the Baltic, the North Sea and the Mediterranean had considerable strategic significance for the economy. These fragile communication webs, often expanded without sufficient long-term consideration and planning, held the economy together.

Dislocation in this area could mean that the economy as a whole would be under severe pressure.

Secondly, it is often argued that, on average, Russian factories were larger than their counterparts elsewhere, as is usually the case with the most recently industrialising economies. Certainly the Putilov Metal Works in St Petersburg with 12,000 employees in the early years of the twentieth century was one of the world's largest factories, but the figures for overall concentration of workers are based on a survey which omitted workshops employing less than fifteen and thus exaggerate the importance of the larger concerns. The figures produced in this way show that concentration of workers in Russian factories was noticeably high. According to contemporary figures, Russia in 1902 had nearly 12,000 enterprises employing 1–5 employees with a total of 27,800 workers, compared to Germany in 1895 which had over 1.1 million such enterprises employing 3 million workers. At the other extreme Russia had 300 enterprises employing over 1,000 with a total of 2 million employees, compared to 296 such enterprises in Germany employing a total of 562,000 employees. While the figures at the lower end of the scale may be distorted by the exclusion from the Russian figures of artisans and many untraced small enterprises — perhaps reflecting the greater lassitude of the Russian bureaucracy compared to its German counterpart — there can be no doubt that the figures do show the existence of numerous large factories in Russia. One should, however, by no means overlook the fact that the characteristic industrial concern in Russia was the smaller factory employing 50–100 people. Moscow in particular was notable in this respect. In St Petersburg, a newer industrial centre, factories were more dominant but workshops were still important. Even in the larger factories the effects of concentration were greatly modified by the fact that such enterprises were divided into smaller shops and sections which were often, in theory at least, rigidly segregated from one another to the extent that fines were imposed on employees found in areas other than the one in which they worked.

The international connections of Russian industry must also be borne in mind in understanding the peculiarities of Russian economic development in these years. Russia's role in European, and eventually world, trade, and its dependence on the outside world to fill critical gaps in its own ability to industrialise, notably its chronic shortages of capital and technical expertise in production and commerce, left their imprint on the Russian economy. Russian grain exports were the bedrock of her position in the international market, enabling her, partly thanks to a tariff system which controlled imports, to build up a trade surplus. This provided a stable foundation for the rouble and the platform which encouraged foreign capital to flow into Russia. The crucial weakness of this system, however, was the steady fall of international grain and other agricultural prices from the late 1870s onwards. This basic feature of the 'Great Depression' hit Russia very hard. In order to maintain the value of grain exports quantities had to rise to counteract falling prices. This put further enormous pressure on Russia's internal agrarian economy and brought a squeeze affecting landowners and many peasants who had to market grain in order to pay their rents and taxes. As a result of this the relatively self-contained Russian economy of the mid-century was becoming much more dependent on the vagaries of the European and Atlantic economy. Its fragility in periods of crisis in the international economy was exposed by the 1905 revolution which had its roots in the post-1899 depression in the European economy.

Finally, the role of the state, presiding over and orchestrating these developments to the best of its ability, must also be taken into account. The absence of the pre-conditions for a self-generating growth of capitalism in Russia meant that, in the absence of energetic entrepreneurship, the state had to shoulder the burden of economic development if it was to 'keep up' militarily and strategically with its great rivals such as France and Britain who had, in the Crimean war of 1854–6, administered a salutary lesson in how far Russia had fallen behind since 1812. This catastrophe had completely wiped away the complacency about strategic security which had characterised Russia since its defeat of Napoleon and its emergence as arbiter of Europe, not to mention its more recent role as policeman of last resort for authoritarian monarchies in Central and Eastern Europe threatened by the revolutions of 1848. Now it was clear that the state needed to industrialise in order to improve strategic communications, to build up the armaments industry, and to bolster other defence-related industries. In addition, it should not be forgotten that all this had to be paid for. The prominence in the industrialisation process of successive Russian Finance Ministers such as Reutern (1862–78), Bunge (1881–6), Vyshnegradsky (1886–92) and, best known of all, Witte (1892–1903) reminds us that the imperative of broadening the tax base in politically acceptable ways (that is, not taxing the wealthy landowners if it could be avoided) meant that the ministry had a vested interest in promoting new and profitable sectors to compensate for the eternally stagnant peasant economy.

No account of Russia before the revolution can ignore the fact that the agrarian economy, and in particular the peasant economy and its associated society, exerted an overwhelming shaping influence in many areas. The most important of these was the stagnation of the peasant economy in the densely populated Russian and Ukrainian heartland, a feature rooted in the impact of serfdom, which was abolished only in 1861. The cheapness of serf labour meant that there was little incentive to mechanise, improve or invest in agricultural land. Production growth could be achieved by extending the area of cultivation into new frontier areas of the southeast and east; or by simply using labour more intensively on the existing estates, leaving however many peasants there were to support themselves from their own allotment areas which they held irrespective of the overall number of peasants in the village, so that a growing population had to be fed from a static amount of land. As a result of this, by the middle of the century the mass of the population lived narrow, circumscribed, near-moneyless lives. Such a situation could not stimulate the growth of an internal market, a development made even less likely by Russia's acute shortage of capital. These two aspects of stagnation — abundant cheap labour and acute shortage of capital — were linked to one another, as is graphically illustrated by the custom of describing the wealth of an estate not by its land value or its size, but by the number of serfs ('souls') who worked on it. This figure was the best guide to an estate's productive power.

This is not the place to assess the impact of the abolition of serfdom, enacted in 1861, but a few remarks about it have to be made. Economically, it was, in the medium and long term, a disaster for both peasant and landowner, the former because he continued to be locked into the same overcrowded land apportionment. Indeed, the peasants appear to have lost land as a result of the settlement, especially in the more fertile areas of the Black Earth zone. But the landowners also found the new conditions hard. Labour had to be paid for and the shortage of capital had severe effects, chronicled by the writers of the late nineteenth century. The novelty of the money economy, and the absence of habits of savings and investment, produced stereotypes, in life and literature, such as the spendthrift landowner who blew all his available money on frivolous pursuits as soon as he received it as did Dmitrii Karamazov (in Dostoevsky's *The Brothers Karamazov*), or the declining gentlefolk trying to hang on to the last piece of property as portrayed by Chekhov in *The Cherry Orchard*. Even those willing to adjust to change and try to improve their estate could share the frustration of Levin in Tolstoy's *Anna Karenina* whose mistrustful and traditional-minded peasants refused to co-operate, sometimes completely rationally from their own point of view, with new machinery and new methods. The number of landowners fell rapidly after 1861 and the total amount of land held in privately owned estates followed suit. In 1877 there were 115,000 landowners with a total of 73 million hectares of land; in 1905, despite the overall population rise, there were only 107,000 with a total of 53 million hectares.

Thus, the agrarian economy was being squeezed in a vice, the jaws of which were rising population and falling international grain and other agricultural prices resulting from the opening up of American and Australian food production for the European market. This was exacerbated by the inexorable demands of the taxman, particularly for the payments owed by peasants to recompense the state for their supposed emancipation (redemption payments). As these were payable in fixed money amounts — as, of course, was indirect taxation which fell on articles of everyday use such as vodka, sugar, matches and kerosene — falling prices had to be met by increased marketing of grain. At the same time, population pressure reduced the amount of land available per head so that the pressure was intense. In the Black Earth province of Kherson the burden of peasant redemption payments rose by 40% in real terms while the land available per head fell by 27%. In the non-Black Earth province of Tver the corresponding figures were 30% and 18%.

The outcome of this situation was a fragile subsistence economy which could collapse in the most adverse circumstances, as was drastically indicated by the 1891–2 famine in which some 400,000 people died. It should, of course, be borne in mind that famine strikes selectively at the poor and is not an indication that an entire population, even in the region where famine rages, is affected.

Although the overall picture of the peasant economy is a dark one, many peasants were able to live comfortable or, at least, tolerable lives. There were enclaves and regions of relative prosperity, often associated with areas where serfdom had had little impact, such as the Baltic region or areas of new settlement like the South-East and Siberia. On the other hand, some of the peripheral regions were among the poorest, for instance Armenia and parts of Central Asia. Most of the ensuing analysis, however, is devoted to the European slavic core of the Russian Empire.

It is within the peasant way of life that the first links between Russian labour and socialism — understood as collective rather than individual ownership of the means of production — are to be found. The two basic units of peasant society, the household and the commune, were both collectivist. Within the household, all resources were shared and all contributed to it in accordance with ability and custom (to the extent that there were fixed roles for individuals depending primarily on age, gender and marital status) and drew from it in accordance with need, once again mediated by custom and tradition. Inheritance law usually backed up joint family ownership. The dividing off of separate households usually came through agreed marriage settlements. Of course, in addition to providing a social framework for existence, the peasant family differs from others in being a basic unit of production, so the same principle of sharing applied to its land and property which belonged to the household as a whole. While the head of the household had a major influence on the distribution of this property the family could, and often did, change the head when he (it was invariably a man, with the exception of some households consisting of widows alone or with children) appeared to be administering family affairs improperly.

In order to achieve such a change, the family would call in the authority of the commune to decide on what action should be taken. A great deal of attention has been given to the peasant commune (the organisation of households in each village) at the expense of attention to the households themselves, so its main features are better known. As it existed in the latter half of the nineteenth century, it had been deliberately strengthened by the Imperial legislators to provide a bulwark of resistance to potential peasant mobility which, they feared, might increase as a result of the emancipation of the serfs. The commune, they decreed, was to be the joint tax-paying institution. It would be up to the commune to distribute the burden among its constituent households according to their ability to pay. The commune also had powers to re-distribute land in accordance with the same set of criteria.

Another of its powers was the granting of permission to leave the commune and it was this which put a brake on peasant mobility since, if the result were to be an added tax burden on the rest of the commune, there would be a reluctance on the part of the commune to allow young, able-bodied males to leave to find employment elsewhere. However, as over-population became chronic the situation was reversed, and poorer households could make ends meet only if some remitted earnings from the city — usually industrial or domestic labour — were available to it.

Taken together the household and the commune provided a very distinctive attitude to production and property, which could be summarised as creating what a former government minister referred to in 1914 as an 'innate socialism'. Wherever one turns, the evidence is overwhelming that the peasantry shared certain instinctive socialist principles. In the first place, they saw no reason why those who did not work should live better than those who did. With the biblical approval, known to them in their highly religious culture, they believed that 'he who does not work, neither shall he eat'. In practice this meant that peasants saw no reason to keep landlords in luxury and, from their own experience, could be said to have derived a version of the idea of surplus value, namely that the work of the poor (i.e. themselves) was the foundation of the wealth of the rich (i.e. the landowners). In opposition to this state of things, the peasants, despite their wide regional, cultural and occupational diversity, had their own naturally socialist values of sharing property and labour. Their chief grievance was the unequal distribution of land. Their constant theme, which was repressed most of the time because of the extremely unfavourable conditions for its possible fulfilment, was re-distribution. It was usually expressed in minor ways — surreptitious gathering of firewood in the landowner's forest, pilfering his crops, using his pasture for their animals — but in times of crisis, either when the situation became unbearable and desperation took over or when, for more complex reasons as in 1905 and 1917, the repressive apparatus of the state was severely restricted or neutralised, this resentment could rise up in ugly, violent and more determined forms including arson, mass encroachment on landlords' property, refusal to pay rents and taxes and, occasionally, physical assault and murder. The ubiquity of such responses, once it was realised the opportunity was there, is eloquent testimony to the continued existence of a deep sense of underlying grievance and hostility towards the landowners. The evidence of 1917 also suggests that those who had taken advantage of the official change of heart about the commune after 1905 — as a result of which the government began to see the commune as a source of collective peasant rebellion rather than as a bulwark of stability — and set up as individual rather than communal farmers were also the object of deep-seated hostility and viewed as traitors to the village. This state of affairs came about because the rural disturbances of 1903–6 had shown the government that the preservation of order would be best served by the weakening of the commune. As a result, in 1907 it began a policy of encouraging peasants who could do so, referred to by the Prime Minister Stolypin as 'the sober and the strong', to consolidate their land, leave the commune and become independent farmers. Some 20% of households are thought to have withdrawn from the commune in this way by 1916 but in the revolutionary years they appear to have been drawn back into it. Like the 'cut-offs' supposedly lost in 1861, the commune land alienated by these reforms was a particular provocation to the peasantry's sense of their own rights.

This vigorous peasant sense of natural rights and social justice has enormous implications for the urban industrial work-force, towards whom we now turn. There are many reasons for this. One of the most obvious is the rural origin of a very high proportion of the urban labour force as a result of migration. Alongside the traditional visitors who trickled through the remote villages — itinerant preachers and holy men, pedlars and tradesmen of various kinds, government officials from the military and tax-gathering organisations — the rural environment became the target, in the late nineteenth century, for a new type of outsider: the industrial recruiter.

As in all newly industrialising societies the countryside provided the necessary pool of labour for the cities. Detailed study of the pattern of labour migration in Russia has been relatively neglected since the official presupposition of Soviet, and some non-Soviet, historiography has been that 'advanced', usually skilled, workers tend to be more revolutionary while workers of rural origin were volatile, ill-organised, tolerant of poor conditions, easily cowed (particularly by the threat of dismissal) and, as a consequence, poor material for constructive socialist and revolutionary activity. In Russia's case it is not at all clear that this conclusion followed from the stated premises, as will be discussed below. However, despite the fact that many historians of the topic prefer to gloss over migrants in favour of other component parts of the working class, enough information is available to form a general picture of the scope and nature of migrant labour in the formation of the Russian proletariat in the last four decades of Tsarism.

In discussing the labour force it must be borne in mind that Russia's various industrial regions did not share identical characteristics. Some were much faster growing, some recruited over a wider area, some were heavily backed by foreign capital and new equipment, some were very traditional. As a result, generalisation is impossible. Fortunately, however, the two most thoroughly studied industrial regions, Moscow and St Petersburg, show the extremes of this process. Their patterns of industrialisation were quite different from one another, resulting in a different social, political and economic climate in each of them. At the root of this distinction lay the fact that the textile industry of Moscow had, until the mid-nineteenth century, been one of the most highly developed industries in Russia but that, in the latter part of the century, it was being rapidly superseded in every respect — size, technology, output, capital investment — by new metal-based, often armaments-oriented industries for which St Petersburg became an important focus of expansion. A rough index of comparative growth is shown by the fact that, in Moscow, output grew by 130% from 1879 to 1900 while the comparable figure for Russia as a whole was 172%; The Moscow work-force rose by 75% in this period whereas in Russia as a whole it tripled. The population explosion in St Petersburg, discussed below, outstripped both of these. Between 1892 and 1902 some 260,000 people migrated to Moscow, its population reaching 1.1 million in 1902 and, eventually, 1.7 million by 1914. The attraction, of course, was employment and Moscow offered a wide variety of opportunities. In 1917 there were 250,000 artisans, 30,000 transport and communication workers, 135,000 in services (about 100,000 of them in domestic service) and 165,000 factory workers. The main groups of factory workers were in textiles, the largest Moscow industry (57,000), and metal-working (25,000). Thus the Moscow work-force presents a picture of great diversity. If one includes the fact that factory and workshop sizes, in textiles, for example, varied from five workers at the lower end to 6,000 workers at the higher, this diversity is even more striking. In Moscow, even in metal-working, 45% of the work-force was described as artisanal. In addition to its overall growth the factory work-force in Moscow was also changing in composition, particularly in terms of the growing population of women employed. In the early nineteenth century the factory work-force had been almost entirely male. By 1912, women represented 50% and in 1918 70% of the work-force in textiles. In cotton spinning almost 100% of the workers were women. The overall picture of the Moscow labour force, then, is one of a wide diversity of occupations with factory workers in large factories a small, but significant, minority.

While some of these features also hold true for St Petersburg, in the main it had a rather different composition. Its population rose from 1.26 million in 1897 to 2.11 million in 1914. It continued to grow during the war. In 1910 some 27% of its population were workers; of these 234,000 were factory workers, 77,000 white-collar workers, 52,000 in transport, 25,000 in catering, 41,000 in public utilities. In addition there were 260,000 servants and 58,000 artisans. In 1890 there had been only 73,000 factory workers in St Petersburg. In 1914 there were 242,000: in 1917 there were 417,000. This represented some 12% of the 3.4 million industrial workers in Russia as a whole. The leading sector in St Petersburg was metal-working. This grew particularly fast during the war: its work-force increased 135% between 1914 and 1917. Employment in the chemical industry doubled in these years. Most other sectors either remained constant, such as textiles, or declined as in food, printing, and paper industries. As a result, in 1917 an overwhelming 61% of the factory work-force was employed in metal-working compared to about 33% in 1908. The proportion employed in large factories employing over 1,000 also went up from 38% around 1900–5 to 50% in 1914 and 68% in 1917. In Moscow in 1900, 57% of the work-force worked in establishments employing fewer than 500. By comparison, the figure for workers employed in factories of 500 or more for Russia as a whole was 54%; the corresponding figure for the United States was 32.5%. Petrograd boasted a number of large factories. The biggest was the Putilov works with 12,000 employees. There were several other factories employing 4,000–6,000 workers, some of them being naval dockyards, which is a reminder that in St Petersburg the state played a much more direct role in control, particularly in the larger and better equipped factories. Even privately owned concerns, like the Putilov factory, were entirely dependent on the state for orders. This has led one historian to describe St Petersburg as 'an island of technologically sophisticated state-monopoly capitalism in a country whose mode of production still consisted, in the main, of rudimentary capitalist and precapitalist forms'.[1] This was naturally accentuated by the war which brought important changes in the social composition of the Petrograd work-force. Many workers were conscripted and their places were taken by women, youths and refugees from occupied areas. By January 1917 there were 130,000 women workers in Petrograd, or 33% of the labour force. In 1900 they had been 20%; in 1914, 26%. This was below the national average of 27% in 1914 and 43% in 1917. The most feminised factory work-force was that employed in textiles (57% were women in 1913, 69% in 1917). Even metal working showed a rise from 3% in 1913 to 20% in 1917. It is likely that these increases reflect, at least in part, a deliberate policy by employers to recruit women in the wake of the disturbances of 1905. Women workers tended to be clustered overwhelmingly in unskilled and badly paid jobs.

The overall picture that emerges of a sizeable and increasingly rapid growth drawing in more and more recruits, should, of itself, point to the importance of migration in the make-up of the urban work-force, particularly in factories. Information related more directly to establishing what ties there were between town and country tends to confirm the importance of such links. In the first place, 68% of the population of Petrograd in 1910 had been born outside the city. By 1917 this had risen to 73.6%. In Moscow in 1902, 73% of the population was migrant. Even allowing for the fact that in Moscow a quarter of these migrants came from Moscow province itself and that in St Petersburg about a quarter of them had lived in the city for ten years or more, the links with the village and its culture, in which they had spent their formative years, remained substantial. Even long-term urban employment did not preclude the maintaining of contact with the village, particularly for poorly paid workers in areas of fluctuating employment for whom return to the village was the final safety net. Various studies show that a wide range of links to the village survived until 1917. Although summer closure of factories was rare by 1900 it still existed and workers were often recruited on eleven-month contracts. Seasonal migration still existed, amounting to 10% of the population of St Petersburg in 1910. But the most substantial ties involved continued ownership of property in the village, the remitting of part of wages to subsidise the inadequate family plot, or the residence of a male worker's wife and family in the village. In 1899 a survey of a Moscow factory

1. S. Smith, *Red Petrograd* (Cambridge, 1983), p.9.

employing 2,000, who had been in the factory for more than ten years on average, revealed that 90% of the workers owned land although only 64% had detailed information about it. Even in 1918 some 20% of Petrograd workers still owned land. If one allows for the fact that women were more or less excluded from land ownership yet were a sizeable proportion of the factory labour force then this figure is even more significant. A factory survey of 1908 revealed that 42% of married workers and 67% of single workers remitted money to the countryside. Marriage, in St Petersburg at least, frequently meant a wife in the village rather than in the city; 87% of married male textile workers in St Petersburg had wives and children in the countryside. The corresponding figures for metalworkers and printers were 69% and 67% respectively. At the Baltiiskii shipyard the figure was 29%. If one adds to this the fact that women workers tended to quit the city when they started to bear children and were replaced by new, younger recruits it becomes even clearer that family ties and population interchange with the countryside remained very strong.

Finally on the question of migration and the persistence of rural links, it should be noted that migrant workers often lived in loose associations of people from the same area known as *zemliachestva*. Within these associations peasants would, to an extent, maintain the culture and traditions of the locality from which they had come and to which many of them would eventually return. The importance of *zemliachestva* in the early stages of industrialisation in Russia is unquestionable. Robert Johnson's study *Peasant and Proletarian* has shown that certain occupations, in the Moscow industrial region and elsewhere, tended to be closely linked to particular villages and areas. Brickmakers came from Kaluga, carpenters from Vladimir, stove-makers and stone-cutters from Tver, bast-matting makers also from Kaluga. At one factory subject to a specially detailed survey in 1899 it emerged that 50% of the work-force came from Riazan, nearly half of them from a single county. This is partly explained by hiring patterns, recruiters feeling happier to find workers in places they knew and where their existing workers had links and connections to ease the task of recruiting, and to continue with known rather than unknown quantities. Also labour was often contracted by gangs, and groups so hired might live in urban communes known as artels in which a cook/housekeeper would be employed and meals and living expenses shared. While these were distinct from *zemliachestva* they, none the less, were often similar in that they were frequently composed of people from the same place of origin. As far as the *zemliachestva* proper are concerned, Johnson claims, from the rather fragmentary evidence, that local cultural traditions were often preserved through institutions such as the Piatnitskii choir which survives to the present day as one of the Soviet Union's best known musical ensembles. Marriages between *zemliakii* (people from the same place of origin) were not infrequent.

In the absence of any alternative worker organisations before 1900 shared place of origin might be the first step towards the mutual confidence necessary for collective action in co-ops, mutual aid societies and artels. There is some evidence of local clustering of signatories of petitions. It would, of course, often be the case that, given recruitment patterns, turbulence among a particular craft or workshop group in a factory would involve people from the same place of origin. There is, Johnson points out, no evidence to show that non-*zemliachestvo* industries had substantially different patterns of unrest, though it may be significant that the 'backward' and turbulent brick industry had a high regional concentration among its work-force. In addition, letters to family members appear to have helped spread trouble. *Zemliakii* also helped protect labour organisers fleeing from the authorities. While it may be rather romantic to say that *zemliachestva* created 'a community of family and friends from home' and that 'friends were ready-made since the urban community was just an extension of the village back home'[2] one can agree with Robert Johnson that local links provided a continuing channel for rural–urban interchange, provided assistance and cultural continuity for migrants and could act as a focus for social and collective protest. One could also add that it preserved the communal instinct and 'innate socialism' of the village within the more threatening and impersonal conditions of the city.

Development of the urban labour movement

The stages of political and organisational development of the Russian urban labour movement are depicted by clear landmarks, placed at approximately ten-year intervals. The first significant strike occurred in 1885. In 1896–7 the textile workers undertook a

2. D. Koenker, *Moscow Workers and the 1917 Revolution* (Princeton, 1981), p.48.

succesful series of strikes. The last two stages represent mass unrest, stretching far beyond the labour force, culminating in the major upheavals of 1905 and 1917. Each of these phases marks a qualitative escalation in the power, aims and cohesion of Russian urban labour. The sequence can leave no doubt in anyone's mind about the militant tradition of Russian workers. For rural labour, the peasantry, only 1905 and 1917 were of major significance but the events of those years can only be understood if one takes their participation fully into account. Apart from these years of crisis, endemic and often astonishing rural rebellions took place. In 1898, for instance, police reported that peasant disorders in southern and south-eastern Russia had led to entire villages carrying out armed attacks on landowners' property, including dwellings.[3] However, while such outbreaks were confined to small areas they were easily contained by the authorities and made no more than a momentary impact on the established system. The urban labour movement, however, was a source of greater concern to the authorities and it is to an examination of its growth and impact that the remainder of this study is devoted.

The first workers' organisations, such as the Northern Union of Russian Workers to which Khalturin belonged, had come into existence in the 1860s and 1870s. They were part of the awakening of lower-middle-class students (*raznochintsy*) and other members of the intelligentsia to the plight of 'the people' (*narod*) at the heart of Russian populism in its formative decades. While it is undoubtedly true that the populists focused primarily on the peasantry, since a clearly defined working class barely existed at that time, they did not spurn contact with workers in factories and workshops who were often, to all intents and purposes, peasants employed in the city. Apart from Khalturin's unsuccessful assassination attempt, however, these first organisations amounted to little. It was in the more repressive atmosphere of Alexander III's reign (1881–94) that the first significant workers' movements got under way, both among workers themselves and in their name among revolutionary (usually émigré) intellectuals. It is, of course, no accident that this conjuncture should be as it is, if only because populist attempts to arouse the peasantry — first by peaceful propaganda and then by terrorist example — had utterly failed by 1881. It was from among former populists that the recently discovered works of Marx, which

---

3. L. Kochan, *Russia in Revolution* (London, 1970), p.52.

identified the proletariat as the chosen revolutionary class, began to find greater acceptability. At the same time as émigrés such as Plekhanov were setting up the first Russian proletarian Marxist revolutionary organisations, such as the Emancipation of Labour Group, workers themselves, quite independently of intelligentsia tutelage, were beginning to make their presence felt, though only in an, as yet, very limited way. None the less, both the Tsarist regime and the radicals knew that great oaks from little acorns grow.

The first little acorn was planted in 1885 when Russia underwent what is generally regarded as its first significant experience of labour unrest. This occurred at the Nikolsky cotton mills in Orekhovo-Zuevo, significantly a large factory set deep in the countryside of Vladimir province in the Moscow region and a typical 'traditional' Muscovite enterprise, in that it had developed as a pure example of native Russian merchant and entrepreneurial capitalism. It was owned by an Old Believer family headed by Savva Morozov. On 7 January 1885, the work-force of 4,000, incensed beyond toleration by the levying of fines running at 30–50% of wages for breaches of work discipline and quality control, and at a wage cut of 25%, walked out and petitioned the Governor of the province for protection against the harsh and arbitrary acts of their employers. Surprisingly, perhaps, their demands were not only listened to but accepted, and by 3 June 1886 the government had even prepared and promulgated what was, in effect, Russia's first labour code. The government's interests and preoccupations were clear from the contents of the new law. Employers were obligated to pay cash wages in full at specified fortnightly or monthly intervals. Workers were threatened with four to eight months' imprisonment for organising a strike and two to four months for taking part in one.

Despite this apparently easy success it was not until 1896 that the next major strike occurred, although there were plenty of minor skirmishes. On 23 May 1896 a strike broke out among 750 workers at the Rossiiskaia cotton mills in St Petersburg. The unlikely sounding pretext for the strike was a demand for payment for the national holiday on the occasion of Nicholas II's coronation. By the end of the month all the major textile factories in the city were at a standstill and on 3 June non-textile factories, including Putilov and Nobel, joined in. Some 30,000 workers were thus on strike, not only Russia's but one of Europe's largest strikes. Even more remarkable, perhaps, is the fact that, after having to make concessions on wages and labour conditions which included the promise of an eleven-and-a-half-hour day to be implemented by the beginning of 1897, the employers, after calculating that such solidarity on the part of their workers could not be repeated, went back on their promises, only to be faced with a recurrence of the strike in 1897. On 16 April 1897 the eleven-and-a-half-hour day and a 7% wage increase for some employees were introduced in the St Petersburg cotton mills. As with the strike in Orekhovo-Zuevo, government anxiety at the public order implications of strikes and a certain distance between state and employers was in evidence, to the extent that a law was promulgated on 2 June 1897 limiting excessive working hours and establishing the eleven-and-a-half-hour working day, though, in the absence of enforcers and penalties, it was largely ignored.

Though such events were encouraging for the radicals and frightening for the authorities they were insignificant in comparison with the great mass movements of 1905 and 1917. It is not possible to give more than a brief outline of labour participation in these events before moving on to an analysis of what were the chief sources of dynamism within the Russian labour movement throughout the period under review.

It would appear that the only valid generalisation about the labour movement in the years around 1905 and 1917 is that all sectors and all regions were heavily involved and that no clear patterns of participation can be discerned. Workers and peasants of different crafts, trades, regions, genders and age groups were involved. Oil workers in Baku, peasants in Saratov, leather workers in Moscow, and textile workers in Ivanovo were all paradigms of militancy. Distant provincial cities like Rostov-on-Don were among the first to experience major strikes in the early twentieth century. A careful study of peasant involvement also shows that different groups participated in different places, the determining factor, one might surmise, being found in local circumstances. According to this account, while it was usually younger, poorer, male peasants who instigated rebellious activity — ranging from the insignificant, such as crop pilfering, to the serious, such as arson — it was not unknown for older peasants, females and richer peasants, who alone possessed the horses and carts necessary to make, for instance, tree-felling worthwhile, to urge on the others. 'Outside agitators' in the form of rurally employed intellectuals such as agronomists, doctors and engineers; or urban-based proletarians whose work, for example on the repair and maintenance of railway track, brought them into contact with the rural population through whose areas they passed; or even returned workers, not to mention returned conscripts from the army and navy engaged in the futile struggle against Japan in 1904 and 1905; all these appear to have had, at best, a marginal influence on the peasantry's activities.[4] Studies of urban activity show a similar diversity. While younger, unmarried workers were often more militant all sectors could be found taking the lead. In a number of places state-sponsored 'police trade unions' played a major role in catalysing worker activities, most notably St Petersburg where the revolution proper was instigated by the volleys of bullets fired by the police into the ranks of demonstrators and bystanders on Bloody Sunday (9 January (old style) 1905). The demonstration had been called within the spirit of the 'medieval' Slavophile myth of the right of all citizens to petition the Tsar when their grievances became intolerable. Within a loyal framework of patriotism and devotion to the Orthodox church, and under the leadership of a government-sponsored priest, Gapon, the Assembly of Russian Factory Workers brought together a mass demonstration of 400,000 people who converged on the Winter Palace from a variety of points around the city. Attempts to sift through the participants have not revealed any identifiable pattern of involvement beyond seeing it as representative of a wide cross-section of the labouring poor of the city and its surrounding districts. Workers from all parts of industry, artisans, even peasants participated. There was also a leaven of sympathetic intellectuals and some middle-class support.

One of the most determined and violent episodes of 1905 occurred in the Polish city of Łodz, where, for five days in mid-June workers controlled the streets and barricades were set up. Here a major motivating force, broadening the revolutionary coalition, was anti-Russian Polish nationalism. Corresponding feelings were present in rebellious activities throughout the other Baltic provinces of the Empire — Lithuania, Estonia, Latvia and Finland. It was also present in the Caucasus and not entirely absent from the Ukraine, where it was frequently diverted by the authorities into violent anti-Semitic pogroms. It is also noteworthy that it was in the twin textile town of Ivanovo-Voznesensk that Russia's first Soviet was

4. See M. Perrie, 'The Russian Peasant Movement of 1905–1907: its Social Composition and Revolutionary Significance', *Past and Present* (November, 1972), 57, pp.123–55.

set up, to co-ordinate a strike there in summer 1905, an event crystallised into myth by subsequent historiography but a rather commonplace occurrence within its actual context. The example was followed later in St Petersburg at the time of its General Strike, accompanied by a railway strike which, given the fragility of Russian communications, presented the government with an unanswerable threat not only to the economy and the food supply lines of the 'grain-importing' cities of north Russia, but also to its control over troop movements. It was this dire emergency which extracted the reluctantly granted concessions of the October Manifesto, which vaguely promised an unspecified form of wide popular participation in government. As soon as the coast was clear the autocracy retracted as much as possible of what it had given away. The final major event of 1905, and one of the most violent, occurred in the more 'traditional' and 'Russian' environment of Moscow where a rebellion in the working-class district of Presnia, once again involving a wide cross-section of the working class and radical sympathisers, was only suppressed by guards' regiments, artillery and cossacks, an event memorably reconstructed in Pasternak's novel (and film) *Dr Zhivago*. Urban and rural violence continued beyond 1905, however, and 1906 was a year of continued suppressed civil war with some 2,000 government agents being killed and hundreds, if not thousands, of 'ringleaders' of rebellion in town and country being summarily executed by roving 'field courts martial'. Again the impact of these events was felt throughout a wide spectrum of the lower ranks of Russian society.

In the light of this it will come as no surprise that the return to labour militancy, in 1912–14, temporarily damped down by the patriotic euphoria of the early days of the war, but getting under way again in late 1915, also refused to stay within easily accessible boundaries and affected a wide spectrum of the urban population; however, in contrast with 1903–6, the rural population remained largely uninvolved until some weeks after the collapse of Tsarism in the February revolution. The economic conditions of wartime, as experienced by the urban population — rapidly escalating prices outdistancing wage rises; long hours; harsh labour discipline; food shortages; disgust at the disastrous outcome of the war — affected a wide range of the population. Strike waves, at particularly acute moments, involved enormous numbers of people. For instance, in the months of September 1915 and January, April, May, June and October 1916 over 100,000 people took part in strikes.

The conventional division of these into 'economic' and 'political' strikes is difficult to sustain in the cold light of actual conditions for almost all strikes in Russia, especially in wartime, had strong elements of both since the state and its coercive powers remained the chief arbiter of industrial relations. Again the safest generalisation is to point to widespread and deep-rooted militancy rather than to claim to discern clearly established patterns within this kaleidoscope of events. Even in 1917, when militancy was a feature of the life not only of almost all workers and peasants, but even, in their own way, of office workers, managers, senior civil servants, university teachers, generals and even Grand Dukes, patterns were submerged beneath the universal struggle to fill the vacuum caused by the unexpected, precipitate and complete collapse of the Tsarist state, an event which let the cork out of a bottle filled with the effervescent aspirations of all parts of society to rejig social relations and social institutions to serve their own interests more appropriately.

Why was Russian labour militant?

How are we to explain this formidable record of militancy on the part of Russian labour? On the face of it, given the rebellious tradition of the peasantry, and its perhaps crudely expressed but none the less deeply held belief in the natural rights of all to a share in property and an innate sense of outrage at the flaunted affluence of the rich (outrage shared even by those who, in a spirit of humility or fatalism, believed that nothing could alter this immutable way of the world), one would expect historians to have turned in this direction to seek an explanation. In point of fact, the view that dominates discussion starts from exactly opposite assumptions. In the most widely prevailing opinion, the further a worker developed *away* from the countryside the *more* revolutionary, the more 'conscious' and the more 'advanced' s/he was thought to become. This progression usually co-existed with a rise up the enormously complex gradations of skill from unskilled to skilled labour and thereby to higher wages. It also often entailed long-term residence and long-term employment in industry and was thought to be likely to coincide with having been born and brought up in an urban working-class environment. As opposed to these so-called advanced workers, those who were left behind in this process, low-paid, short-term, frequently female labourers, were thought to be 'backward', lacking in 'consciousness' and even potentially counter-revolutionary. At best they were thought to be capable of actions described as 'spontaneous', by which was meant chaotic, ill-organised, ill-led and, perhaps, riotous activities of a reactive nature, that is as a protest against an immediate grievance. As opposed to this, conscious workers were supposed to show greater organisa-tion, more subtle appreciation of longer-term questions (in other words, a higher level of political consciousness) and to be more disciplined. As a result of all these characteristics advanced workers were thought to be 'revolutionary' where backward ones remained 'spontaneous' and volatile.

This theory of advanced and backward workers was a very prominent one among revolutionary intellectuals in Russia at the turn of the century. Its origin is clear: it was derived from the orthodox interpretation of Marx. The proletariat, Marx had argued, would become radicalised by the constant frustration it would face in trying to overcome the effects of exploitation which it was bound to feel as a result of its place in the capitalist system. Its conscious-ness would be raised from that of the uncomprehending, narrow-minded and potentially petty bourgeois peasant, who dreamed of individual ownership of land, not the collective ownership which was the hallmark of socialism. Its consciousness would thereby, Marxists concluded, rise to the recognition that only a complete transformation of property relations, releasing the means of pro-duction (machines, land, capital) from the shackles of private own-ership and placing them instead under the liberating control of collective ownership, could fulfil their hopes. In the broadest terms, the activities of the revolutionary parties were aimed at hastening this process. The trouble is, however, can one identify a substantial body of advanced workers in Russia and do those who most closely fit the bill act in the way the theory expects them to do?

It was an axiom of Russian revolutionary thinking that the Russian working class was a long way from fulfilling the criteria for revolution derived from Marx's writings. It was, as was the case for Marx himself, to countries like Germany, France, and Britain that radicals looked for signs of the development of an assault on private ownership of the means of production. Lenin's views on the level of development of the Russian working class did not change substan-tially on this point. Writing in early 1917 Lenin had asserted that

We know perfectly well that the proletariat of Russia is less organised, less prepared and less class-conscious than the proletariat of other countries. It is not its special qualities but rather the special conjuncture of historical circumstances that *for a certain, perhaps very short, time* has made the proletariat of Russia the vanguard of the revolutionary proletariat of the whole world. Russia is a peasant country, one of the most backward of European countries. Socialism *cannot* triumph there *directly* and *immediately*. (Emphasis in original.)[5]

Lenin was not alone in this. The Mensheviks were equally insistent on it. In the 1905 revolution, for instance, a major resolution had talked of the 'weak organisation of the leading ranks of the proletariat'. It is interesting to note that they believed, like Lenin in 1917, that power might none the less pass to the proletarian party. The conditions under which this might happen — namely that they should remain 'the party of extreme revolutionary opposition' and not get involved in any possible Provisional Government, and that the revolution must spread to Western Europe — are closer to Lenin's policy in 1917 than to that of the majority of the Mensheviks themselves.

Curiously it was Trotsky who constantly emphasised the strength of the Russian proletariat. Writing in 1906 in *Results and Prospects* he explained that this did not contradict its backwardness. Indeed, it was in part because of it, since the same process of retardation affected the bourgeoisie even more severely. As a result, when measured against the bourgeoisie, the Russian proletariat was in a more powerful position than, say, the American proletariat where capitalist forms of production were much more highly developed. 'In an economically backward country', he concluded, 'the proletariat may come to power earlier than in an advanced capitalist country.' In this way, Trotsky did not deny the backwardness of the Russian proletariat but believed that this position bestowed certain advantages on it.

All this would seem to suggest that the notion of an advanced working class was clearly seen to be inapplicable to Russia at that time. However, if this were accepted, one would then have to conclude that the militancy and innate socialism of the Russian labour movement came from elsewhere. Rather than accept this, most radicals then and since have sought alternative explanations. Some have followed Trotsky's view of the supposed advantages of

5. V.I. Lenin, *Farewell Letter to the Swiss Workers* (26 March 1917); in *Collected Works* vol. 23 p.371.

backwardness. More commonly, however, others have sought to identify sub-groups within the working class which more closely resembled the advanced proletariat and which might be seen to have played a leading role in this militancy. While the class as a whole was indubitably backward, according to this terminology, its leaders and militants might, perhaps, be advanced. Extensive recent research had made it possible to give a more detailed picture of the composition of the Russian working class.

Clearly there were imperfect degrees of differentiation in the Russian labour movement and working class. In addition to the mass of fairly recent migrants who made up the bulk of it there were cores of more urbanised skilled workers and artisans. While skilled workers have been studied in depth it is more difficult to delineate the characteristics of the Russian artisanat and its contribution to the labour movement. In the first place, there was a multitude of small, scattered workshops in which a high proportion of the artisans were employed and which eluded, in the circumstances of the time, reliable information-gathering. Even government figures before 1900 ignored establishments of fewer than sixteen employees (double that if unmechanised) and after 1900 defined a factory as a workshop employing twenty or more. Secondly, artisan labour could shade into skilled factory and craft labour and it is difficult to draw the line between them. Despite these handicaps, however, one can make a number of comments about artisans.

First of all, they were very numerous, probably outnumbering the factory labour force in Moscow and not being far behind in St Petersburg.[6] Over the country as a whole they far outweighed the factory labour force. Secondly, migrant artisanal labour appears to have differed very little in its social profile from other parts of the migrant urban labour force. However, the artisans in the cities were slightly more urbanised than the labour force as a whole and therefore comprised a lower proportion of migrants. To draw further distinctions would be to split hairs. As far as their political behaviour is concerned generalisations are rather hazardous. As in Western Europe some of the earliest and strongest unions were formed by defensive-minded artisans fearful of the mechanisation and de-skilling of their crafts. However, they did not stand aloof from the rest of the working class and were enthusiastic participants

---

6. V. Bonnell, *Roots of Rebellion: Workers, Politics and Organisations in St Petersburg and Moscow 1900–1914* (Berkeley, Calif.: 1983), p.23.

in institutions such as the Soviets which brought together a wide range of workers. Even so, no clear correlations between them and behaviour supposedly typical of advanced workers can be drawn. For instance, among the workers most closely fitting the profile of advanced workers the largely artisanal printers tended to be moderate and economistic rather than forthrightly revolutionary. In October 1917, for instance, they protested at the Bolsheviks' closing down counter-revolutionary and bourgeois newspapers on the grounds that this deprived them of work. One historian has attributed this moderate behaviour to the fact that the nature of their work brought them into contact with intellectuals and the middle classes and this made them more deferential.[7] This dubious sounding proposition would appear, on the face of it, to be equally applicable to other artisan groups, notably tailors, except that the Tailors' Union showed a higher propensity to support the Bolsheviks and to be in the forefront of militant activity in 1905 and in 1917. Thus the role of the artisans, though clearly of great importance, is hard to generalise about and provides very mixed evidence in support of the theory of the avant-garde role of advanced workers. The artisanat is a key area requiring further detailed research.

The category most frequently claimed to fulfil this advanced role was that of the skilled workers. Even here, though, considerable caution is necessary. The most widely favoured candidates as advanced workers, the metalworkers, were, in Moscow, made up 45% by artisanal labour. Victoria Bonnell has shown quite convincingly that craft and workshop patriotism dominated the self-image of metalworkers.[8] There were some 100 skill gradations in St Petersburg metalworking and the differences between them were jealously guarded by those who had risen up this hierarchy. The propensity which some of them showed to form unions, the Metalworkers being one of the strongest unions in St Petersburg and Moscow in the period in which unions were allowed to function after 1905, was often motivated by the desire to protect differentials and privileges and to improve working conditions rather than from any sweeping political aims and objectives.

None the less, many historians have pointed to a crucial division within the workers, particularly of St Petersburg. According to this

---

7. Koenker, *Moscow Workers*, p.299.
8. Bonnell, *Roots of Rebellion*.

view there was a relatively well-educated, settled and organised layer of skilled workers, who were thought to be more politically aware and sympathetic to revolution. The attitudes and way of life of this group contrasted sharply with that of the mass of recent rural migrants who were raw, ill-organised and transient and who, despite their uniformly poor conditions of life and tendency to sporadic outbreaks of protest, were considered unpromising material by radical organisers. The fact that these unskilled workers were dominated by allegedly fatalistic rural attitudes, tended to return home to the village after a few years and, supposedly worst of all, were often women who were particularly looked down upon by male union and political organisers meant, it is often argued, that they were more of an obstacle to socialism and to revolution than an asset. This argument has been frequently put forward by Soviet historians, not least because it appears to tally with Lenin's views on the subject. Even though, as we have seen, he was aware of the overall backwardness of the Russian working class, this did not prevent him from differentiating between more and less advanced sectors of it. Although this interpretation emphasises one aspect of Lenin's argument at the expense of his overall caution about the nature of the Russian working class as a whole and of its situation in an overwhelmingly peasant country, it has been echoed by non-Soviet historians as well.[9]

The evidence for the importance of this division comes, especially, from anecdotal evidence presented in worker memoirs. For instance, according to A. Buiko, a worker of rural origin: 'In the first years, before I outgrew my still peasant attitudes, I felt myself alone and constantly experienced fear before other people. But once I grew close to my comrades, I began to feel unshakeable ground beneath my feet.'[10] As far as unskilled and female labour is concerned the view expressed in a newspaper of 1914 that 'The majority of women workers, including our mill, drag behind at the tail end of the labour movement'[11] is typical of many. While it would be foolish to ignore the mass of such evidence it has to be used critically. Much of it comes from committed Bolshevik sources, whether it was published at the time or subsequently. Many of the volumes of memoirs reflect the party line of the period in which

9. A good example of this is D. Mandel, *The Petrograd Workers and the Fall of the Old Regime* (London, 1983), pp.9–43.

10. Quoted in ibid., p.22.

11. Ibid., p.26.

they were published. Most of them came out in the years 1925–35 and reflect the growing emphasis on the theme of socialism in one country, an ideology which, among other things, required the Russian working class to be portrayed as confident, independent and self-sufficient. The degree to which they claim the workers were hostile to other classes — especially peasants and intellectuals — frequently varies according to the changing requirements of party policy. Sometimes the explanations sound rather mechanical. It is necessary, for instance, to explain why many workers in 1917 supported the Socialist Revolutionaries rather than the Bolsheviks. One memoirist, A. Shotman, says of such workers in one district of Petrograd that:

> The main mass of workers consisted of a settled element that had worked at the factory for several years. There were, for example, some who had worked 20 or even 30 years consecutively . . . Many workers had their own small houses; there were even some who had several houses which they rented out. Naturally, among this category of worker it was useless to conduct any sort of agitation for the overthrow of the existing order . . . Only the youth, and even so, not the sons of the old-timers, but the outsiders, were more or less receptive to agitation.[12]

To describe Socialist Revolutionaries as supporters of the old regime is quite wrong. The real issue of why these workers were not Bolshevik is skated over. Interestingly, the hint at the end that perhaps migrants were more receptive to revolutionary agitation than settled, skilled workers would not normally appear except that, at this point, it serves the current, rather slender argument. By and large, awkward workers like these Socialist Revolutionaries tend to be dismissed as a labour aristocracy. Whatever value this term may have in other connections it is hard to avoid the view that in Leninist and Bolshevik usage an advanced worker is a skilled worker who supports the party whereas one who does not belongs to the aristocracy of labour.

In addition to exercising caution engendered by the convenient way in which this anecdotal evidence serves later purposes, it is also necessary to measure it against the rather sparse systematic material relating to this question. While it is, no doubt, the case that there are great differences of outlook and attitude between skilled and unskilled workers and between male and female workers, this does

12. Ibid., p.39.

not necessarily mean that there was a linear progression from peasant to proletarian similar to that from chrysalis to butterfly, nor that skilled workers were always the conscious revolutionary acti-vists and leaders of the unskilled. In reality, the evidence is more ambiguous. Perhaps the most striking evidence which casts doubt on the correlation between advanced workers and radicalism and militancy is the information about their activities in the critical year of 1917. Many historians have concluded that strikes and similar demonstrations of militancy tended to emanate first and foremost from the better-paid, more urbanised and more highly skilled workers in larger factories, pointing, for instance, to the fact that large factories provided 82% of strikers in Moscow in 1917 even though they employed only 74% of the work-force.[13] However, a number of important qualifications have to be made. First, some of the most militant groups in 1917 (as in 1896) did not come from this category. Secondly, some workers best fitting the category had rather low rates of militancy. Thirdly, the recorded figures can be assumed to have under-reported strikes in smaller enterprises while those in larger ones were much harder to overlook. On this last point, a good example of under-reporting is provided by figures gathered by Diane Koenker for the activities of the Tailors' Union in early 1917.[14] Press reports provided information about seventeen strikes in 1917 and 742 strikers in the first three months of the Revolution, where the union records showed there had been 119 strikes and 1,706 strikers in the first three months of the Revolution alone. Thus the, in any case, rather small disparity of 74% of the workers providing 82% of strikers in Moscow might, in reality, be reversed if fuller information were available.

With respect to the other two points, Diane Koenker's careful study of the evidence of participation in strikes in Moscow in 1917 shows very clearly that while metalworkers had the second highest propensity to strike (though how this was distributed between artisanal and large factory metalworkers is not given) the highest propensity to strike was demonstrated by wood-workers who, though only 2.5% of the work-force, accounted for 10% of strikers. In addition the leather workers had the longest and most bitter strike of the year in Moscow, and neither of these groups fits the pattern of advanced workers. It is interesting to note that this was

13. Koenker, *Moscow Workers*, p.31.
14. Ibid.

also the case in the 1896/7 strike wave in St Petersburg. The 'backward' women workers of the La Ferme cigarette factory went on strike earlier than the 'advanced' metalworkers of the Putilov and other factories.

Textile workers appear in the middle of the table for strikes in Moscow in 1917, but one of the least militant groups of workers, the printers, are among the most advanced, by criteria of pay, skill and urbanisation. The opinion that this anomaly is explained by 'their unique position in society' which made them 'less adamantly opposed to co-operation with the bourgeoisie'[15] would, to say the least, raise a few eyebrows among their equivalents today in Fleet Street and Wapping. Be that as it may, the evidence of correlation between advanced workers and militancy, and even more tenuously with higher political and class consciousness, is very ambiguous and the case cannot be said to have been proven. The evidence seems to show that at least some of the 'advanced' sectors of the working class were following the path charted out by their counterparts in Western Europe, where higher pay and better conditions of employment led away from class solidarity and revolution and towards labourism and 'economistic' activities. Indeed, one could argue that the strike pattern of 1917 is better explained in terms of 'economistic' demands since 92% of all strikes in Moscow included demands for higher pay. Disputes over hiring and firing, holidays, pay during shut-downs and the eight-hour day account for almost all strikes in Moscow (for which the most thorough figures are available) leading the historian to the conclusion that 'the overwhelming majority of strikes in Moscow in 1917 centred on economic issues' and thus reflected worker/management rather than worker/regime tensions.[16] There is nothing to suggest that the picture was substantially different elsewhere. Indeed, it has been convincingly shown by Steve Smith that even apparently highly 'conscious' activities such as worker take-overs of factories in St Petersburg in 1917 were prompted by the desire to protect employment and as a last desperate gesture to keep production going in the face of fuel shortages (real or contrived by the management), lock-outs and cash flow crises.[17]

Bearing these different types of evidence in mind, can one satisfactorily resolve the question of the role of different sections of the

15. Ibid., p.299.
16. Ibid., p.293.
17. Smith, *Red Petrograd*.

Russian working class in revolutionary activity? The memoir evidence suggests, overwhelmingly, that the advanced 'cadre' workers were to the fore in factory committees, trade unions and so on, though, as we have seen, this was in accordance with the theory many of these memoirists subscribed to anyway. On the other hand, as Smith points out, 'quantitative data to bear out this contention are lacking'.[18] Unfortunately, the same is true with respect to any other contention. However, a critical reading of the best quantitative approach to the question so far (Koenker) suggests the issue is by no means as straightforward as Bolshevik memoirists and others have suggested. But until there is a really thorough and comparative study of artisans, skilled and unskilled workers the case has to remain not proven.

Given these ambiguities which make the simple correlation between advanced workers and high revolutionary class consciousness rather unsatisfactory, one is still left with the problem of accounting for the Revolution, the emergence of a socialist and supposedly proletarian society in Russia and the high, unprecedented degree of participation of the labouring classes in these processes. Can one provide a more satisfactory and comprehensive explanation?

A number of important components making up such an explanation can be identified. In the first place, the extensive links between the urban industrial labour force — factory and artisanal — and the countryside with its communal and rebellious traditions surely has to be given more weight. A second structural feature is the existence of a brilliant, creative and, in many cases, heroically self-sacrificing intelligentsia devoted to the eradication of social injustice in Russia. Beyond these a number of contingent circumstances also have to be given due weight. First, labour discipline in Russia was exceptionally harsh and working conditions were often insupportable. Secondly, the authorities were extremely unaccommodating in the face of the legitimate complaints raised about these conditions. Thirdly, the overall conjuncture of events has to be taken into account to the extent that the growth of a turbulent 'unmade' (to adapt E.P. Thompson's phrase) working class of Russia coincided with a period of increasingly threatening external crisis for Russia culminating in the catastrophe of the First World War. A number of other features also have to be taken into account. For example, the aspirations of nationalists on the periphery of the Russian Empire

18. Ibid., p.190.

gave an added impetus to change, though the degree of influence they exerted on labour is a matter of dispute.

In the front rank of these factors comes the traditional peasant roots of the Russian urban labour force. Despite the fact that the major twentieth-century revolutions — Mexico, China, Algeria, Vietnam, Kampuchea, Angola, Mozambique, Nicaragua and so on — have been largely peasant-based, and that the Russian Revolution itself had a peasant dimension of crucial importance, many observers have tended to see the peasantry as a conservative force. At best, certain theorists have used concepts such as 'alienation' (in the psychological sense) to describe the feelings of the rural migrant moving to a large city. This leads, it is argued by writers such as Chalmers Johnson and Neil Smelser, to a sense of confusion and disorientation which makes such migrants a ready prey for radical political agitation and predisposes them to revolution. Unfortunately, in the case of the revolutions referred to above and of the Russian Revolution itself, the evidence to support such a thesis is exceedingly thin. In the first place, peasants who did not migrate, who remained in their family villages working their family plots, proved themselves to have an extensive, not to mention violent and brutal, revolutionary streak which had nothing to do with psychological disorientation and a great deal to do with the primitive peasant sense of social justice and deep-rooted resentment against the idle rich. Similarly, all the evidence suggests that urban protest did not arise from a sense of personal insignificance and bewilderment at a complex and misunderstood urban environment; rather it was a rational, focused activity aimed at righting elementary wrongs, usually sparked off by particularly insupportable acts such as lock-outs or pay cuts by the employers. In any case, an important distinction should be borne in mind. Unlike the contemporary Third World and particularly Latin American model of an uncontrolled drift to the city and its accompanying shanty towns by a desperate and hungry peasantry, in Russia the system of industrial recruitment, the construction of workers' barracks and the internal passport system meant that arriving in the city and the factory without a job or a place to live and having to search for them was relatively rare. Being recruited to a factory was certainly not an easy experience for the Russian peasant, no doubt, but it was no more bewildering than military service (indeed, less so, since it was likely to be shorter-term for many) and is not directly comparable to the contemporary Third World experience.

Even when the rationality of labour activity has been recognised its existence has caused a certain amount of puzzlement among historians. 'Where', asks Victoria Bonnell, 'did workers find the bases of commonality necessary to undertake such activities?' In reply to her own question she points to 'shared position in the skill hierarchy' and craft-consciousness.[19] Others have, astonishingly, treated the Russian labour force as a kind of *tabula rasa*. While it is one thing to point to the absence of pre-existing guilds and craft unions and other established bureaucracies and organisations the equivalent of which, it is claimed, held the revolutionary cutting edge of Western European labour in check, it is another to argue that in Russia there was 'an emergent working class that was quite devoid of strong traditions of thought and organisation'.[20] In fact, the reverse was the case. The peasant brought to the city or the factory the communal traditions and sense of social justice developed in rural society. It is a mistake to imagine that the peasant voided his mind and jettisoned his world-view on the journey from village to factory or underwent a long-lasting sense of bewilderment and disorientation once he arrived. To overlook the aspects of her or his experience as a peasant which contributed *positively* to protest activities is to misunderstand the world of the Russian peasant. A sense of solidarity was instilled in peasants by their common experience of oppression by landowners and the state, and also by their attachment to the Orthodox church which gave them equal dignity as Christians, as people created by God, with those who oppressed them.

Few scholars have even toyed with the question of the growth not of separate 'class' consciousness but of a sense of solidarity embracing the 'labouring masses' as a whole, or even of being part of the *narod*, the people. The term 'labouring masses' or 'the people' and their derivatives and synonyms are much more frequent in the documents, slogans and debates of the labour movement in this period than more refined class-based terms such as 'proletariat' or even 'worker' (as distinct from 'working masses' which has a more populist ring to it). Where more overtly ideological phrases appear they are often the product of the intelligentsia leaders rather than the members of such organisations. In 1917, the sense of general solidarity found its expression in soviets where the diffuse popular

19. Bonnell, *Roots of Rebellion*, pp.442–6.
20. N. Harding, *Marxism in Russia: Key Documents 1879–1906* (Cambridge, 1983), p.2.

mood fitted into a matrix of commonality and shared goals and interests of quite extraordinary proportions. Even after October, the new 'proletarian' government often found continued instinctive resistance to repressions aimed at fellow members of the *narod*, whereas there was toleration of almost any kind of brutality against the former ruling class. To overlook this basic framework of solidarity and to ignore its origin in the shared experience of Russian rural life and traditional Orthodox society is to miss one of the most potent forces of the Russian Revolution. One cannot but feel here the effects of Western European and North American ethnocentricity getting in the way of understanding a culture in its own terms. Curiously, Russian intellectuals, often dazzled by West European thinkers and showing a tendency to denigrate their own traditions, have sometimes shared this short-sightedness.

In the case of Russia, at least, these considerations suggest there is a need to modify theories based on the assumption that peasants are 'conservative', even 'reactionary', and that there is a linear progression from their 'backwardness' to 'advanced', working-class, revolutionary consciousness via urbanisation, literacy and organisation. Rather it would appear that in Russia there was a more acutely revolutionary phase in the early stages of industrialisation when peasant values, including rebelliousness, met up with the acute exploitation characteristic of early industrialisation, greater literacy, the growing possibilities of organisation and contact with pre-existing artisan and petty bourgeois radicalism. If this phase had been overcome perhaps a greater stability based on improved living standards might have come about. It would follow from this that as the features of an 'advanced' working class began to prevail and the migrants became more urbanised, better educated, more orientated towards 'craft' and 'class' consciousness and towards labourist aims, then the prospects for revolution, far from advancing, might be thought to have been receding and the Russian labour movement be seen to be replicating the path of development of the British or the German labour movement. However, Russia was nowhere near reaching this higher stability in our period. Development in this direction was being impeded by the powerful factors mentioned earlier — intelligentsia radicalism, state intransigence, the historical conjuncture and the influence of nationalism among the minorities — which combined to ensure that labour in the Russian Empire would, for the time being at least, retain its radicalism. In order to complete our picture, then, it is necessary to examine the importance of these crucial factors, starting with intelligentsia radicalism. Almost by definition socialist theory is the preserve of intellectuals. Given the very limited (albeit widening) access to education that characterised nineteenth-century Europe in general and Russia in particular, this could hardly have been otherwise. The resulting separation of theoreticians of socialism from its putative practitioners is visible in all socialist movements, but of all the major states it was particularly prevalent in Russia. This was, above all, attributable to the existence of a small intelligentsia, divorced from the élite and from the people, which played an important role in the Russian revolutionary movement. While the Russian intelligentsia has always eluded succinct definition (and this is certainly not the place to correct this), a number of its characteristics have to be borne in mind. First, its members were normally university graduates. Exceptions to this did exist but it was a prerequisite of membership that a person would be highly literate and articulate even if self-taught. Secondly, opposition to Tsarism was an essential feature. This could, however, comprise liberal, socialist and, arguably, even slavophile critiques of the autocracy as it actually existed. Thirdly, the intelligentsia had a sense of self-sacrifice and devotion to the cause of the emancipation of the people. This feature has led some commentators to compare it to a monastic order or a religious sect and, indeed, one could see some limited parallels. Within these basic criteria a wide variety of Russian intellectuals considered themselves to be part of the intelligentsia. Not all of them were socialists. The following remarks apply largely, though not exclusively, to the socialist intelligentsia.

Russian socialist theory and the Russian revolutionary movement have often been thought of, by people as widely separate from one another as Lenin and Solzhenitsyn, to be an imported movement vehemently opposed to backward, superstitious Russia. It should be remembered, however, that it retained certain distinctively 'Russian' features throughout its existence. Two in particular are relevant to our discussion. In the first place, the first socialist ideas of any influence enunciated in Russia were formulated by Alexander Herzen and, although he had little direct knowledge of the Russian peasantry, he emphasised their potential socialism. His socialism defined itself in debate with Western socialists, for whom it was axiomatic, particularly given the experience of France in 1848, that peasants were reactionary and petty bourgeois. Herzen's idealised view of the Russian peasant commune, drawn from literature about it rather than from direct observation, was one of the main sources flowing into the populist movement of the 1870s which attempted to realise the revolutionary potential of the peasantry by propaganda or, failing that, by terrorist acts. It was in pursuit of the latter strategy that Khalturin exploded the bomb in the Winter Palace. Although neither of these strategies brought immediate results the loose current of 'populism' (that is, a largely, though by no means exclusively, peasant-based version of socialism) remained the most widespread political movement in Russia. Even after the October revolution the successors of the populists, the Socialist Revolutionary Party, captured some 50% of the votes.

A second persistent feature of Russian socialism is what might be called its 'Bakuninism'. Above all, Bakunin gave top priority to the struggle against the state and against the church as the main oppressors of the people. For this, he came into bitter conflict with Marx and the First International split irretrievably as a result. Yet, although Russian socialists looked to Marx rather than to Bakunin, the themes of the latter echo much more strongly in Russian socialism than they do in German or British socialism. This was attributable not so much to the intellectual influence of Bakunin as to the peculiarities of the Russian political and social structure in which the state and its subservient church were direct and prominent organs of repression, often outweighing and not always being equated with the power of landowners and capitalists. In Russia the state, through various historical accidents, remained a relatively independent force in Russian life. It was not in the pocket of any class. If anything it was the executive arm not of the landowners as a class but of the Romanov family. The question of giving priority to 'political struggle', that is the attack on the state, echoes through all the pronouncements of a wide variety of Russian revolutionary thinkers, and it was because they weakened this commitment in favour of more 'economist' demands (better wages and working conditions) that the Russian equivalent of the Bernsteinian revisionists were attacked vehemently by Bolsheviks and Mensheviks alike in the early twentieth century. From the time of its origin under Plekhanov, Russian Social Democracy never weakened in pledging that the first priority of the movement had to be the overthrow of the Tsarist state and the convening of a Constituent Assembly. In this, they were at one with the populists from whom Plekhanov had derived some of his ideas.

Another important, and specifically Russian, feature of intel-

ligentsia socialism was its search for a revolutionary class to implement its ideas. The intelligentsia, small and isolated as it was,
stood no chance of realising its revolutionary dreams on its own.
Having developed its own revolutionary consciousness in the mid-
nineteenth century it saw its task thereafter as being one of grafting
its revolutionary ideas on to a more powerful class better equipped
to make a reality of them. The populists saw hope in the rebellious
tradition of the peasantry; but their initial efforts in this direction in
the 1870s were frustrated, not least because of all the periods in the
nineteenth century they could have chosen, this decade was the one
in which the political and economic conditions of the peasantry, still
enjoying the brief honeymoon of the emancipation of 1861, made
them less disposed to revolution. By the end of the century the
peasantry, under the pressures described earlier, had once again
become turbulent. None the less, the failure of populism to raise the
peasantry led some populists, like Plekhanov, to argue, under the
influence of Marx, that the working class rather than the peasantry
should be the group to which the hopes of revolution should be
attached. Though the proletariat was small and weak in Russia at the
time he first enunciated these ideas, in the mid-1880s, it was, he
argued, destined to grow as Russia modernised and was, in any case,
already a powerful force on the European scale.

It followed from this relationship — intelligentsia revolutionary
consciousness seeking a revolutionary class to implement its ideas
— that some mechanism would be needed to effect the necessary
transfer and raising of consciousness. In the 1870s, the populists had
first tried direct propaganda, 'going to the people', as it was called
and, later in the decade, a minority of perhaps no more than two
hundred formed a conspiratorial network, the People's Will (*Narodnaia volia*), aimed at carrying out terrorist actions against the
agents of the state. After 1881 they settled down to a mixture of
both which was institutionalised in the Socialist Revolutionary
Party. When it was founded in 1901 it still had a political wing and a
terrorist wing.

Eventually, Russian Social Democracy also had to face the same
problem. While it remained a small émigré group, able, as Plekhanov joked, to fit into a rowing boat on Lake Geneva, the issue was
not pressing but as the working class and as Social Democracy
began to challenge populism, questions of party organisation began
to emerge from the mid-1890s on. The best known aspect of this
process — Lenin's view that a party of conscious militants was

needed to instil revolutionary ideas into a recalcitrant and persistently 'economist' and 'trade unionist' working class — had been a
stock-in-trade of the Russian revolutionary movement since the
1870s (except, of course, that in the early stages it was peasants
rather than workers who were to be the target). His energetic
arguments in defence of this in *What is to be done?* (1902) were not
particularly original and shared many important features with other
attacks on economism and the threat it posed of diverting the
workers' movement away from direct confrontation with the state
and into reformism.

While it was all very well to defend the role of the party in this
way, various attempts to implement such ideas had run into a series
of practical snags, in the front rank of which was the problem of
bridging the vast religious, educational, social and economic gulf
that separated the intelligentsia from the people for, although the
intelligentsia was despised and feared by the establishment, the
masses often saw it as part of the élite. The problem was compounded by social geography. The intelligentsia was urban, the
peasantry rural. Any intrusion of urban strangers into the world of
the village was likely to have predictable results — misunderstand-
ing, suspicion and fear. This was exactly the response aroused by
the 'going to the people' in the mid-1870s. As a result, the populists
began to approach peasants who had greater contact with the city —
seasonal workers, migrants — with a view to using them as a
transmission belt to the countryside. Thus, even for peasant-
orientated populists, urban workers very quickly became a key
spearhead. In this conception, however, workers were not thought
of as qualitatively distinct from the peasantry, rather they were
simply the most accessible part of it.

Surprisingly, the Social Democrats shared some of these presuppositions. It would be quite wrong to picture them, Menshevik or
Bolshevik, closing their minds to the wider exploited population in
favour of narrow concentration on urban workers. Party programmes
and manifestos show this time and time again. Once again one can
surmise that the vanguard nature of the urban workers arose, at least
in part, because of their relative accessibility. The majority were still
close to the peasants and it was, as we have seen, axiomatic, among
Russian Marxists, that the Russian working class was 'backward',
particularly in comparison with Germany, Britain and, to a lesser
degree, France.

The chief route to overcoming this backwardness was, it was

generally thought, through raising their consciousness. The populists had themselves come to this conclusion as long ago as the 1870s. The view of Lenin was not totally divergent from that of his rival Martov on this point. For both, the centrepiece of the party was its newspaper, because only through such publications could the life-blood of propaganda and education circulate through the movement. For all Social Democrats in the years before 1905 the production and distribution (illegally) of the newspaper absorbed most of the party's energy. In the somewhat easier conditions after 1905, when it was possible to organise legal trade unions and to have at least a little legal immunity for some party members, broader aims and objectives were pursued. However, compared to political parties, trade unions never assumed a predominant role. Even in 1905, when they were at their peak, unions only represented 10–11% of St Petersburg and Moscow workers. In the years of reaction their numbers fell considerably.

The degree to which this process of raising consciousness can be seen to have been actually taking place in Russia in the early twentieth century is difficult to measure. In his valuable memoirs, recently translated into English, the Social Democratic worker-organiser Semen Kanatchikov diminished the significance of the intelligentsia, claiming that they lived in a different world from that of the workers, and had little in common with them. At the same time, however, his memoirs show that such worker organisations and circles as were able to exist in the period before 1905, about which he was writing, often revolved around intellectuals. This is borne out by other evidence. Almost all the leaders and organisers of radical parties were intellectuals. Parties, circles and workers' groups tended to consist of a small intellectual nucleus around which clustered a group of workers, themselves a tiny minority of the labour force. Undoubtedly intellectuals played a crucial role as the yeast in the dough of these early organisations and were particularly valuable in articulating demands, writing programmes and manifestos and, to a limited extent, politically educating potentially radical workers. The intelligentsia core of radical political parties was never diluted. Intellectuals continued to lead all the major Soviet-based parties during the 1917 revolution. In a sense, rather than transferring consciousness to the workers themselves the intellectuals *were* that consciousness. They stood by and, when the opportunity arose, became the articulators and leaders of the mass labour movement.

The revolutionary potential of the Russian labour movement, then, is not to be explained as the result of a gradual increase in consciousness transferred to it from the intelligentsia. Certainly, the existence of the revolutionary intelligentsia meant that there was a conscious leadership available at moments of crisis. But it was not the intelligentsia which provoked those crises. Many of them sought to exert such control but the degree to which they achieved it is debatable. A recent study[21] of the relations between Social Democratic trade unions and parties between 1906 and 1914 shows that the émigré intelligentsia party leaders were often out of touch with organisers in Russia. The former pursued sweeping strategic objectives while the latter were more involved in day-to-day issues of survival and piecemeal advance.

All this would suggest that, in place of the intelligentsia model of revolution coming about as the outcome of a steady rise in working-class revolutionary consciousness as a result of propaganda and the greater urbanisation of workers, it should be recognised that the radicalisation of the Russian worker was, paradoxically, a consequence of the experience of labourism itself.

Labour discipline and working conditions in Russia at the turn of the century were uniformly harsh. Wages were low, hours were long, accidents frequent, job security non-existent for many, sickness benefit and compensation unheard of. Housing was overcrowded, fines for absenteeism and unpunctuality were frequent. An impression of these problems can be obtained from the fact that, according to official figures, 245 people were killed and 3,508 injured in metal-working factories in 1890. In 1904, 556 people were killed and 67,000 injured, that is over 10% of the labour force in that sector. Only in June 1903 were employers made liable for medical and welfare costs arising from accidents in their factories.[22] Housing, particularly for rural migrants, was appalling. Many lived in dormitories the beds of which were occupied at different times of day by workers on different shifts. Artisans often slept in their workshops. Overcrowding was common. In one case a room thirteen feet square was shared by four couples. Slightly smaller family rooms might house up to twelve people. One apartment block in Moscow had one kitchen with a single stove for eighty inhabitants.

21. G. Swain, *Russian Social Democracy and the Legal Labour Movement 1906–1914* (London, 1983).

22. H. Seton-Watson, *The Russian Empire 1801–1917* (Oxford, 1967), p.541.

About 50% of a worker's income went on a Spartan diet composed largely of black bread which provided 55% of calories consumed.[23] Many more examples of the harshness of working life and the associated living conditions could be given.

Given the conditions under which women and men worked in the mines, factories and workshops of the Russian Empire it is not surprising that extensive protest existed. Other industrialising countries had faced similar problems. What made the situation more serious in the case of Russia, however, was the fact that, in the absence of any mediating institutions (before 1905, at least, and partially thereafter) the state was in the front line of any serious disturbance in industrial relations, as, indeed, it had been for centuries in the event of equivalent rural disturbances. This meant that any serious strike brought a risk of escalating rapidly into a direct confrontation with the police. Thus a strike, no matter how trivial, was treated as a minor rebellion. Political parties, trade unions and the like being illegal, political organisations and activities of any kind being outlawed by the autocracy, arbitration tribunals being practically non-existent, labour relations in Russia were a simple matter of the state backing up (not always whole-heartedly) the authority of the employers. In these circumstances, the distinction between 'economic' and 'political' strikes becomes so thin as to be meaningless in most cases since strikes usually broke out in protest against specific grievances, often of a very provocative kind, such as fines, wage cuts or lock-outs. If they were well supported and the employers refused to compromise the police would be called in to restore order. The strikers thus came into direct conflict with the state and the distinction between the 'economic' and 'political' aspects of the strike were obliterated. Since they were illegal before 1905, all strikes in Russia were, *ipso facto*, political. The advantage of this was recognised early in his career by Lenin who, with characteristic energy, urged workers to hit out at the employers and the regime in the manner of the strikers at the Semiannikov factory in 1895. 'You know', he wrote,

> there's a toy where you press a spring and up jumps a soldier with a bayonet. That's what happened at the Semiannikov factory and that's what will happen all over the place. The factory owners and their toadies are the spring. Push it and the puppet that it activates will appear — the

23. Koenker, *Moscow Workers*, pp. 54-6.

public procurator, the police, and the gendarmes.[24]

Constant pressure, he concluded, would weaken the whole mechanism.

It would be easy to conclude from this that Tsarism should have taken steps to de-politicise industrial relations. But in the prevailing conditions nothing could have been more difficult to implement. The dominant position of the central state, the very keystone of the autocratic system, the framework of the Empire and the guarantee of its territorial inviolability, would have to be substantially altered. In an atmosphere where even slightly reformist government ministers such as Witte and even Stolypin were suspected by the court camarilla of being near-revolutionaries, there was little hope of changing this fundamental situation. Such attempts as were undertaken at providing a legal framework for labour relations were half-hearted, partial and ineffective. What is worse, they sometimes seemed to be a sign of weakness. The first labour code, promulgated in 1886 was, as mentioned above, something of a panic reaction to the first serious strike in Russia. The enactment of the eleven-and-a-half-hour day was a similar response to the St Petersburg disturbances and remained a dead letter as there was no agency to enforce it. Before 1905 Tsarist labour legislation was of minimal importance.

As a measure of the antiquated mentality of Tsarism the only semi-acceptable avenue of complaint open to workers, as to peasants and all other citizens, was the vestigial right of petition to the Tsar. Some clever policemen had the bright idea of using this opening as a way of luring the dissatisfied workers away from contact with atheistic radicals. Instead, they would set up loyalist workers' organisations which would contain protest within acceptable bounds. Wherever these experiments in 'police socialism' were tried they blew up in the faces of the organisers for the simple reason that there were no acceptable bounds for organised protest in Tsarist Russia. This was demonstrated at its clearest in the Bloody Sunday demonstration in St Petersburg on 9 January 1905. All the elements of typical Tsarist labour protest were there. The demonstration was rooted in specific economic grievances, it chose the ancient right of petition to the Tsar as its channel of expression, it

24. V.I. Lenin, 'To the Workers of the Semiannikov Factory' (January 1895); quoted in Harding, *Marxism in Russia*, p.140.

expressed fundamental loyalty to Tsar and country and it was broken up by a fusillade of bullets that left hundreds of casualties, many of them bystanders, and crystallised the total incompatibility of Tsarism and popular protest with greater clarity than could a thousand revolutionary pamphlets. In a few hours economist protest had been turned into revolution, not by agitators but as a result of the inner logic of the situation and the prevailing structures.

Even after the emergency of 1905 passed the state failed to take (indeed, still could not take) serious measures to de-politicise labour relations. The years after 1905 show an insistent and irreversible erosion of concessions forced out of the autocracy in its year of crisis. The Duma was hemmed in, freedom of the press restricted and manipulated where possible, unions harassed, radical parties driven back underground. It is no surprise then that, when industrial turbulence blew up again in the wake of an economic slow-down, the state returned to direct intervention. In 1912, a massacre of some 200 workers in the goldfields was a signal that nothing had changed and by July 1914 there were barricades in the streets of St Petersburg once again. Direct confrontation between labour and the state was as explosive as ever. If anything, wartime conditions made this even worse. The rising tide of urban unrest in 1915 and 1916 pitted workers of all categories against the authorities. If such action was considered rebellious in peacetime it was verging on treachery during a war such as that in which Russia was engaged. Martial law, which had been extended to an ever-increasing proportion of the country after 1905, is seldom a suitable instrument for negotiating a settlement of labour problems.

Conclusion

We are now in a position to draw together the various threads making up the specific texture of the relations between labour and socialism in Russia. In the first place, although serfdom had been abolished in 1861, no deep-rooted political, legal or cultural structures had developed in its place. With respect to relations between state and population Russia remained, in many respects, a serf state without serfs. The expectations of the government that it should retain absolute power, material and spiritual, grew rather than weakened, particularly after 1881. In many other respects the imprint of serfdom remained. The commonality of peasant life and the instinctive sense of natural justice arising within the villages was carried over into the cities. The clarity of class relations in Russia resulting from the peasant–landowner/state and the worker–employer/state divides showed no sign of being changed. No rising tide of affluence or burgeoning intermediate classes and groupings of sufficient weight were emerging to modify the stark polarisation of Russian society. In such a society the invitation to class war and the preaching of collective ownership were simply the formulation of age-old truths known to a wide variety of the population in their everyday lives. The continued existence of a radical intelligentsia selflessly dedicated to the service of the people ensured that there would, when necessary, be a general staff to lead the army of the discontented. Given time, perhaps this polarisation might have weakened and the pressures might have been contained; after all, a comparable period of turbulence can be detected in early nineteenth-century England, but the outcome was not revolution. In Russia, however, the conjuncture of this internal crisis with her weak position in the international economy — her vulnerability in the wake of European depression being a major factor contributing to the build-up of unrest in 1900–5 and again in 1912–14 — plus the outbreak of the fatal war with Germany meant that no time for internal change was left to her. Thus, the road to the establishment of the world's first self-proclaimed proletarian and socialist state was opened up by its serf and peasant background as much as by any other of the many contributory factors. The peculiar distortions of that new state were also rooted in the same soil.

BIBLIOGRAPHY

V. Bonnell, *Roots of Rebellion: Workers, Politics and Organisations in St Petersburg and Moscow 1900–1914* (Berkeley, Calif., 1983)

L. Engelstein, *Moscow 1905: Working Class Organisation and Political Conflict* (Stanford, Calif., 1982)

P. Gatrell, *The Tsarist Economy 1850–1917* (London, 1986)

R. Glickman, *Russian Factory Women: Workplace and Society 1880–1914* (Berkeley, Calif., 1984)

P. Gregory, *Russian National Income 1885–1913* (Cambridge, 1983)

N. Harding (ed.), *Marxism in Russia: Key Documents 1879–1906* (Cambridge, 1983)

R. Johnson, *Peasant and Proletarian: The Working Class of Moscow in the Late Nineteenth Century* (New Brunswick, NJ, 1979)

L. Kochan, *Russia in Revolution* (London, 1970)

D. Koenker, *Moscow Workers and the 1917 Revolution* (Princeton, 1981)

D. Mandel, *The Petrograd Workers and the Fall of the Old Regime* (London, 1983)

M. Perrie, 'The Russian Peasant Movement of 1905–1907: its Social Composition and Revolutionary Significance', *Past and Present* (November, 1972), 57, pp.123–155.

W. Sablinsky, *The Road to Bloody Sunday* (Princeton, 1976)

H. Seton-Watson, *The Russian Empire 1801–1917* (Oxford, 1967)

T. Shanin, *The Roots of Otherness: Russia's Turn of Century*, Vol. 1, *Russia as a 'Developing' Society* (London, 1985); Vol. 2, *Russia 1905–1907: Revolution as a Moment of Truth* (London, 1986)

S. Smith, *Red Petrograd* (Cambridge, 1983)

G. Swain, *Russian Social Democracy and the Legal Labour Movement 1906–1914* (London, 1983)

S. Turin, *From Peter the Great to Lenin* (London, 1935)

R. Zelnik, 'The Peasant and the Factory', in W.S. Vucinich (ed.), *The Peasant in Nineteenth Century Russia* (Stanford, Calif., 1968), pp.158–190.

—— (ed.), *A Radical Worker in Tsarist Russia: the Memoirs of S.I. Kanatchikov* (Stanford, Calif., 1986)

5

SOCIALISM AND THE WORKING CLASSES IN ITALY BEFORE 1914

John A. Davis

The origins and politics of Italian socialism

In 1892 an Italian Workers' Party was founded at Genoa which three years later took the name of the Italian Socialist Party (PSI). By 1900 the Party had achieved electoral support comparable to that of the two main opposition groups in the Italian Parliament, the Republicans and the Radicals. By 1913, in the last elections held before Italy entered the First World War in 1915 and the first to be fought under the terms of universal male suffrage, the PSI was the largest of the opposition parties, although this election also saw the first appearance of a second political party with a mass following, the Catholic Popular Party.

In the two decades before the First World War the PSI played a central role in Italy's political history, and its very presence bore witness to the steady incursion of mass politics into a parliamentary system which at the time of Unification had been remarkable for its narrowness. In 1870 barely 2% of Italy's 26.8 million population had the right to vote. The narrowness of the electorate was at least in part a result of the open rift between the Church and the new state. Italy's political unification had been achieved through the destruction of the old Papal States and the Vatican remained openly hostile towards the Liberal state. Given the influence exercised by the clergy in many parts of Italy, this ruled out any attempt to imitate the experiments in conservative democracy pioneered by Napoleon III in France and Bismarck in the new German Reich.

The dangers of this narrow electoral base were understood by critics on the political right as well as the left. In 1882 the parliamentary suffrage was broadened, and although the Radical Party's proposal for universal suffrage was not carried the electorate was trebled and virtually all those who were literate obtained the vote. Six years later male suffrage was introduced for local government elections. The extension of the franchise was hedged around with qualifications that were designed to ensure that the widened electorate would strengthen rather than challenge the established structure of power. But this proved less than effective, and the enlarged electorate opened the way for the rapid expansion of mass politics in a political world that had previously been dominated by closed and exclusive élites of notables and landowners.

The birth of the Socialist Party was the most important, although not the only symptom of the incursion of the masses into Italian politics, and it was no coincidence that the decade in which the new Party first came into being witnessed a concerted attempt to reverse this process. But like Bismarck's earlier anti-socialist crusade in Germany, the politics of repression in Italy proved at best unsuccessful and at worst counter-productive. At the moment when the crisis seemed most acute at the turn of the century, the political climate underwent a marked change and the politics of repression gave way to a new search for accommodation with the masses and with organised labour. The initiative for this change in the tactics of the Italian conservatives came from Giovanni Giolitti, the joint leader of the administration that came to power in 1901 and the most influential force in Italian politics until the War.

The changed political climate after 1901 necessarily thrust the PSI and the labour movement into the forefront of Italian politics. It is with the Party's political role and strategy in these years, therefore, that any discussion of the relationship between the Party and the Italian working classes, between the Party and the labour movement, and between political socialism and popular socialism must begin.

The immediate inspiration for the founding, at Genoa in 1892, of an independent Workers' Party committed to a programme of class struggle and the socialisation of the means of production came from the massive successes of the German SPD in the elections of February 1890. But the nascent Italian socialist movement was also deeply rooted in the tradition of democratic politics that had grown

out of the struggles for Italy's national independence and unification earlier in the century and in the steadily expanding labour
organisations that had taken form in the following decades.

In an intellectual climate that was strongly influenced by positiv-
ism and the theories of Darwin and Spencer, it was natural that the
early Italian Socialists should have seen Marxist socialism as a
logical evolution from earlier democratic and socialist movements in
Italy. But the reality was perhaps less tidy.

The Republicans were the most important and influential of the
democratic movements that had originated in the struggles for
national independence earlier in the century. But although most
Republicans maintained their opposition to the monarchist state,
their political ideas were largely drawn from Mazzini, with the
result that their attitude towards socialism was either ambiguous or
hostile. Mazzini's nationalism had been republican and radical, but
he had always been vehemently opposed to socialism which he saw
as a continuation of the Jacobin tradition of the French Revolution.
Mazzini believed socialism to be a materialistic doctrine that failed
to comprehend the spiritual dimensions of nationalism, and as a
nationalist he could hardly welcome the divisive theories of class
war. Like St Simon, from whom he drew many of his central ideas,
Mazzini's concern was to stress the unity of interest and purpose
that bound the individual to the nation.

Belief in the virtues of inter-class co-operation was one of the
corner-stones of Mazzini's politics, and strongly influenced the
Workingmen's Associations which spread rapidly in northern Italy
after 1848. Mazzini's denunciations of the evils of socialism became
more outspoken and culminated in the condemnation of the Paris
Communards in 1871. Together with his subordination of social
issues to the overriding priority of creating the nation state, this
alienated many more radical Republicans.

Although the struggles for independence had produced a variety
of alternative democratic programmes, none had left a clear legacy.
Giuseppe Ferrari, Carlo Pisacane and Garibaldi himself were all
convinced democrats, but had never established coherent political
programmes. Yet concern over the social evils and inequalities of
the new Italy did provide the basis for the formation of a loose
alliance of democrats who rejected Mazzini's programme and under
the leadership of Felice Cavalotti formed a parliamentary group
known as the Radicals.

Others turned to socialism in the 1870s, but in Bakunin's libertarian interpretation of the International rather than what was frequently described as Marx's 'authoritarian German socialism'. This enthusiasm for the ideas of his arch-enemies explains Marx's characteristically unflattering description of the first Italian socialists as 'a gang of drop-outs, the dregs of the bourgeoisie . . . All the so-called Sections of the International in Italy are run by lawyers without clients, by doctors without training or patients and by billiard playing students . . .'[1]

The first Italian sections of the International were formed in the South after Bakunin's stay in Naples in 1865–6, but then quickly spread throughout the country. Many Italian anarchists came from the affluent middle classes, but anarchism also achieved a strong popular following in a number of areas. As in Spain in the same period, separatist feelings and anti-clericalism provided fertile soil for the libertarian programme. In the Romagna, for example, anarchism took root in the autonomist and anti-clerical prejudices that the experience of priestly government from Rome had bred in the region, and began to compete with the staunchly established Republican tradition. The anarchists also found popular support in parts of Tuscany. Anarchist hostility to the state was warmly received by Florentine artisans, for example, who were enraged when the seizure of Rome in 1870 ended the city's brief but commercially advantageous spell as capital of the new state. But the workers in the marble quarries of Massa and Carrara on the coast to the north of Pisa provided anarchism with an equally committed but sociologically different following. It was not only skilled workers with strong craft traditions and a sense of collective autonomy, like the marble-workers of Massa and Carrara, who rallied to the anarchist programme, however. In Rome, for example, the anarchist movement found its strongest following amongst the workers and navvies who came in their thousands to rebuild Italy's new capital in the 1870s and 1880s.

Support for the anarchist programme waned after the failures of attempted insurrections at Bologna in 1874 and near Benevento in 1877. In 1879 Andrea Costa, who had been a prominent anarchist activist in the Romagna, renounced the anarchist programme in favour of legalitarian socialism and his highly publicised conversion was symptomatic of a broader shift. While an exile in Paris, Costa had

---

1. Quoted in R. Michels, *Storia Critica del Movimento Socialista Italiana* (Florence, 1926), p.30.

established close contacts with Jules Guesde. But the most important influence was the Russian exile Anna Kuliscioff, from whom first he and then Filippo Turati learned the principles of Marxism. On returning to Italy in 1881, Costa helped found the Revolutionary Socialist Party of the Romagna (PSRR). This was a local movement with a strong following in the towns of Imola and Ravenna, but the PSRR did also succeed in attracting support from the landless farm labourers of the region, illustrating the important part which the agricultural labourers of the Po Valley were to play in the development of Italian socialism. Even within the Romagna, however, the PSRR's influence was very localised and the Republicans remained the most influential political force in the region.

Costa's party campaigned in the 1882 elections, the first under the extended suffrage, and he was elected at Ravenna with support from the Republicans and Radicals to be the first Socialist in the Italian Chamber of Deputies. But the 1882 electoral campaign also saw the formation of another important democratic initiative, the Milanese Italian Workers' Party (POI) which successfully campaigned to return Antonio Maffi as the first working man to enter the Italian Parliament.

The POI had emerged from earlier attempts to co-ordinate the activities of the numerous workers' leagues and associations that existed in Milan and in Lombardy, and was founded with the object of achieving direct representation for working people. The product of Milan's craft-based tradition of independent and direct workers' action, the POI constituted one of the major strands from which political socialism in Italy drew its roots. The POI was banned by the government in 1886, but was re-established at the end of the decade and continued to press for direct workers' action. Its leaders looked with suspicion on middle-class democrats like Costa, while the founders of the new Socialist Party in turn looked with mistrust on the POI's working-class exclusiveness which Turati and others interpreted as an outdated overhang from an earlier corporate craft mentality.

The rapid growth of strikes and protest movements provided a wider dimension to these political developments during the 1880s. The first Parliamentary Inquiry into industrial disputes was held in 1878 following a successful and prolonged strike by the woollen weavers in the region around Biella in Piedmont. In the following decade the number of strikes and of workers taking strike action greatly increased. The official statistics recorded 263 strikes between

1880 and 1886, the most important being those staged by printing workers in Milan (in 1880), textile workers in Como (1880), building workers in Turin (1881 and 1883), leather workers in Milan (1883), and by farm workers at Reggio Emilia, Cremona, Mantua, Catania, Treviso and Taranto between 1880 and 1883.

There were a number of reasons for the growth in strikes and protests. In the cities unrest reflected the consequences of rapid urban expansion, which brought poor living conditions, chronic housing shortages and extremely precarious conditions of employment. There were also more specific grievances, and the introduction of new factory regulations, of piece-rate systems and new methods of production began to feature amongst the causes of disputes, while the workers' demands concentrated increasingly on shorter hours and protection against wage cuts.

The parallel growth in rural protest also pointed to the broader impact of the agricultural crisis. Similar effects were being felt throughout Europe in these years, but in Italy the prevalence of small peasant farms and the extremely precarious conditions in which the greater part of the rural population lived greatly aggravated the impact of the crisis. It was in these years that the first massive exodus of Italian emigrants from northern Italy began. While many peasant farmers from Lombardy and the Veneto set sail for Argentina and Brazil, others sought to resist. At Mantua, for example, a General Association of Workers was formed with 2,000 members in 1879. In the province of Ravenna 15,000 farm labourers joined co-operatives in the 1880s, while mutual aid societies, producer and consumer co-operatives spread amongst many other groups of urban and rural workers. The unrest culminated in the strikes that were staged in the Mantua district in 1885, to which the government responded with heavy-handed military repression, the arrest of suspected leaders and the banning of the Milanese POI that had shown solidarity with the striking farm labourers and peasants.

Repression was not effective, however, and the charges brought against the Mantuan strikers were thrown out by the Appeal Court in a way that was particularly humiliating for the government. This setback strengthened the position of those conservatives who wished to imitate Bismarck's tactics and who believed that a strong but paternalist state was the best protection against social unrest. Proposals were put forward in Parliament to legalise labour organisations and strikes and to introduce legislation to protect women and child workers and to provide compulsory industrial accident insurance schemes. But in the rapidly deteriorating economic situation after 1890 these attempts to alleviate the appalling conditions in which Italian workers lived, and to encourage rather than deter labour from organising were all unsuccessful.

The immediate cause of the crisis of the 1890s lay in the collapse of the speculative boom on which the massive urban rebuilding programme had been based, combined with the commercial repercussions following Italy's adoption of high protective duties on manufactured and agricultural imports in 1887. The result was deep commercial recession, widespread bank failures and heavy unemployment. When food prices also rose steeply, protest and discontent spread throughout Italy.

It was against this background that the Italian Socialist Party was created. But although it drew on tendencies that were already present in Italy the new party was not so much a synthesis of these tendencies as the explicit victory of one over the rest. The supporters of legalitarian socialism were the victors, while the losers were the anarchists and the advocates of direct workers' action.

The founders of the Socialist Party deliberately tried to exclude both these rival tendencies. The Party's ideology and political strategy was shaped primarily by Filippo Turati and Anna Kuliscioff, whose role was critical although less public than that of her companion. Their socialism had much in common with the socialism of Bebel, Jaurès, Keir Hardie and Max Adler, and drew its inspiration from democratic and humanitarian traditions that were much older than Marx. Yet it was Marxism that provided the Italian democrats for the first time with a coherent political programme that proved capable of achieving a broad following amongst both the Italian middle and working classes.

The Party grew from the Socialist League which Turati and Kuliscioff had founded in Milan in 1889. Their programme had gained much wider publicity through the newspaper *Lotta di Classe* and the periodical *Critica Sociale*, which in the 1890s became one of the most fashionable and influential forums for intellectual and political debate in Italy. They saw the struggle for socialism in evolutionary rather than revolutionary terms, and they believed that the class struggle should be fought through the institutions of the bourgeois state. They also stressed the need to achieve strength through organisation.

The model was quite consciously that of the German SPD, and the emphasis on the need for organised political action through and under the leadership of the Party caused the members of the Milanese POI to secede from the Party at its foundation. This was to be only the first of many subsequent divisions and secessions, and the alternative tendencies that Turati and his supporters, had tried to exclude thereafter constituted the platforms around which the internal debates within the Party evolved.

Internal conflicts were later to loom large, but in its early years the new Party was exposed to an onslaught that threatened its existence yet also helped impose unity. The economic and commercial situation deteriorated rapidly in the early 1890s, and successive governments invoked emergency powers and suspended civil and political liberties in response to popular protest and rioting. Many suspected that these measures were only the pretext for a more concerted attempt to reverse the progress of mass politics. As the crisis reached its height in the closing years of the century, fears grew that a military or monarchist coup was imminent and even constitutional conservatives openly proposed substantial reductions in the powers of the Chamber of Deputies.

There were two peaks to the crisis. The first came in 1894, when military law was invoked in response first to protests by peasants and workers in Sicily and then by the workers in the marble quarries of Massa and Carrara. A wave of anarchist outrages during the summer, including an attempt on the life of the prime minister, Francesco Crispi, and the assassination of the French President by an Italian anarchist, led to the introduction of sweeping emergency laws. These made strikes, public meetings and assemblies illegal and effectively suspended the right of association and the freedom of the press, as well as giving the police wide powers to arrest and detain suspected persons.

Although Crispi fell from power in 1896 his successors did not relax the emergency laws and the second peak of the crisis came when protests against high food prices and unemployment occurred throughout Italy during the autumn, winter and spring of 1897–8. Attempts to placate the unrest by lowering import duties on wheat were unsuccessful and the government again invoked military law. Following a strike at the Pirelli rubber factory in Milan in May the government ordered the military occupation of the city to restore order and stop what it described as a revolution. The occupation was followed by the wholesale arrest of those held responsible for fomenting public disorder, which included most of the leaders of the Socialist Party as well as leading Catholic opponents of the government.

But the politics of repression proved counter-productive. The military courts that were set up in the aftermath of the so-called 'Milan revolution', the existence of which even conservatives found highly dubious, gave the Socialist Party particularly valuable publicity. Those suspected of plotting the revolution that had patently never occurred received a total of over 1,500 years in prison sentences. Turati, who had tried to dissuade the Pirelli workers from demonstrating, was given a twelve-year sentence, while Anna Kuliscioff who had taken no direct part in the disturbances was sentenced to two years.

Since leading Radicals and intransigent clerical opponents of the government were also victims of these measures, the defence of civil liberties provided the Socialists with a platform on which they could ally with other democratic and progressive liberal opponents of the government. This soon provided the base for a broad anti-authoritarian opposition movement that offered an excellent means for publicising the Party's programme of reform as well as giving the Socialist movement a legitimacy and respectability that it had previously lacked.

The strong support that the Socialists received from the professional middle classes in these years led the German sociologist Robert Michels to dismiss the Party as an extension of the Italian university system. But although the professional middle classes were an important constituency, the Party's electoral base was already becoming much wider and grew in almost direct proportion to the scale of the measures deployed against it.

In 1892 the Socialists had six representatives in the Chamber of Deputies and received 27,000 votes. In 1895 the numbers were respectively 12 and 75,000; in 1897, 16 and 130,000; in 1900, 32 and 216,000. While these figures were not high in comparison with other major European socialist parties at this time, they did represent a significant share of an electorate which in 1900 numbered 2.24 million (less than 7% of a total population of 32.47 million), and of whom only 59% of those eligible actually voted. The traditional opposition groups, the Republicans and the Radicals, had 28 and 34 Deputies respectively in the Chamber in 1900.

If the repressive policies of the 1890s strengthened the solidarity of the Socialist Party, the more subtle tactics of accommodation and conciliation that followed proved more divisive. Following the elections in 1900, a general strike in Genoa in protest at the closure of the city's Chamber of Labour caused the government to fall. Few other European workers could claim such a success, and from the start labour held an important place in the programme of the next administration.

The new government was headed by Giovanni Giolitti and Giuseppe Zanardelli. In place of the overtly repressive policies of the past, Giolitti advocated the state's neutrality in disputes between capital and labour, and greater state intervention to provide minimum welfare support for the working classes. Whether or not he really intended to make concessions of substance remains open to question, but Giolitti made no secret of his belief that the creation of an infrastructure of welfare institutions was first and foremost an antidote to socialism. If Italy was to develop a modern capitalist economy he believed that would be done '. . . not by shooting the workers, but rather by instilling in them a deep affection for our institutions so that we ourselves and not the socialists will be seen as the promoters of progress and as the ones who are trying to do eveything possible in their favour'.[2]

The practical results were tangible enough since at the turn of the century Italy had been remarkable for the virtual absence of even the most rudimentary forms of social legislation and welfare institutions. The final years of the century saw the implementation of earlier proposals to regulate the employment of women and children in factories and mining and introduce compulsory industrial accident insurance, but it was not until Giolitti came to power that a wider programme of welfare and regulatory measures were introduced that marked a definitive break with the *laissez-faire* liberalism of the past.

The package included sickness and old-age pension schemes, regulation of women and child labour, the nationalisation of life assurance companies to fund a range of pension and insurance schemes, the introduction of statutory weekly rest periods, and a national Maternity Fund. Assistance was given to workers' co-operatives and mutual aid societies, while government agencies with special responsibilities for labour, notably the Labour Bureau (Ufficio del Lavoro) and the Higher Labour Council, were created.

2. Quoted in I. Barbadoro, *Storia del Sindicalismo Italiano* (Florence, 1973), vol. 2, p.161.

Labour representatives were nominated to these bodies, although they remained a minority. The national industrial arbitration service that had first been introduced in 1893 (Probiviri) was also strengthened.

Many questioned the effectiveness of these measures and institutions and there can be little doubt that the main beneficiaries were Northern workers in full employment. Non-compulsory insurance schemes offered few benefits for the unskilled and nothing at all to the rural masses who constituted the overwhelming majority of the Italian labour force, while in the South most of this legislation remained a dead letter.

Politically the outcome of Giolitti's attempts to broaden the base of Italian politics was also ambiguous. It proved extremely difficult to reach a working relationship with the Socialists in Parliament, not least because the government's decision not to intervene in labour disputes produced a massive increase in strikes in industry, public services and agriculture after 1901. The wave of strike action culminated in an attempted national strike in 1904, which placed Giolitti under heavy attack from the right. This forced the government to abandon its own policies when it threatened to conscript major groups of public service employees like the railway and postal workers to deprive them of the right to strike.

The escalation of labour militancy after 1901 posed almost as many problems for the Socialist Party, and brought the reformist leadership under increasingly strong attack. The reformist slate was based on the Party's 'minimal' programme of 1895 which included demands for universal adult suffrage for men and women, the payment of Deputies and members of local councils, liberty of the press, speech, of public meetings and association, the state's neutrality in industrial disputes, religious equality, and a national militia in place of the standing army. There were also demands for more specific reforms, including more effective regulation of women and child labour in mines, factories and industry, a statutory weekly rest period, reform of the existing and inadequate legislation on industrial accidents and old age pensions, tax reform, provision of adequate school facilities for the poor, the municipalisation of local services, the eight-hour day and minimum wages.

In Turati's view the Party's objective was to transform the state from within through the organised action of the working classes. To achieve this end, a temporary alliance with the more progressive Liberals and with the democrats and radicals was justified on the grounds that Italy's bourgeois revolution was as yet far from complete. Power was still in the hands of reactionary landlords, of the monarchy and — through the monarchy — the aristocratic Piedmontese officer corps. Against this reactionary and semi-feudal power structure, the reformists argued, the Party should work with the progressive capitalist bourgeoisie to speed up the process of industrial expansion and the modernisation of Italian society.

Turati's strategy was premised on grounds that were quite different from Bernstein's revisionism, and took its cue from the relative backwardness of Italian society. As late as 1913 he argued that '. . . our country is still at the beginning of a transformation that will carry it from an essentially agrarian phase of development to the industrial phase, but as yet it is still in large part a fundamentally rural society'.[3] But many saw this as a betrayal of revolutionary socialism. In the 1890s Turati's main opponent was Enrico Ferri, but in 1902 the opposition acquired greater ideological consistency when Arturo Labriola moved from Naples to Milan to challenge Turati on his home ground. Labriola had been strongly influenced by the ideas of Sorel, and played a major role in introducing syndicalist ideas in the Italian movement. Like the French syndicalists, Labriola and his followers saw the tradition of workers' direct action through the trade unions as the principal revolutionary force in Italy. It was natural, therefore, that the syndicalists should have looked to the Milanese workers' action movement as allies in their attempt to seize control of the Party.

This they did in 1903. Riding the wave of labour militancy at home and condemnation of Bernstein's revisionism at the Dresden Congress of the International, the syndicalist and revolutionary socialists successfully challenged Turati and gained control over the Party and its newspaper *L'Avanti*. In the following year they gave their backing to the general strikes that were declared throughout Italy in sympathy for Sardinian miners massacred by the army during a strike at Buggerru.

The victory proved short-lived. Giolitti took the opportunity of the strikes to call a general election in which the Socialists, the Republicans and Radicals all lost seats. The government's majority was greatly increased, thanks in no small part to support from the Catholics who had participated in the elections for the first time

3. Quoted in B. Vigezzi, *Il PSI, le Riforme e la Rivoluzione 1898–1915* (Florence, 1971), p.67.

since Unification. The reformist Socialists now counter-attacked and the formation of the Confederazione Generale del Lavoro (CGL), Italy's first national trade union federation, in 1906 was designed to stop the syndicalists increasing their support amongst organised labour. But although the leaders of the CGL were hostile to the syndicalists, they were also jealous of their own autonomy and deliberately distanced the CGL from the Party. In 1911 the General Secretary of the CGL, Rinaldo Rigola, went as far as to support an initiative to establish a separate and non-revolutionary workers' party on the lines of the British Independent Labour Party (ILP).

This illustrates both the gap that existed between the Party and the organised labour movement as well as the unduly optimistic nature of the syndicalists' belief in the revolutionary character of the unions. The principal groups of organised labour repeatedly demonstrated their preference for reformist policies, and although the syndicalists did establish strong followings in certain areas they remained a minority. Their most loyal supporters were the railwaymen and the farm labourers in the Po Valley, both of whom enthusiastically endorsed the syndicalist strategy of spontaneous action but without showing much willingness to accept the syndicalists' leadership.

The syndicalists also had strong support in the South, where the authorities made little pretence of adhering to the principles of non-intervention that Giolitti's government had tried to adhere to in the North. In Sardinia, in Sicily and in the Mezzogiorno, strikes invariably led to violence and the tragic list of 'proletarian massacres' that punctuated working class history in these years occurred mainly in these regions. But the violence of labour relations in the South and the willingness of the authorities to protect the interests of the propertied classes by force placed a major question mark against the validity of reformist tactics and gave new force to the syndicalists' opposition to the Party leadership.

The tensions within the Party increased when the syndicalists deliberately flouted the Party leadership by calling for general strikes in Milan and Turin in October 1907, and by setting up a National Direct Action Committee at Parma to lead a prolonged strike by the farm labourers. Despite the violence of the landowners' reactions on this occasion, the CGL refused to support the strike. The failure of the strike discredited the syndicalists and at the Florence Congress in the following year the reformists were able to regain control of the Party. The strategy of the general strike was condemned as 'a dangerous weapon in present circumstances' and the syndicalists were expelled. In 1912 they set up their own trade union movement, the Italian Syndicalist Union (USI).

Defections from the left were mirrored by moves in the other direction. Ivanoe Bonomi, one of the more prominent reformists, came out openly in support of Bernstein in 1907, and launched the proposal for an Italian equivalent of the British ILP. But worse was to follow. In the years after 1907 economic conditions rapidly declined as the long upswing in industrial expansion gave way to recession. Unemployment grew rapidly in the major industrial centres and countryside, and even formerly conciliatory industrialists and landowners adopted more hard-faced attitudes. Growing support for the still small but none the less influential Nationalist movement was an indication of deeper shifts that were occurring in the cultural as well as the political climate. The pragmatic socialism of Turati and Anna Kuliscioff was rapidly losing its intellectual appeal and writers and theorists like Sorel and D'Annunzio were the new fashion leaders. The beneficiaries of the changed intellectual climate were the syndicalists and the new right.

Italy's invasion of Libya in 1911 brought the internal crisis of the Party to a head. For the reformists, Italy's involvement in an imperialist war was an unmitigated disaster, and Turati saw the invasion as an attempt to shift power to the right. He accused Giolitti of embarking on the war with the intent of 'preparing to bring back to power those reactionary forces which in the past you yourself, Prime Minister — and it will remain your great historical achievement — did so much to disarm and disperse'.[4] But while Turati and Kuliscioff remained firm in their opposition to a colonial adventure which they believed served to distract attention away from the programme of internal reform, other colleagues followed Leonida Bissolati and rallied to the patriotic cause.

The Libyan War shattered the reformist group, but there were also many on the left of the Party who supported the invasion, especially in the South where colonial expansion seemed preferable to mass emigration. Although one of the most eminent southern Socialists, Gaetano Salvemini, was a withering critic of the impracticality of Italy's projects for colonisation in Tripolitania and Cyrenaica, nearly all the leading syndicalists, including Labriola, supported the war.

4. Quoted in G. Manacorda, *Il Socialismo nella Storia d'Italia* (Bari, 1966), p.377.

The divisions within the Party were reflected more widely in the labour movement. In September 1911 the CGL had called a twenty-four-hour strike in opposition to the war, but support had been patchy and localised. However, the war caused unemployment and food prices to rise and provoked a new wave of strikes and demonstrations. Some were directed against the war and conscription, while other disturbances were directly related to economic issues. In 1912 and 1913 Turin and Milan were the theatres of major industrial struggle, in which the car-workers and the Metal Workers' Federation (FIOM) played a leading role. The syndicalists increased their efforts to channel this militancy towards a general strike in the summer of 1913 and as a result came into open conflict with the CGL which was using its influence to stop sympathy strikes which the unions were finding very costly to support.

The fresh wave of militancy in the industrial cities and the countryside was reflected in the ascendancy of the revolutionary socialists and their most extravagant spokesman, Benito Mussolini. At the Party's congress in Reggio Emilia in 1912 the extremists ousted the divided reformists, and the Congress rejected parliamentarism in favour of direct revolutionary violence. Mussolini became editor of *L'Avanti* and pronounced the funeral oration on Italian reformism: 'Italy is certainly the country in which parliamentary cretinism — that disease of which Marx provided such a penetrating diagnosis — has reached its most critical and mortifying dimensions'.[5] But the new leadership was scarcely less divided than its predecessors, and while the rhetoric of revolution responded to the militancy of the rank and file the Party's strategy and policies became increasingly unclear.

In the elections of October 1913, however, the Socialists obtained 17% of the vote and returned seventy-four deputies, although twenty-two of these were followers of Bissolati who had supported the invasion of Libya and were therefore denied recognition. In this first election by male suffrage in Italy the conservatives lost ground, while for the first time thirty-three Catholic deputies were returned to the Chamber (although some claimed that at least 200 others owed their seats to Catholic votes). The Socialists also made heavy gains in the local government elections in the following year. Socialist administrations were formed for the first time at Milan, Bologna, Mantua, Cremona, Novara, Verona and Reggio Emilia.

5. Ibid., p.378.

This was a sign of real strength that struck perhaps even more directly than the Party's parliamentary representation at the power and interests of the old élites, many of whom now no longer concealed their impatience with the politics of conciliation.

If these successes created new enemies, the Party's ability to control events also became increasingly doubtful. This was to be evident in the events leading up to the *Settimana Rossa* or Red Week in June 1914, when protests against the treatment of Socialist conscripts led to clashes with the police, rioting and strikes that spread first through the Romagna and then to other regions. The syndicalists and anarchists attempted to exploit the situation by encouraging sympathy strikes, and the strength of the protests forced a reluctant CGL to call a general protest strike.

The *Settimana Rossa* left sixteen dead and over 400 wounded, and revealed the extent to which both the Party and the CGL were at the mercy of local initiatives over which they exercised only the most tenuous control. Mussolini scathingly attacked the CGL for supporting only a token sympathy strike for those killed by the army in the Romagna, yet he carefully avoided pressing matters to a real confrontation. The rhetoric of revolution served to mask rather than resolve divisions, while the Party's leadership became increasingly divided and indecisive.

It was almost inevitable that the outbreak of the European war should have magnified these internal divisions even further. Turati and his followers held fast in their neutralist principles and ensured that the Italian Party alone in the Second International maintained its opposition to the war, but each of the principal factions into which the Party had become divided split again into pro- and anti-interventionist groups. Mussolini's conversion to 'revolutionary interventionism' on the grounds that the imperialist war was the beginning of the end of capitalism and the first step towards the revolution provoked a crisis on the left of the Party which was just as divisive as that which the defections of Bissolati and Bonomi in 1911 had caused on the right. But the war was the occasion rather than the cause of these divisions, whose roots lay both within the Party and also in the relations between the Party and its followers.

The Italian working classes

What was the relationship between the PSI and the Italian working

classes in this period? Did the deep divisions that were evident
within the Party reflect differences that were present within the
Italian working classes, or were the links between political socialism
and the Party's electoral base less direct? These questions are still
easier to pose than to answer, and in many areas current research
has at best ambiguous and at worst flatly contradictory answers to
offer.

Contemporaries were no less concerned than later historians to
answer these questions, and the development of a major new mass
party in the context of an economy that might be considered
backward in comparison with the more advanced Western European states raised questions that were far from academic. The
political strategies of opposing groups within the Party were of
necessity based on different interpretations of the nature of the
relationship between the Party and the working classes. Just as
those strategies were often diametrically opposed to one another, so
too were the interpretations on which they were based.

For the reformists, the heterogeneous structure of the Italian
working classes constituted a fundamental constraint on the Party
and the central premise of their political strategy. Because they
believed that in class terms the Italian workers were as yet 'immature' and embraced a wide range of different occupational groups,
from urban artisans and industrial workers to rural labourers and
tenant farmers, it was argued that only the Party could provide
leadership and impose unity. The Party's function was to establish a
political programme capable of creating unity and achieving the
socialisation of the means of production and the conquest of the
institutions of the bourgeois state. The Party was also seen to be the
principal instrument for propagating socialist ideas and values
amongst the masses through organisation, education and example,
so that unco-ordinated proletarian protest might be transformed
into a cohesive socialist movement.

These arguments were, of course, rejected by the revolutionary
socialists and the syndicalists. Without denying the heterogeneity of
the Italian workers, they argued that the industrial expansion in
certain regions of North-eastern Italy in the final decades of the
nineteenth century had created a new industrial proletariat and
provided the labour movement with its shock-troops. The German
sociologist Werner Sombart was one of the first in the 1890s to
argue that the formation of the PSI signalled the emergence of a new
industrial proletariat in the most advanced sectors of the Italian

economy. Such arguments offered valuable support to those in the Party who believed that socialism came not from above but from below, from the rank and file of the true proletariat, and reinforced their belief that socialism was best pursued through direct action by the workers.

Another German sociologist, Robert Michels, made a similar point in a different way when he castigated the predominantly bourgeois background of the Socialist deputies and claimed that the Party's main purpose seemed to be to provide jobs for the unemployed and unemployable sectors of Italy's professional middle classes. The description of the Socialist deputies was not inaccurate, but Michels' claim that the Party was composed of university professors and their students was a polemical caricature that reflected his own sympathies with the syndicalists' belief that the Party was a bureaucratic artifice which stood in the way of the innate revolutionary instincts of the workers.

The second interpretation, with its Leninist overtones, attracted much attention in Italy in the 1960s, and found strong support in Stefano Merli's massively documented study of the development of the factory system in Italy.[6] Merli argued that in Italy, as earlier in England, the proletariat and socialism were born in the factory, and in the textile factories in particular, where an artisan work-force was transformed in the decades after Unification into an industrial proletariat with a new consciousness of its shared interests in the face of capitalist exploitation. In Merli's view, this new class awareness provided the humus in which the socialist programme of collective resistance to win control over the means of production by the workers themselves took root.

Merli's study remains a major contribution to the relatively neglected problem of the formation of the Italian working class, and at an empirical level catalogued the particularly brutal conditions to which Italian workers were subject. Yet for many critics his conclusions greatly over-estimated the importance of large-scale factory production in Italy before the end of the century. Although the textile industry was the largest employer of industrial labour until 1914, large factories remained rare while factory production co-existed with outputting and domestic production until the turn of the century.

---

6. S. Merli, *Proletariato di Fabbrica e Capitalismo Industriale: Il Caso Italiano 1880–1900* (Florence, 1972; 2 vols).

In a recent study the German historian Volker Hunecke has attempted to overcome certain of the objections directed at Merli's analysis by concentrating on the workers in Italy's first industrial city, Milan. Hunecke argues that the enormous gaps in the timing of industrial development in different parts of Italy means that the formation of the working class must be approached on a regional basis. The fact that the socialist movement first developed a following in Milan was not an accident, he claims, but a direct consequence of the expansion of new industries like engineering, ceramics and rubber that made Milan Italy's first industrial city during the 1880s.[7]

By the end of the 1880s, Hunecke argues, Milan's work-force of artisans and craftsmen had been transformed into a new proletariat composed of industrial workers and sweated labourers in the rapidly declining craft trades. The new proletarian workers ousted the older artisan and craft workers from the leadership of the city's labour institutions, and their political outlook and values were typified in the exclusive workers' action programme of the Milanese Workers' Party (POI) that was founded in 1882, and in the 'resistance leagues' (*leghe di resistenza*) that were formed by other groups of workers in these years in place of older mutual aid and cooperative associations.

These conclusions differ widely from those of an earlier study of the Milanese working class in the same period by Louise Tilly, who has emphasised the continuing dominance of craft trades in the city's economy down to the end of the nineteenth century.[8] Tilly claims that despite the appearance of the newer industries, the city's expansion before 1900 had more to do with demography and immigration than industrialisation. As a result the older craft and artisan trades dominated the Milanese labour movement. Tilly also stresses the lack of unity amongst the city's labour force, the majority of whom were immigrant workers who lived concentrated in new suburban settlements outside the city walls. The city's entire demographic expansion between 1870 and 1900 was concentrated in the new suburbs, whose inhabitants remained segregated in terms of occupation, location and origins, while establishing little contact with the traditional working classes of the old city. Although

7. V. Hunecke, *Classe Operaia e Rivoluzione Industriale a Milano 1859–1892* (Bologna, 1982).

8. L. Tilly, *The Working Class of Milan 1881–1911* (Unpublished PhD Thesis; University of Toronto, 1972).

contemporaries considered that the immigrant workers were the principal source of labour unrest, Tilly's study suggests that this was untrue. There were important exceptions, but in general the immigrant workers lacked unity and played little part in industrial disputes, whereas control over the city's labour movement remained firmly in the hands of the artisans and craft workers down to the end of the century.

Did the minority of industrial workers in Milan perhaps exercise a leadership in the labour movement that far exceeded their numerical strength? A recent study of Sesto San Giovanni, one of Milan's principal industrial suburbs, by Howard D. Bell suggests that this was not the case.[9] Sesto San Giovanni was transformed from a small agricultural and silk-spinning community into one of the main centres of steel-making and heavy machine-building in Italy in the two decades before 1914. It was here that the A.F.L. Falck steel combine built the first Siemens-Martin furnaces and the first automated rolling-mills in Italy, while the Breda heavy engineering company moved to Sesto in order to completely reorganise, departmentalise and specialise production units and processes. Other engineering and chemical industries followed in their wake, making Sesto a show-piece of Italy's industrial revolution. By 1911 Sesto's total population had grown to 13,000, of whom 6,600 were industrial workers together with another 1,000 managerial and white-collar workers.

The fact that companies moved to Sesto from Milan in order to modernise the organisation of production and to break with the decentralised and artisan-based workshops of the city questions Hunecke's insistence on the modernity of the Milanese companies. Secondly, although the work-force in Sesto was transformed in a very short space of time from skilled craft workers into a factory proletariat, there was virtually no labour unrest in Sesto in these years. Bell argues that management supervisors, machine tools, new centralised plant and production processes completely undermined the traditional role of the skilled metalworkers, while craft differentials and control of apprenticeship and labour recruitment by the workers were quickly eroded and destroyed. But the workers did not resist, Bell argues, because the multitude of different leagues and unions into which the skilled workers were organised made collec-

9. H.D. Bell, *Sesto San Giovanni: Workers, Culture and Politics in an Italian Town 1880–1922* (New Brunswick, NJ, 1986).

tive responses more, not less, difficult.

Bell's study also suggests that when they moved to Sesto the workers quickly lost contact with their colleagues in Milan. Indeed, the contrast between Milan, which could claim the highest rate of industrial disputes in Italy between 1900 and 1910, and nearby Sesto where there were virtually no strikes, is remarkable. Although Sesto was barely four miles from Milan, it remained almost completely untouched by the latter's socialist movement. This inevitably questions the nature of the 'leadership' that has been ascribed to the Milanese workers in the labour movement, and Bell argues that it was not the factory but the community that was the midwife of socialism in Sesto. A section of the PSI was not founded in Sesto until relatively late, but long before they adopted socialism the Sesto workers had already established an alternative proletarian culture that was, in Bell's view, rooted in the independent and secular values of artisan culture and tradition.

The studies that have concentrated on the newer industries have revealed one important dimension of the complex mosaic that made up the Italian working classes, and have demonstrated that the most advanced sectors of the Italian economy were adopting forms of production and organisation comparable with the most advanced in Europe. As early as the 1880s the larger engineering firms in Milan began to adopt more specialised forms of production and to copy new German techniques of company organisation. The Breda workshops where railway locomotives were built were reorganised in the mid-1880s along the lines of the German *Platzarbeit* system, and the management also carried out detailed studies of new production techniques in the American engineering industry.

After 1900 these tendencies became more pronounced. The advent of electrical energy made possible a massive reorganisation of textile production, especially in the cotton industry. But the most striking changes came in the engineering and automobile industries, particularly in response to the recession after 1907 which encouraged restructuring operations in nearly all the more vulnerable industries. It was against this background that Giovanni Agnelli reorganised the Fiat motor company, along lines which were pioneered on the small factory that Fiat opened at Poughkeepsie (New York) in order to study American car manufacturing techniques 'hands on'.[10]

10. See esp. V. Castronovo, *Giovanni Agnelli* (Turin, 1971), and S. Ortaggi,

After the turn of the century the engineering and metalworkers in Milan and Turin played a very prominent role in the labour movement. Their numbers expanded very rapidly, and by 1910 rose to 28,000 in Turin alone, seven times more than in 1900. They constituted a third of the city's total labour force, and 6,500 were employed in the car industry, nearly half of them in the Fiat factory in the Corso Dante. The dependence of other industries and workers on the car industry gave them even greater influence. Yet despite this compactness important differences separated the car workers from other groups of workers, while they were also divided amongst themselves. But despite the rapid expansion of Turin and Milan in these years, the part of the 'industrial triangle' that was most densely industrialised was still the pre-Alpine zone where the older industries (especially textiles) were concentrated. The new industrial proletariat was an important element of the Italian labour movement, but it was only one of its many and varied constituent parts.

One of the weaknesses of the attempts to explain the rise of socialism in Italy exclusively in terms of the emergence of a new industrial proletariat is that this assumes that Italy followed a pattern of economic growth that progressed by clearly defined stages to culminate finally in an industrial take-off. But few historians would now endorse Alexander Gershenkron's description of Italy's industrialisation as a sudden big spurt that occurred at the close of the nineteenth century,[11] and recent research has placed much greater emphasis on the length, the complexity and the often contradictory nature of the process of growth in Italy over the course of the preceding century. In the words of one leading Italian historian, by 1914 Italy was still not yet an industrialised nation although it had acquired a strong industrial base.

This meant that economic growth was imbalanced in regional terms, although the effects of change were felt even in those areas that were not themselves directly involved in the process of growth.

'Cottimo e Produttività nell' Industria Italiana del Primo Novecento', *Rivista di Storia Contemporanea* (1978).

11. See A. Gershenkron, *Economic Backwardness in Historical Perspective* (Cambridge, Mass., 1962); and cf. L. Cafagna, 'The Industrial Revolution in Italy 1830–1914', in C. Cipolla (ed.), *The Fontana Economic History of Europe* vol. 4 (London, 1973).

But even in regions where economic growth occurred throughout the century, the patterns of growth were very specific and left distinctive imprints on the structure and the experiences of the Italian working classes.

One striking feature of the 'Italian road to industrialisation' was that for most of the nineteenth century the factory system was a rural rather than an urban phenomenon. In a recent study of the textile industries, the French historian Alain Dewerpe has argued convincingly that in Italy the 'factory system' was not only first established on the countryside but co-existed for a long period with the peasant family economy in many areas of northern Italy.[12] This was not really a case of 'proto-industrialisation', since it made possible an effective and rational utilisation of the existing factors of production (plant, materials, labour) in ways that played a major role in generating the capital accumulation by which Italy's commercial, financial and ultimately industrial economy was eventually transformed.

The most important branch of the textile industry was silk and none demonstrated better how different forms of production could be combined. Silk worms were raised on peasant farms throughout these northern provinces, but although the production of raw silk was decentralised, the initial manufacturing operations had from early in the century become centralised in 'factories'. Silk cocoons were ready for reeling (the process of extracting silk thread from the cocoon) in the spring, and this operation was carried out in mills that were soon converted to steam-power and mechanised. Labour was provided by women and children from the peasant families of the neighbourhood, and even at the end of the century over 90% of the silk reelers and spinners in Piedmont and Lombardy were women and children.

Although wage levels were lower in rural areas than in the cities, skilled labour was by no means superabundant and the textile manufacturers constantly complained about the shortage of labour and the difficulty of maintaining a skilled labour force. The peasant families put their womenfolk into the mills in order to maximise family incomes, but because the work in the reeling mills was seasonal the women were free to rejoin the men for the summer harvest. The predominance of women and children in the silk industry was a sign that the industry's development depended

---

12. A. Dewerpe, *L'Industrie aux Champs*; Collection de l'Ecole Française de Rome (85) (Rome, 1985).

heavily on the exploitation of the rural labour force, but it was also 'a consequence of the way in which the peasant family managed the employment available for the members of the family'.[13]

The prevalence of these mechanised and capitalist forms of production in the North Italian countryside meant that many sections of the rural population had long been accustomed to factory production. The integration of factory-based manufacture with the peasant economy in many cases provided workers with a degree of independence and militancy. One of the earliest theatres of collective resistance to the employers' attempts to change the organisation of production was the Biella region in northern Piedmont. This was Italy's principal woollen manufacturing region, and the scene of the first protracted strikes after Unification which in 1877 gave rise to a Parliamentary inquiry into industrial relations.

Contemporary observers were quick to link the weavers' militancy to their relative autonomy and close-knit social structures. Each family owned a small plot of land, which although insufficient to sustain the family on its own provided an additional income and an alternative in times of recession or strike. The economic and social unity of the weavers' families was preserved by a structure of rigid patriarchal controls. The head of the household decided which sons would emigrate, which daughters would marry, when and to whom, while the weavers jealously controlled the apprenticeship system. The authority of the male weavers was in turn reinforced by the community as a whole, enabling them to maintain a tight control over the labour market and over the labour process.

The Biellese weavers were able to preserve their control over the labour market and the process of production despite the mechanisation of the primary phases of woollen production. There was little resistance to the mechanisation of spinning in the 1820s because the weavers' daughters entered the mills while their earnings remained in the family. Hand-loom weaving remained largely untouched, although any challenge to this was fiercely resisted. When the employers tried to impose new regulations on production or to interfere with the apprenticeship system resistance was also immediate and spread throughout the whole region.

The weavers' resistance continued even after the employers began

13. Ibid., p.348; see also F. Ramella, *Terra e Telai: Sistemi di Parentella e Manifattura nel Biellese dell'Ottocento* (Turin, 1984), and the excellent recent essay by Anna Cento Bull, 'The Lombard Silk Spinners in the 19th Century; An Industrial Workforce in a Rural Setting', *The Italianist* (1987) 7, pp.99–121.

to invest in mechanical looms in the 1880s. Mechanisation of weaving was acknowledged to be uneconomical, but was done explicitly to break the weavers' control over the labour market. None the less, weavers were still able to draw on a powerful substructure of co-operative associations and collective solidarity, and despite growing losses through emigration their resistance continued until the end of the century.

The Biellese weaving communities established a reputation for militancy and a tradition of collective solidarity underpinned by a network of social relations and co-operative associations which made an important contribution to the development of a distinctive working-class consciousness in Italy. Their actions were not simply directed at preserving old craft privileges and obstructing mechanisation, but were aimed at resisting attempts to weaken the workers' control over the organisation of production or access to the labour market.

The circumstances that lay behind the militancy of the woollen workers were in many ways peculiar to the Biella region, however, and textile workers in the neighbouring province of Bergamo were as famed for their docility as the Biellesi were for their militancy. However, thanks to the stimulus of high protective tariffs cotton production began to expand rapidly from the early 1880s, and rapidly outpaced woollen production in terms both of the numbers of workers employed and the level of mechanisation.

Although cotton production was factory-based from the start, strikes were relatively few and rarely successful. The reason may have been that the continuous nature of cotton spinning reduced the integration between factory work and the peasant family economy. The labour force in the cotton mills was divided and segregated by gender in ways that made collective action difficult.

It was by no means the case, however, that the use of female labour was a guarantee against strikes. Particularly where the women could rely on close support from their communities they often played an important part in labour struggles. This was evident not only in the militancy shown by women woollen spinners, but also in the strikes that took place in the Tuscan straw-plaiting industry in 1896 which aroused great public interest. Straw-plaiting was a domestic industry that employed nearly 60,000 women in Central Italy, and the impact of the strike was all the greater because the action was organised entirely by the women, most of whom had little previous experience of organisation. The strike was organised in protest at wage cuts, the introduction of new plaiting machines and at exploitation by male outputters, and attracted great public attention and concern.

However, workers' behaviour was more often affected by the nature of their relations with the community than by gender alone. But community values did not necessarily contribute to militancy. The textile employers preferred to employ women from 'respectable' peasant families, for example, because the patriarchal values that existed within peasant society were reflected in the strict discipline to which the women workers were subjected. The severity of the factory regime was in turn also a guarantee of moral protection without which peasant families might have been less willing to allow their womenfolk to enter the mills.

Nor was there any simple correlation between factory employment and militancy, and the textile industry offers evidence that militancy declined as factory production advanced. After 1900 the adoption of electrical power enabled employers for the first time to move their mills away from the pre-Alpine valleys, where supplies of water power were abundant, to areas where labour was more plentiful. This opened the way for a major reorganisation of production. Between 1891 and 1907 the numbers employed in the woollen industry in Piedmont rose from 7,333 to 15,068, for example, and in the same period wages fell by 30%. But apart from an unsuccessful strike in 1901, there were few disturbances in the industry, while attempts to unionise the predominantly labour force were not successful. Contacts with the old artisan culture and also with the institutions and associations that had underpinned the militancy of the Biellese weavers were lost.

The experience of the textile industry, the largest single industrial employer of labour, illustrates both the complexity of the process of industrial development in Italy and the very different ways in which the process of economic change affected different groups of workers. Industrial relations did not develop along neat unilinear paths, but were determined by circumstances that were particular to each industry, place and time in which discontinuities were at least as evident as continuities.

At the turn of the century nearly 40% of Italy's active population were still engaged in agriculture, which provided almost 50% of Gross National Product; by 1913 agriculture's share of GNP had only fallen to 45%, in contrast to 27% from industry and 30% from services. Agriculture necessarily played a crucial role in Italy's economic development, but once again in ways that differed sharply from region to region. The expansion of intensive capitalist farming was most advanced in the Po Valley which had long been amongst the most productive agricultural regions in Europe. In the late nineteenth century massive irrigation and land reclamation schemes extended the cultivated area eastwards into regions that had previously been swampland and marsh. The poorer rural communities that depended on the meagre resources provided by these common lands were destroyed, and the emigration from the Venetian hinterland to Brazil in the 1880s foreshadowed the later proletarian emigration from the South.

The advent of intensive farming in the central and eastern Po Valley destroyed many older communities, but it also created a new rural work-force of wage labourers. Huge armies of labourers were drawn into the region during the 1880s and 1890s. Some were former peasants, some were migrants from other regions. They worked and lived in conditions that were at best precarious but became even worse once the reclamation projects were finished and the demand for labour fell. Unlike the share-croppers and peasants, the hired hands (or *braccianti*) had no contact with the land and were completely dependent on wage labour. A later observer described them as '. . . a true agricultural proletariat, whose livelihood was always uncertain, which lacked any form of attachment to the land and was constantly subject to changes of residence and vulnerable to changing economic conditions. . . . In certain seasons of the year unemployment was like a chronic disease.'[14]

The labourers' vulnerability derived in part from the seasonal character of agriculture which imposed long periods of unemployment, and during the winter in particular the labourers were mainly dependent on public works for a livelihood. But their vulnerability was aggravated by the structural over-supply in the labour force, which the landowners were eager to maintain and exploit because it kept wages at minimum levels. From the 1880s onwards the labourers attempted to respond to these conditions by organising collectively in order to establish some control over the labour market. The first initiatives took the form of co-operatives which tendered

14. A. Serpieri, *La Guerra e Le Classi Rurali in Italia 1930*; quoted in S.J. Surace, *Ideology, Economic Change and the Working Classes: The Case of Italy* (Berkeley, Calif., 1966), p.63.

collectively for work with private landowners or the public authorities. From an early stage many of these co-operatives had a strong utopian socialist colouring, and Nullo Baldini, for example, who formed the Ravenna Labourers' Co-operative in 1883, was an enthusiastic disciple of Cabet's *Icarius*.

By the turn of the century the farm hands of the central and eastern Po Valley were amongst the most militant and organised groups of workers in Italy, and they provided the Socialist Party with its firmest electoral strongholds. But rural unrest and organised protest were evident in many other regions as well, especially in the South where the agricultural depression and the consequences of the trade war with France lay behind the demands of the Sicilian peasants for fairer leases in 1893/4. The violent repression that followed marked the beginning of the massive waves of emigration from Sicily and the Mezzogiorno in which hundreds of thousands of southerners sought work in the expanding cities of America's eastern seaboard. Mass emigration was a consequence of the failure of the agrarian economy in the South to adopt new methods of production, although ironically it was the money which the emigrants sent back in remittances that kept Italy's foreign trade account balanced and permitted further industrial investment.

Despite the distances involved, emigration was usually only temporary but it did serve to reduce the excess in the labour supply in certain areas. This had particularly dramatic consequences on the vast wheat farms of the arid Apulian plains to the north of Bari, which were one of the few areas in the South where large concentrations of rural labourers comparable to those in Emilia were to be found. Here Italy's finest durum wheat was grown on vast estates known as *latifundia*. The estates were worked by landless labourers who lived in the teeming company towns that dotted the plain. As in the Po Valley, the system relied on the structural over-supply of labour which kept wages at the barest minimum.

When emigration began to redress the balance in their favour the Apulian workers also began to organise. In a recent study Frank Snowden has argued that the absence of a significant class of peasant farmers gave the Apulian labourers' leagues greater cohesiveness than those in the Po Valley, and in particular gave the syndicalist emphasis on direct action a particularly strong appeal.[15]

15. F.M. Snowden, *Violence and Great Estates in the South of Italy. Apulia 1900–1922* (Cambridge, 1986).

The close of the nineteenth century saw rural unrest and organised protest spread to other regions which had in the past been proverbial for their tranquillity. None more so than Tuscany, whose famous share-cropping tenancy (*mezzadria*) had throughout the nineteenth century been held up as a model of the partnership between capital and labour. Yet the opening years of the twentieth century saw the first strikes by Tuscan share-croppers in protest against the landowners' abandonment of established customs and the imposition of new contractual obligations and exactions.

These developments provide clear evidence of the tensions and unrest that were generated by the transformations that were taking place in Italy's agrarian, industrial and urban economies in these years. Yet the impact of economic change was rarely the same in any two parts of Italy or in any two occupations. At moments of crisis, such as during the 1890s and in the recession after 1907, unemployment, low wages and high food prices could give urban and rural protest a degree of unity which certainly alarmed the authorities. But did these protests provide the basis for a broader and more unified labour movement?

Trade unions and organised labour

The occupational profile of the Italian working class at the turn of the century gives a clear indication of the problems facing the development of an organised labour movement. The 1901 census put the total population over nine years of age at a little over 25 millions. The number of workers in small artisan shops (including the owners of these small enterprises) was around one million, with a further 300,000 spinners and weavers. The total number of wage earners in manufacturing industry was about two and a half million, and of these 27% were women and a further 17% children. Although there was rapid growth in industrial employment during the following decade, the numbers employed in manufacturing or mining expressed as a percentage of the total population still remained much lower than in other industrial European countries (4.7% in Italy in comparison with 12.9% in the UK, 10.1% in Germany, 7.7% in France). However, the industrial work-force was also highly concentrated: over 58% of workers in companies employing ten or more people were in the North-West (the so-called 'industrial triangle' formed by Milan, Genoa and Turin). The same area contained nearly 50% of the total mechanised power in Italy (measured in hp), but hardly more than 20% of the total population. Yet even in this dynamic area, textiles remained the principal employer and continued to account for 60% of Italy's non-agricultural exports down to the First World War.[16]

Almost half the labour force was under the age of 21, implying a very high turnover of labour which would have made effective collective organisation extremely difficult. In addition, rigid hierarchies of skill and status survived amongst the craft trades which made organisation across different occupational categories just as difficult. The greater the skill the higher the pay and shorter the working day, creating a descending hierarchy dominated by old craft trades like the printers, followed by state employees, railwaymen and metalworkers. The highly skilled and the totally unskilled were the two principal categories, with few intermediaries. The size and nature of the differentials that separated these two groups, as well as the internal differentials (of gender in particular) within each group made collective action in pursuit of shorter working hours or better pay highly problematic.

Giuliano Procacci has argued that these structural features made the establishment of industry-wide union federations extremely difficult, whereas the organisations developed on a more local basis often showed considerable strength and solidarity.[17]

Before 1900 the only forms of organisation which were both permitted and indeed encouraged were mutual aid societies, but although these were widespread their objectives were generally limited to providing help to members in times of sickness and unemployment, contributions towards funeral expenses and so forth. The 1870s and 1880s saw the expansion of similar forms of association in the countryside where the collapse in agricultural prices in the 1870s and 1880s brought widespread ruin to small farmers. In rural areas of northern Italy the parish clergy played an important part in establishing popular savings banks and producer co-operatives in these years, but many Liberals also came to accept that such ventures were needed to encourage working-class self-

16. The data are taken from G. Procacci, *La Lotta di Classe in Italia agli Inizi del Secolo XIX* (Rome, 1970), pp.9–18; and L. Cafagna, 'The Industrial Revolution in Italy', pp.305–324.

17. See G. Procacci (1970): his arguments are summarised in his 'The Italian Workers' Movement in the Liberal Era', in R.J.B. Bosworth and G. Cresciani (eds), *Altro Polo: A Volume of Italian Studies* (Sydney, 1979).

help and avert the worst consequences of the agrarian depression.

During the industrial and agrarian conflicts of the 1870s and 1880s many of the mutual aid societies were transformed into 'resistance leagues'. This has been seen as a crucial turning point in the history of labour institutions in Italy, in which older traditions of craft organisation gave way to new and broader forms of resistance. The new leagues were formed to resist de-skilling, new piece-rate systems, longer hours and lower wages, and served to establish a new collective and proletarian awareness amongst the workers and provided them with a means to assert their own control over the work process and production.

The reality was probably less tidy. Even after 1900 most industrial leagues or unions were small and localised. The liberalisation of the government's policy towards labour disputes led to the formation of a spate of new union federations after 1901, but few of these had any real strength and membership often fell heavily in the years that followed.

The skilled and craft workers remained predominant within the new federations, the largest being the railwaymen, the printers, building workers and metalworkers. Attempts to establish a federation of textile workers proved unsuccessful, and although the Metalworkers' Federation (the FIOM) grew rapidly it was rarely able to impose its authority over its constituent parts. In Milan alone the FIOM was divided into sixty-seven different sections and strike initiatives tended to come from individual sections and the shop-floor. This was something that the American labour leader Samuel Gompers noticed when he visited the city in 1911: 'Subdivision of industries even to the smallest seems to be the rule in Milan. Whereas in some European cities that I have visited a whole industry would be bulked together — as the "metalworkers" or the "wood workers" — in Milan they are separated in their constituent parts.'[18]

The General Confederation of Labour (CGL) was founded in 1906 with about 200,000 members. Thereafter membership rose to slightly less than 400,000 in 1911, before dropping back to about 300,000 in 1914. Membership was affected by the growth of unemployment in these years, while the secession of the syndicalists, who established their own union confederation (USI) in 1912 with about

18. S. Gompers, *Labor in Europe and America* (New York, 1912), p.162 (quoted in I. Barbadoro, *Storia* (1973), vol. 2 p.82).

100,000 members, also played its part. A further 100,000 workers were also enrolled in Catholic unions in 1910, most of them being agricultural workers and farmers. But nearly half the members of the CGL were also agricultural labourers and peasants.

The farmworkers had been amongst the first in Italy to form a union federation in 1901, which in the following year had more than 200,000 members. Although membership oscillated from year to year, the farm labourers remained one of the largest groups within the CGL, constituting 32% of the membership in 1907 and 48% in 1913.

Support for the rural leagues and unions that formed the basis for the Fedeterra (the Federation of Land Workers' Leagues) came mainly from farm labourers, although in some areas tenant farmers and share-croppers were also involved. But there was a clear correlation between the areas in which the rural unions were most militant and those with the highest concentrations of landless labourers. These were regions around Mantua, Ferrara, the Polesine, the south of the province of Verona, the Lomellina and the rice-growing plains of eastern Piedmont. Between 1901 and 1905, 239 rural strikes involving 106,000 workers were recorded while a further 247 rural strikes between 1906 and 1910 involved 123,000 workers. The comparable figures for industrial disputes in the same periods were respectively 732 strikes and 147,000 workers, 312 strikes and 219,000 workers. One contemporary noted that strikes in the Emilian and Romagnuol countryside were almost permanent after 1907.

Yet despite the prevalence of rural workers in the unions, the trade unions did represent over a third of organised labour in Italy, and in 1910 and 1911 the figure came closer to a half. Within certain industries, especially the railways, printing and paper-making, rates of unionisation were much higher, and indeed amongst the highest in Europe. Yet there were also many industries in which the unions were negligible, while throughout most of the South the national unions had very scant following.

The structural imbalances revealed by national or 'horizontal' labour organisation were in some cases compensated by the strength of more localised confederations, and in particular those that gravitated around the Chambers of Labour. The Chambers of Labour were one of the most distinctive institutions of the Italian labour movement, and reflected the real solidarities that could exist between different groups of working people at a local level. The first

Chamber was established in Milan in 1890, but the Chambers rapidly spread to other cities and other parts of Italy. From 57 in 1900 their number grew quickly and by 1910 their collective membership was greater than that of the CGL (504,841 and 165,192 respectively), while unlike the union federations they had also succeeded in establishing a reasonably strong presence in the South as well, where over 100,000 members were registered.

The model was the French Bourses du Travail and the Chambers had first been introduced with the support of many municipal authorities to complement the Chambers of Commerce. In the context of the commercial and industrial recession that gripped Italy after 1889, they were intended to function as labour exchanges, but in many cases — like Milan — they were quickly taken over by workers' or democratic organisations.

In many towns and cities the Chambers came to provide a focus for the activities of the different unions, leagues and associations that existed in the locality, and because of the local character of many industrial disputes they were often much more effective than the union federations in providing leadership, co-ordinating the actions of the different unions and establishing collective bargaining procedures with employers. In Milan, for example, the Chamber's 43,192 members were divided in 165 different leagues, and in Turin the picture was much the same with 8,083 members from 58 different leagues — the most powerfully represented being the printers, railwaymen and engineering workers.

Another strength of the Chambers of Labour lay in the fact that the unskilled and unemployed could also obtain representation. This enabled them to establish a broad-based popular following not only in the major industrial cities but also in cities like Rome and Naples where the unions were weak. The Chambers of Labour provided wide opportunities for cultural and recreational activities as well, and often sponsored the activities of the Casa del Popolo, popular leisure and recreation centres that provided a focus around which an alternative proletarian culture could take shape not only in the cities but also in rural villages.

The strength of labour movement at a local level was also evident in the development of 'Factory Commissions' in some of the leading industries. The first Commissions appeared in the engineering industry, with the approval of the more progressive employers who believed that it was easier to negotiate with organised workers and that better organisation at a factory level reduced the risk of spontaneous and wildcat strikes. This was illustrated by the attitude of the cotton entrepreneur, Bonnefon Crappone, the first leader of the Turin Industrialists' League that was formed in 1906. Crappone paid warm tribute to the ability and dedication of the workers who represented their colleagues on the Factory Commissions: 'I must confess my admiration for these men who after a full day's hard labour proved themselves able not only to defend the interests of their comrades with skill and tenacity, but also to debate even the most complex of the issues with which the industrialists confronted them'.

Through the internal Factory Commissions the engineering workers were able to negotiate with the employers not only over wages but also over the technical aspects of production and the organisation of labour. But although the Factory Commissions marked an important step forward in organised wage-bargaining, they were limited to a very small number of industries and even then aroused fierce opposition from other groups of workers. In the case of the car workers, for example, the syndicalists repudiated the agreements reached by the Commissions on the grounds that they were in the hands of the bosses.

The Factory Commissions, the unions and union federations, and the Chambers of Labour all illustrated the ways in which working people in Italy were becoming organised and each of these institutions contributed to the development of a self-conscious proletarian awareness. Even though the vast majority of working people, not to mention the more precarious categories that made up the urban and rural poor, lacked any form of organisation, the number and significance of those who were becoming organised in both formal political and less formal associations was growing, and growing rapidly.

Although there was considerable overlapping between organised labour and political socialism, the institutions of the labour movement jealously preserved their own identity and autonomy. Of the leading union confederations, only the Fedeterra and the FIOM consistently supported the PSI, and in the second case this led the syndicalists to break away and form their own union. The railwaymen were more open in their hostility to the Party, especially when they became locked in a prolonged struggle to resist Giolitti's attempts to ban strikes by public employees. Yet the union was unwieldy, and despite its sympathy with the syndicalists it did not support the independent syndicalist union federation (USI). The Printing-workers' Federation also jealously retained its own independence from the Party. This explains both why the CGL's guarded support for the reformist leadership grew steadily more distant, and the enthusiasm shown for the project of an independent Labour Party probably reflected accurately the wishes of the majority of organised workers.

The presence of a number of critical conflicts of interest was another major obstacle to the formation of a more cohesive labour movement. Even in the most advanced sectors of the economy there was no broad agreement on the issue of tariff protection, for example, which since the abandonment of free trade in 1887 had been one of the main political targets of the democratic opposition in Italy. The PSI had taken a leading part in blaming high food prices, low domestic living standards and a stunted consumer market on high import duties. But workers in heavily protected industries like cotton, steel and shipbuilding were understandably reluctant to take up the anti-protectionist cause, and it was not until 1913 that the CGL formally supported the return to free trade. These and similar conflicts also contributed to the CGL's preference for confining itself to industrial and trade union matters and avoiding politics.

Amongst the rural unions the sources of conflict were even more dangerous. The PSI's policies towards the countryside and peasant questions were quite different from those of its French and German counterparts. Guesde and Lafargue had persuaded the French Parti Ouvrier in 1892 to abandon its programme of proletarianisation of the countryside and to work instead to protect the peasantry from the incursions of agrarian capitalism. In Italy, the militancy and strength of the labourers' unions in the Po Valley was interpreted as evidence that the capitalist transformation of the countryside was well advanced and irreversible. The Party sided with the labourers in what was believed to be the inevitable and rapid process of capitalist transformation.

By identifying exclusively with the landless farm labourers, and in particular by adopting a programme of collectivisation of the land, the Party risked cutting itself off from the share-croppers, the tenant farmers and the peasants. Although the Socialists were unlikely to make inroads into the peasant heartlands of the Veneto and North-Eastern Lombardy, the situation was very different in those regions of the Po Valley where share-croppers and tenant farmers were numerous. In an attempt to broaden its appeal, therefore, the Party's policy was modified after 1902 and opposition to the co-operative movement, which had originally been seen as a means of preserving rather than overthrowing agrarian capitalism, was dropped.

This opened the way for an alliance between the labourers' leagues and those of the share-croppers in certain areas. The Land-workers' Federation of the Romagna that was formed in 1901 included both the share-croppers' Republican leagues and the Social-ist leagues of the labourers; similar alliances were also formed at Reggio Emilia. But the balance of power between the two groups was always delicate, and the situation was further complicated by the presence of many intermediary categories like farm servants with annual contracts who lived in and considered themselves quite different from the hired hands.

Where the *braccianti* were in a clear majority, as was the case in the area around Mantua and in the southern part of Bologna province, they remained hostile to the share-croppers. When the labourers gained control of the local federation in Mantua they excluded all share-croppers and denounced co-operatives as a threat to the labourers. Since this was counter to the Party's agrarian policy, it was natural that many of the labourers' leagues should have given their support to the syndicalists. But although the emphasis which the syndicalists placed on direct workers' action was well suited to the realities of rural unionism, the labels were ultimately more important than the ideological differences which they were supposed to express.

After the general strike of 1904 the Party and the Fedeterra attempted to exert firmer control over the agrarian unions, but this did not prove very successful. The strike that was called in 1907 by the syndicalist leadership of the Parma Chamber of Labour revealed both the strength of syndicalist support amongst the labourers' unions and also the tensions that existed between the autonomist tendencies of the leagues and Party's hopes of achieving strength through organisation. These tensions easily spilled over into open conflict.

An important factor in the escalation of violent conflict in the Po Valley region was the introduction of mechanical threshing ma-chines, which began to appear in part because of the labourers' success in obtaining better wages and organising the casual rural labour force. The landowners responded by investing in machinery to reduce their reliance on labour, and in particular began using steam-powered threshing machines. These machines not only exacerbated the conflicts between the labourers and the landowners, but also set the labourers and the share-croppers at one anothers' throats. Many tenant farmers were obliged to use wage labour during the harvest period, so that they were also hit by the increase in wage rates and by the attempts by the leagues to monopolise the supply of labour. The threshing machines offered the share-croppers a way of avoiding these increased wage costs during the harvest periods, and through their co-operatives the machines could be leased at economic rates.

The labourers claimed that the machines were taking away their work, and in this they were supported by the mechanics and stokers. The share-croppers and small farmers were more vulnerable than the larger landowners and were the first targets of the systematic campaigns of intimidation and machine-wrecking adopted by the labourers in an attempt to assert their exclusive right to work the new machines. In many areas the conflicts soon became very violent and often the machines had to be protected by armed guards. Arson attacks and reprisals by both sides became the order of the day, and were symptoms of a collision of unreconcilable interests that were soon to plunge much of the Po Valley into virtual civil war.

These conflicts illustrated vividly the antithetical nature of the interests that had briefly been accommodated within the ranks of the Fedeterra and under the banner of the Socialist Party. But it was not only in the Po Valley that the Party's attitude towards socialism in the countryside was in danger of shipwreck, and the conflicting interests of the North and South also came to a head over the Party's agrarian policies.

When the labourers on the cereal estates of the Apulian plain began to organise, the landowners' response differed only to the extent that it was more nakedly violent than in the Po Valley and could rely on more open support from the authorities. The result was an interminable series of massacres as troops clashed with strikers in unequal combat, providing the Italian labour movement with its largest cohorts of martyrs in these years. But whatever the internal strength of the collectivist programme adopted by the Apulian labourers, the PSI showed little interest in them. In fact, many of the Party's supporters in the South looked with suspicion on the rural disturbances and argued that the peasants were counter-revolutionary by nature. But there were others who saw in the violence that was unleashed on the Southern countryside undeniable evidence of the failure of reformist policies to bring any benefits to the South.

Amongst these was Gaetano Salvemini, who had become a leading spokesman of this Southern opposition within the Party. Salvemini bitterly denounced the Party's agrarian policies which he claimed were determined entirely by conditions in the Po Valley and sacrificed the interests of the Southern rural population to those of the urban and rural workers of the North. For the same reason he dismissed the Party's support for rural co-operatives and legalitarian reform on the ground that: 'So long as the law is controlled by the great landowners and the lower middle classes the prospects for reform in Italy remain nil'.[19]

In short, the divisions within the Party were more than fully reflected in the different and often contradictory interests that were embraced within the organised labour movement in these years. Different interest groups gravitated towards different political and ideological tendencies. But this was as often a matter of convenience as of deeper commitment, producing some puzzling contradictions. Amongst the opponents of reformism, many of those who were most vocal in support of the syndicalists were in practice themselves reformists. This was the case not only of the railwaymen, for example, but also of many of the agrarian leagues in Emilia. It was also the case of many of the syndicalist leaders, whose rhetoric often owed more to jockeying for position within the Party than to ideological commitment.

To conclude that the labour movement was deeply divided at a national level or that organised labour represented only a very small minority of the total labour force would be true not only of Italy but of every European society in this period. Far from broadening our understanding, national comparisons may simply serve to reinforce well-worn stereotypes, not least because of the artificial image that 'national aggregates' suggest. Generalisations at a national level may grossly distort local realities, particularly in a country like Italy were local conditions varied greatly. It only needs a slight change of perspective to draw attention to the strength of socialist support in many localities in contrast to the apparent weaknesses of nationwide forms of association, or to acknowledge that the levels of

19. Quoted in I. Barbadoro, *Storia* (1973), vol. 1 p.113.

unionisation amongst certain groups of workers in Italy were amongst the highest in Europe.

Political commitment and mobilisation are always difficult to assess, and external indicators such as trade union membership or the membership of political parties provide only the roughest of guides to how people behaved and thought. However, the growth in popular support for socialist politics that was expressed in both national and local elections indicates that socialism did succeed in representing the interests and aspirations of a significant and growing section of the Italian working classes before 1914. Whatever its apparent weaknesses, Italian socialism had acquired a national following and in many localities socialism had become the dominant political force before 1914.

Why was this? There are no simple answers, and older traditions need to be considered as well as newer influences. Throughout much of rural Italy the vestiges of older communal ways of life had by no means disappeared and collective forms of ownership and agriculture survived to the end of the century. For those who lived in the countryside and also for many of the immigrants who poured into Italy's expanding cities in this period, collectivist values were part of a familiar world. Similarly, the self-consciously independent and secularist traditions of many of the old craft and skilled trades were also an influential source of collectivist and separatist values.

The language of politics was another important influence. Ever since Unification, denunciation of the materialist values on which political Liberalism was based had been part and parcel of political dialogue and gave the language of class wide currency in Italy long before the coming of the Socialists. The conservative critics of the new state were the first to take up the attack on the values that underpinned the Liberal revolution. During the debates on the 'Social Question' that dominated Italy's domestic politics in the late 1870s the conservative critics of the new state held up the misery and despair that stalked the cities and countryside of the new state as evidence of the egotistical political and economic theories on which it was premised. In denouncing the self-centred materialism of Liberal dogma as the cause of these evils, the mainly Catholic conservative critics of the new Italy gave their imprimatur to the language of class, and their message was readily taken up more widely from the pulpit and through a variety of cultural, devotional and recreational associations.

The Catholic Church played a leading part in denouncing the

materialism of Liberal Italy. Once Leo XIII's encyclical *Rerum Novarum* (1892) had committed the Church to win back the imperilled souls of the European working classes, the Church's attempts to intervene in an ever widening range of social and cultural activities in Italy became even more evident. In the countryside the Church's initiatives were directed mainly at small peasant farmers, at domestic workers and artisans, and took the form of sponsoring consumer and producer co-operatives and savings banks. There were also moves to extend Catholic influence in local government. From the time of Unification Catholics had been forbidden to participate in national elections, but local government had always been considered as a part of 'civil society' and therefore separate from the state. Yet in contrast to the steady expansion of rural co-operatives and savings banks, Catholic initiatives in local government remained more uncertain, not least because of the doubts they aroused within the Catholic hierarchy.

The increased zeal with which parish priests sought to intervene in the daily lives of the working classes in the decades before 1914 was often strongly resented. In the case of Sesto San Giovanni, Howard Bell has shown how a distinctive proletarian culture developed directly out of workers' attempts to emancipate themselves from the influence of the parish priest.[20] The independent recreation and social activities that were launched to counter those sponsored by the parish priest provided the nucleus around which an independent proletarian culture developed and which was only later grafted on to socialism.

But socialism was never the only means through which an independent working-class awareness might find expression. Individual families could turn to a variety of alternatives in their attempts to adapt to changing conditions, of which emigration was perhaps the most obvious. Even when this involved crossing the Atlantic, emigration was in most cases a temporary rather than a permanent choice, and although it brought changes to existing family structures it did also enable family economies to remain intact. But to emigrate was a choice that related to other alternatives as well, and it has been suggested that where labour organisation was strong — for example amongst the farm-hands of the lower Po Valley — the tendency to emigrate was weak.

Even where labour was organised, however, this could and did

20. H.D. Bell, *Sesto San Giovanni* (1986).

take a variety of different forms and political colours. In many regions of Italy, for example, the co-operative movement had established strong roots and provided an important alternative source of collectivist ideas and values. Even after the Socialists dropped their hostility to the principle of co-operation, Republicanism remained the dominant influence and the National Co-operative League not only retained its separate identity but also continued to expand its membership down to 1914.

Although 'outside' the socialist sphere, the co-operative movement played an important part in the struggle to establish popular control over local government. The reform of the local electorate in 1889 had made popular local government possible, but the Socialists were relatively slow in coming round to the concept of municipal socialism. It was not until 1904 that a full programme for the conquest of local government was put forward, and this was furiously opposed by the syndicalists and revolutionary socialists.

The Radicals and the Republicans were the first to set out to conquer town halls, while many of the earliest initiatives in popular local government were also quite independent from the socialist movement. This was the case of the Milan Humanitarian Society, for example, which was founded as a private charity in 1893. The Society soon embarked on a broader programme of activities designed to improve the conditions of the Milanese working classes through the provision of direct assistance and a range of educational and cultural facilities. The Society gave its backing to the establishment of a Popular University, technical training schools for workers, People's Libraries and a Social Museum, as well as plans for a workers' institute along the lines of Ruskin College at Oxford. Initially the Party was critical and Turati considered the Society's activities to be well intentioned but politically misguided. It was not until after 1900 that the Party gave its support to the Humanitarian Society, but although the number of Socialists on the Society's executive council increased the Society continued to act with and through independent institutions, notably the Chamber of Labour and certain industrialists.

Even when it had won the Party's blessing, municipal socialism necessarily involved alliances with other political groups and labour organisations that made it anathema to the opponents of reformism within the Party. Yet in contrast to the rhetoric of the revolutionaries, local administration provided the Italian socialists with the opportunity to establish and in certain cases implement a clear and practical programme of reforms, in particular the municipalisation of public services and utilities, improved educational and health facilities, tax reform and the honest management of local finances. In 1910 Turati wrote: 'It is primarily as an Economic Corporation that the Popular Town Council differs from its predecessors. Just as the national government was formerly the management board of the bourgeoisie, so the town council was its local equivalent.'[21]

The advance of municipal socialism became possible when in 1903 Giolitti introduced legislation which permitted the municipalisation of local services and opened the way for a rapid expansion in the range of services run by the council. Municipal tramways, bakeries, clinics and schools all formed part of a new institutional context in which the language and values of collectivism were realised. Even though the first major conquests did not come until the eve of the War, it was in the small but gradually growing number of socialist municipalities, like the Florentine suburb of Sesto Fiorentino, and in the larger number of townships where socialists had a voice in the local administration, that Italian socialism was translated into administrative and social reality before 1914.

The practical example of municipal socialism was an important factor in the diffusion of a broader collectivist sub-culture amongst working people, but there were others of a quite different nature working in the same direction. In a recent study of the behaviour and structure of the new working-class districts of Turin, Maurizio Gribaudi has shown how socialism could provide newly immigrant families with a sense of collective identity which they otherwise lacked, as well as a valuable network of contacts.[22] In circumstances of rapid labour turnover, of precarious conditions of employment and chronic shortage of housing, the street or district came to replace the family as the principal element of support, while the network of socialist clubs, cafés and recreational facilities provided individuals and families with social contacts as well as a constant supply of information about jobs, vacancies and housing.

The spread of socialist ideas was also facilitated by changes in educational and literacy rates. In comparison with other European

21. Quoted in G. Sapelli, *Comunità e Mercato: Socialisti, Cattolici e 'Governo Economico Municipale' agli Inizi del XX Secolo* (Bologna, 1986), p.169: see also E. Decleva, 'Socialismo e Etica del Lavoro: La Società Umanitaria', in M. Degli Innocenti (ed.), *Filippo Turati e Il Socialismo Europeo* (Naples, 1985).

22. M. Gribaudi, *Mondo Operaio e Mito Operaio: Spazi e Percorsi Sociali a Torino nel Primo Novecento* (Turin, 1987).

countries, illiteracy rates in Italy at the turn of the century were high (48% as opposed to 18% in France, 19% in Belgium and 23% in Austria-Hungary), while less than 8% of Italian children attended primary schools (15% in Austria-Hungary and 17.5% in Britain). But as always national aggregates seriously distort local realities, and while literacy levels in the South and in the countryside were way behind European averages, those in the North and in the cities were probably well above average. Virtually all urban workers could read, while in the countryside the children of landless labourers — unlike those of peasants and share-croppers — generally attended school.

This was reflected in the rapid expansion of the popular press after 1900, although the reading public remained highly differentiated. A survey carried out in 1906 suggested that printing workers, engineering and electrical workers were avid readers, while butchers, grocers and milkmen, as well as shoemakers, smiths and building workers were not. Yet although improved literacy rates may have contributed to political awareness, more informal social institutions and meetings seem to have remained the most effective means for transmitting political ideas and values. Through the workers' recreational clubs and societies, as well as cafés, hostelries and taverns a distinctive and alternative proletarian culture could take shape. Although this might become synonymous with socialism, this was by no means always the case. If in a 'purist' perspective this might be seen as a sign of the eclecticism and hence weakness of Italian socialism, it also made socialism particularly open and accessible in Italy and enabled the Socialists to find a following amongst widely different categories of working people and ensured that it was never the preserve of the urban industrial working class alone.

Conclusion

Despite the emergence of a strongly collectivist sub-culture in many parts of Italy in the years between 1890 and 1914, the extent to which popular politics and socialism overlapped remains uncertain. In those areas where socialism had found its strongest following, the collectivist values on to which socialism was grafted had often developed quite spontaneously. Political loyalties remained mixed and even in a new working-class community like Sesto San Giovanni there were many groups of workers who remained loyal to the Church, to older Republican associations, or else took little part in organised political or social activities. Even when they did exist political affiliations might express other identities as well. Regional identity was not diluted by migration, for example, and in Sesto it was not accidental that the small group of syndicalists came from Emilia.

Nor did the acceptance of socialist politics necessarily change individual patterns of behaviour. The language of equality and emancipation does not seem to have changed gender relations amongst the Turin workers, whose families continued to reflect older patriarchal divisions of labour. If socialist clubs and associations provided new opportunities for women to participate in social activities, this did not enable women to break into the older preserves of male sociability; while women and children from socialist families often continued to attend Mass although externally rejecting the influence of the Church. Even where support for socialist principles was strong, sympathy for the ethics of socialism was not necessarily always a sign of political commitment. The purchase of a socialist newspaper, for example, might be no more than an external gesture of group membership.

Despite these reservations there can be no doubt that in many parts of Italy socialist policies and ideals had developed a strong popular following before 1914. This was most evident in local administration, but the gap that separated local from natonal socialism should not be overdrawn. As in other European countries in the same period, the politics of personality played a very important part in bridging the gaps between local and national socialism. In many ways the Party can be seen as an agglomeration of individual leaders with their own personal following and regional base. Camillo Prampolini, Enrico Ferri and Leonida Bissolati were all examples of this, although it is not difficult to spot their counterparts in other European (and North American) socialist movements in this period. In an age when personalities dominated politics much more than parties in the public mind this was arguably a source of strength not weakness, and when Robert Michels stressed the importance of rhetorical skill for success in the Party he was paying a compliment to the ability of the Socialist deputies. But personal influence was not simply a matter of individual charisma, and was often underpinned by firm institutional ties. Turati, for example, owed much of his influence over the Party not only to his close contacts with the leading intellectual milieu of the day, but to his equally close

connection with a major union confederation, the post and telegraph workers.

Political socialism, municipal socialism, ethical socialism, industrial socialism, rural socialism, personality politics: these were all
component parts of Italian socialism. Yet no matter how distinctive
each of these components was, none could exist alone. But apart
from a growing sympathy for the principles for which the Socialists
stood, for the ethics of socialism, what was it that held the Italian
socialist movement together?

The answers to that question probably have more to do with the
political contexts within which Italian socialism developed rather
than its more internal and inward-looking features. As was argued
at the start of this essay, the repeated attempts to halt the advent of
mass politics in the 1890s gave the Socialist Party the opportunity to
establish itself as the legitimate voice of the Italian working classes
with a broad-based political programme. Although drawing support from the professional middle class, the Party succeeded in
establishing itself as the champion of a wide range of working
people.

Politically the Party's task became much harder once the politics
of repression gave way to the new climate of consensus and conciliation after 1901. But these changes were accompanied by other
developments which added to the difficulties facing the Party.
Popular unrest and discontent in the 1880s and 1890s derived a
degree of unity from the fact that high food prices and low wages
provided rural and urban workers with common grievances, and
throughout the 1890s these were the themes that unified rural and
urban unrest. But as the Italian economy began to recover from the
recession and entered into a new and rapid phase of industrial
expansion between 1896 and 1906 many of the elements of unity in
working-class protest were unhinged. Real wages rose for many
groups of workers, particularly when the contraints on industrial
action were slackened after 1901. But this gave greater prominence
to the pursuit of sectoral interests while at the same time widening
the differences between different groups of workers, between the
skilled and the unskilled, the urban and the rural, the employed and
the unemployed, between Southerners and Northerners.

These were problems that faced every Second International
Socialist Party, and they explain in part the insistence on retaining
allegiance to the maximalist programmes of revolutionary socialism
despite the realities of reformist politics. The rhetoric of revolution

was conveniently abstract and avoided the awkward demarcations of skill and wages that were posed by more specific proposals for reform.

Yet in Italy it was particularly difficult to adopt that option. The Socialists entered the political arena not in the wake of Bismarck's state socialism but as inheritors of a Liberal revolution that had set its face resolutely against interference in the market-place. Unlike Germany, Italy in 1900 had only the most meagre structure of welfare institutions or social legislation. Observers of all political colours were agreed on the extremely wretched conditions in which the bulk of the Italian working population lived and on the massive gaps that existed between levels of development in different parts of the country.

The Socialists were not alone in perceiving the threats that this neglect posed for the future of the Italian state. Progressive Liberals and the new Catholic Democrats both adopted programmes of institutional reform, and in these circumstances the PSI could hardly have done otherwise. But in so doing the Party inevitably became identified with the protection of certain interests, most notably those of the Northern skilled and employed workers, at the expense of others, the unskilled, the unemployed and the Southerners.

While the political and economic context in which the Party found itself after 1900 tended to increase internal divisions and made it difficult to establish clear lines of policy, the Party's very presence encouraged others to organise and seek unity where previously there had been none. The political theorist Gaetano Mosca had earlier voiced the fears of many sections of the Italian propertied classes when he observed that:

> In Italy the masses are amongst the most impoverished in Europe, and the rural populace in particular lives a life of degrading and unremitting toil. . . . Nonetheless they continue to suffer and toil because hitherto they do not believe that there can be any simple answer to their plight and because they are as yet untouched by subversive theories . . . Yet we should not assume that they will not one day begin to organize . . .[23]

Following the general strike of 1904, first the landowners and then the industrialists began to respond to what was perceived to be the challenge from organised labour. In Turin the engineering employers played a major part in founding the Industrial League in

23. Quoted in G. Sapelli, *Communità e Mercato* (1986), p.26.

1906, which by the following year represented 250 employers and sought to co-ordinate negotiations with the workers in each sector. Amongst the landowners of the Po Valley even more aggressive associations were spreading with the explicit purpose of destroying the power of the labourers' unions by whatever means possible. These tendencies became more pronounced in the recession after 1907. Many sectors of Italian industry were hit by major problems of overproduction, leading to company mergers and restructuring which brought about a greater concentration of industrial capital, and giving new muscle to collective action by the employers.

The new spirit of organisation and collective defence that was evident amongst the employers and landowners was also reflected in political changes. The emergence in 1913 of a new Catholic Party with a mass popular base in many ways marked the end of the structure of parliamentary government within which the PSI had developed. Although the Catholic Popular Party had been called into being to defend the old political order and ward off the evils of socialism, it was soon to make the parliamentary system inherited from the time of Unification unworkable.

The formation of the new Catholic Party was one political consequence of the fears aroused by the growth of the Socialist Party. But perhaps even greater fears had been aroused by the Socialists' successes in local government. It was here that the most serious and direct challenge was made to the power of the old élites that had dominated Italian politics since Unification, and it was no accident that in the crisis that followed the First World War Socialist control over local and municipal administration was to be the first target of the fascist counter-attack.

In response to these developments, whose longer-term implications could not have been predicted before 1914, the Party at first seemed to gain a new breath of unity. The rapid deterioration in Italy's economic situation as recession began to bite after 1907, together with the political divisions provoked by the Libyan War, seemed for a moment to restore some unity to working-class protest in response to rising unemployment, rising prices, wage cuts and lay-offs. The new air of militancy was reflected in the victory of the maximalists. But rather than offer a means for solving the sectoral and regional divisions that had spread through the Party, the maximalist programme was little more than a means for avoiding and shelving these issues. The appearance of unity could be maintained only by substituting rhetoric for intent. The events of the

Settimana Rossa in June 1914 revealed all too clearly the contradictions and hesitations which the maximalist programme attempted to mask, and placed an indelible question mark against the internal coherence and unity of both the Party and the Italian labour movement. Whether the sympathy for the ethics of socialism that was shared by a considerable number of working people in Italy meant commitment to a programme of political socialism, and if so what form of socialism, remained very open questions.

BIBLIOGRAPHY

F. Andreucci, 'The Diffusion of Marxism in Italy during the late 19th Century', in R. Samuels and G. Stedman Jones (eds), *Culture, Ideology, Politics* (London, 1983)

G. Are, 'Economic Liberalism in Italy: 1845–1915', *Journal of Italian History* 1 (1978)

H.D. Bell, *Sesto San Giovanni: Workers, Culture and Politics in an Italian Town 1800–1922* (New Brunswick, NJ, 1986)

A.C. Bull, 'The Lombard Silk Spinners in the 19th Century: An Industrial Work-Force in a Rural Setting', *The Italianist* (1987) 7, pp.99–121

L. Cafagna, 'The Industrial Revolution in Italy 1830–1914', in C. Cipolla (ed.), *The Fontana Economic History of Europe* vol. 4, part 1 (London, 1973)

A. Cardoza, *Agrarian Elites and Italian Fascism* (Princeton, 1982)

G. Castronovo, 'The Italian Take-off: a critical re-examination of the problem', *Journal of Italian History* 1 (1978)

M. Clark, *Modern Italy 1871–1982* (London, 1986)

P. Corner, *Fascism in Ferrara* (Oxford, 1975)

S. Discala, *Dilemma of Italian Socialism: The Politics of Filippo Turati* (Amherst, Mass., 1980)

S. Gompers, *Labor in Europe and America* (New York, 1910)

M. Gonzales, *Andrea Costa and the Rise of Socialism in the Romagna* (Washington, DC, 1980)

W. Hilton-Young, *The Italian Left* (London, 1949)

D. L. Horowitz, *The Italian Labour Movement* (Cambridge, Mass., 1963)

R. Hostetter, 'The evangelical socialism of Camillo Prampolini', *Italian Quarterly* xviii (1975)

—— *The Italian Socialist Movement, Origins 1860–1882* (Princeton, 1958)

A. A. Kelikian, *Town and Country under Fascism* (Oxford, 1986)

B. King and T. Okey, *Italy Today* (London, 1901)

A. Lyttelton, 'Landlords, Peasants and the Limits of Liberalism', in J.A. Davis (ed.), *Gramsci and Italy's Passive Revolution* (London, 1979)

M.F. Neufeld, *Italy: School for Awakening Countries* (Ithaca, NY, 1961)

G. Procacci, 'The Italian Workers' Movement in the Liberal Era', in R.J.B. Bosworth and G. Cresciani (eds), *Altro Polo: A Volume of Italian Studies* (Sydney, 1979)

D.D. Roberts, *The Syndicalist Tradition and Italian Fascism* (Manchester, 1979)

A.W. Salamone, *Italy in the Giolittian Era: Italian Democracy in the Making 1900–1914* (Philadelphia, 1960)

C. Seton-Watson, *Italy from Liberalism to Fascism* (London, 1967)

D.M. Smith, *Italy: A Modern History* (Ann Arbor, Mich., 1969)

F.M. Snowden, 'From Share-Cropper to Proletarian: the Background to Fascism in Rural Tuscany 1880–1920', in J.A. Davis (ed.), *Gramsci and Italy's Passive Revolution* (London, 1979)

—— *Violence and Great Estates in the South of Italy. Apulia 1900–1922* (Cambridge, 1986)

S.J. Surace, *Ideology, Economic Change and the Working Classes: The Case of Italy* (Berkeley, Calif., 1966)

R. Sykes, 'Revolutionary Socialism in the Italian Labour Movement: the Agrarian Strikes in 1907–8 in the Province of Parma', *International Review of Social History* xxi (1976)

L. Tilly, 'I Fatti di Milano: the Working Class of Milan and the Rebellion of 1898', in R.J. Bezucha (ed.), *Modern European Social History* (Lexington, Mass., 1972)

B. Vigezzi, 'Italian Socialism and the First World War', *Journal of Italian History* 2 (1979)

S.J. Woolf, 'The Poor, Proto-industrialization and the Working Class: Italy (sixteenth to nineteenth century)', in *The Poor in Western Europe in the 18th and 19th Centuries* (London, 1986)

6

THE LABOUR MOVEMENT IN SPAIN BEFORE 1914

Paul Heywood

Anarchism and socialism in Spain prior to 1914

The central feature of the Spanish labour movement prior to the First World War was its weakness. Although it has become commonplace to refer to the strength of Spanish anarchism, particularly as contrasted to anarchist movements in other European countries, such an emphasis can be highly misleading. In fact, the apparent strength of anarchism in Spain derives in large measure from its juxtaposition to an even weaker socialist movement. Whereas in most of the rest of Europe the struggle for control of the First International between the followers of Karl Marx and Mikhail Bakunin had been settled by the early 1870s in favour of the former, leading to the emergence of important Marxist socialist parties, in Spain it was the Bakuninites who prevailed. Thus, while in Germany, Austria, France and Italy, socialist parties had by 1914 achieved real political significance, in Spain by the same date the socialist movement was barely established at a national level. The following statistics provide an illustration of the Spanish socialist movement's comparative weakness. In 1913, the year of the greatest number of labour conflicts in Spain up to that point, the Socialist Party had one deputy, its union had 147,729 members, there were 284 strikes and 84,316 strikers. In that same year there were 42 socialist deputies in Italy, 75 in France and 110 in Germany: there were 810 strikes, with 384,725 strikers, in Italy; 2,404 strikes with 887,062 strikers in Russia; and 1,459 strikes with 664,000 strikers in Britain; both the French and the Italian socialist union movements had around 500,000 members.[1]

On the Spanish working-class stage it was the anarchists who had captured the periodic flashes of a generally guttering limelight. Through occasional spectacular outbursts, such as the 1892 invasion of Jerez, the 1903 Cordoba strike, or the Semana Trágica (Tragic Week) of 1909 in Barcelona, the anarchists maintained a public presence which was generally denied to the essentially cautious and legalistic socialist movement. In actual fact, though, Spanish anarchism was marked by a cyclical pattern of brief moments of glory followed by failure and repression.

Any analysis of the Spanish labour movement prior to the First World War must emphasise the significance of regional variations. In rather schematic terms, the organised labour movement evolved during the latter part of the nineteenth century into two distinct groups, divided along both geographical and ideological lines. On the one hand, socialism became established principally in Madrid, and later on in the mining regions of the Basque Country and in the heavy industrial sector of Asturias; on the other, anarchism and anarcho-syndicalism took root in the predominantly agrarian province of Andalusia and in the so-called 'revolutionary triangle' of Catalonia, Zaragoza and Valencia. Regional diversity, which forms a central focus of the following analysis, provides a crucial clue to the differential development of working-class organisation and strength in Spain. In attempting to trace that development up to 1914, however, this chapter will also concentrate on three further factors which are generally accorded insufficient attention in the existing literature: the role of the state within the political structure of the Spanish Restoration Monarchy (1875–1923); the respective organisational structures of the anarchist and socialist movements; and the significance of the poverty of indigenous Marxist theory to the development of Spanish socialism.[2]

1. Figures in Juan Pablo Fusi, 'El movimiento obrero en España, 1876–1914', *Revista de Occidente* (1974), 131, p.204.

2. A major drawback facing the historian of modern Spain is the lack of detailed statistical information available before the twentieth century. Strike statistics were not published until 1903 in Barcelona, and 1905 in the rest of the country; moreover, such statistics must be considered of questionable accuracy, as must the very few population censuses which exist for the nineteenth century. With regard to the workers' movement, statistics for both the socialist and anarchist movements are uneven: there is little information on either before 1900, except in a few local areas. In addition, the restrictions on academic freedom which prevailed until the death of General Franco in 1975 contributed to the relatively unsophisticated state of current

An emphasis on these factors will demonstrate why the most widely favoured explanations for anarchist primacy over the socialist movement are inadequate. Three of these in particular have enjoyed widespread currency. First, and least convincing, is the view propounded initially by Anselmo Lorenzo, a committed anarchist militant, in his 1901 publication, *El proletariado militante*. Lorenzo's argument, often repeated since, was that the Spanish workers were won over to anarchism mainly through the strength of character and personality of Giuseppe Fanelli, Bakunin's personal emissary, who arrived in Spain in October 1868. Fanelli, who spoke no Spanish, supposedly captivated his audiences through 'expressive mimicry' and served as the 'catalyst . . . for the most widespread workers' and peasants' movement in modern Spain'.[3]

Second, and of almost equal implausibility, is the perennial chestnut of Spanish idiosyncrasy: quasi-metaphysical speculations about the innate anarchism of the Spanish national character. Thus, Salvador de Madariaga, the influential liberal essayist, argued in his widely acclaimed history of Spain, 'By temperament and psychology the Andalusian tends to the philosophical anarchy of Kropotkin; environment and experience tempt him to follow the violent path of Bakunin'.[4] In similar vein, the philosopher Miguel de Unamuno attributed the success of the disciplined Socialist Party in the Basque Country to the 'seriousness of the Basque character'.[5] Linked to this assessment is the idea, outlined by Juan Díaz del Moral in 1928 and widely accepted since, that the appeal of anarchism to southern peasants was essentially emotional: a 'religious heresy' reacting against the claimed hypocrisies of the Catholic Church. The dissident German communist, Franz Borkenau, observed 'Anarchism *is* a religious movement, in a sense profoundly different from the sense in which that is true of the labour movements of the progressive countries'.[6] However, although anti-clericalism

---

labour movement historiography in Spain. This chapter can only aim to serve as a general overview: much detailed research remains to be done.

3. Anselmo Lorenzo, *El proletariado militante* (Madrid, 1974; first published in two vols, 1901 and 1923), pp.38–44. For a recent example, see Murray Bookchin, *The Spanish Anarchists. The Heroic Years 1868–1936* (New York, 1977), pp.12–16.

4. Salvador de Madariaga, *Spain* (London, 1942), p.115.

5. Miguel de Unamuno, 'El socialismo en España', *Obras completas* (n.d.), IX, p.737.

6. Juan Díaz del Moral, *Historia de las agitaciones campesinas andaluzas, Córdoba* (Madrid, 1929), pp.182–224, esp. pp.207ff; Franz Borkenau, *The Spanish Cockpit*

undoubtedly played a significant role in anarchist motivations, especially in Catalonia, the pervasiveness of the Catholic Church's influence should not be exaggerated. Throughout much of rural Andalusia and Extremadura, in the south, the Church appears never to have re-established an institutional presence after the fifteenth-century expulsion of the Moors.

Slightly more sophisticated is the third and most widely favoured explanation of anarchist success in Spain. Expressed succinctly by the historians Pierre Vilar and Jaime Vicens Vives, this view stresses economic variables, laying emphasis on the industrial backwardness of the Spanish economy as compared to those of northern European countries. The appeal of anarchism, strongest in rural Andalusia, can be seen as the logical consequence of social and economic backwardness, while its penetration of the more industrially advanced region of Catalonia is explained by the small unit structure of Catalan textile industry which allowed the class struggle to retain 'a personal note'.[7] Although this theory is commendably parsimonious, it falls down through its inability either to account for the lack of anarchist penetration in other areas where there were small unit industrial structures, such as Guipúzcoa in the Basque Country, or to explain regional diversity *within* Andalusia.

It can hardly be overstressed that Spain in the late nineteenth and early twentieth centuries was predominantly agrarian. In 1900, over 4.5 million people out of a population of some 18.5 million were directly dependent on the land; between 1900 and 1914, some 65 to 75% of the active population was employed in the agricultural sector of the economy, as Table 6.1 shows, industrial production accounting at best for just 15% during this period.[8] The wealth generated by agriculture and industry was rarely invested in basic infrastructural provision to support a burgeoning population. Although the rate of growth of the Spanish population was lower than that of its European neighbours, it none the less far outstripped the country's capacities in terms of health and housing. Living condi-

---

(London, 1937), p.22. See also: Gerald Brenan, *The Spanish Labyrinth* (Cambridge, 2nd edn, 1950), pp.188ff; E.J. Hobsbawm, *Primitive Rebels* (Manchester, 1971), pp.74–92; Raymond Carr, *Spain 1808–1975* (Oxford, 2nd edn, 1982), p.444.

7. Jaime Vicens Vives et al., *Historia social y económica de España y América* (5 vols, Madrid, 1972), Vol.5, p.327; Pierre Vilar, *Spain. A Brief History* (Exeter, 2nd edn, 1977), p.79.

8. Fusi, 'Movimiento obrero . . . ', p.206; J. Harrison, *An Economic History of Modern Spain* (Manchester, 1978), pp.21–3.

Table 6.1 Occupation of the active Spanish labour force according to census data, 1877–1910

Year	Agriculture	Industry	Services
	%	%	%
1877	70	11	19
1887	66.5	14.6	18.7
1900	66.34	15.99	17.67
1910	66	15.82	18.18

Source: J. Harrison, *An Economic History of Modern Spain* (Manchester, 1978), p. 69.

Table 6.2 Spanish population statistics, 1861–1920

Period	Births		Deaths		Increase		Pop.
	a	b	a	b	a	b	
1861–1870	605	37.9	491	30.7	114	7.2	15.5m
1881–1890	628	36.2	551	31.4	77	4.8	17.5m
1891–1900	633	34.8	536	30	97	4.8	18.1m
1901–1910	657	34.5	481	24.4	176	10.1	18.5m
1911–1920	615	29.8	483	23.5	132	6.3	19.9m

a: absolute figures (in thousands)
b: per 1,000 inhabitants

Source: Jaime Vicens Vives *et al.*, *Historia social y económica de España y América* (5 vols, Madrid, 1972), Vol. 5, p. 16.

tions for the Spanish work-force were usually appalling: levels of hygiene were abysmally low; concomitantly, the mortality rate was very high. In 1900, for instance, the mortality rate in Spain stood at 30 per 1,000, compared with an average of 18 per 1,000 in other European countries. (See Table 6.2)

Within the general pattern of agricultural dominance, one area was of particular significance. The massive southern province of Andalusia, where the size of the agrarian labour force matched that of the industrial work-force in the whole of the rest of Spain, was the principal site for the early implantation and development of anarchism. At face value, the appeal of anarchism in Andalusia is easy to understand. The region had long been characterised by the widespread existence of *latifundia*, massive estates which relied upon the systematic exploitation and oppression of an underclass of landless day labourers, the *braceros*. Conditions of life for the mass of the *braceros* were brutal in the extreme: food shortages and long periods of unemployment were the norm.

The appalling hardships of their daily existence helped make Andalusian peasants receptive of anarchism's seemingly straightforward promise to break the stranglehold of the *latifundistas* through seizure of the land followed by the destruction of state power. The implied violence of the anarchist message held an obvious appeal: its millenarian promise of the complete destruction of the existing order. Incendiarism, insurrection and assassinations became endemic throughout the province of Andalusia in the latter part of the nineteenth century. Beguilingly simple, this image of a millenarian mass of landless Andalusian peasants drawn to anarchism by its messianic promise of salvation through revolution has enjoyed considerable influence. In fact, the reality of rural anarchism in Andalusia was rather more complex than this.

Two points in particular merit emphasis. On the one hand, the correlation between *latifundia* estates and anarchist strength is less than clear-cut. Although the incidence of *latifundia* estates in Ciudad Real, Huelva, Granada and Cáceres was similar to that in the anarchist strongholds of Cordoba, Seville and Cadiz, the penetration of rural anarchism in these four provinces was very limited. Moreover, in Cordoba and Seville, rural anarchism was strongest in those municipalities where *latifundia* accounted for just 35–40% of the cultivated land. Indeed, only Cadiz demonstrated a clear relationship between the incidence of rural anarchism and the proportion of cultivated land in the hands of *latifundistas*.[9] On the other hand, recent studies of support for anarchism in Andalusia undermine the view that it was the near exclusive preserve of unskilled, landless *braceros*. Research by Temma Kaplan has suggested that the extent to which small producers and skilled workers were involved in the Andalusian anarchist movement, above all in Cadiz, has been underplayed. Kaplan has concentrated on the sherry-producing areas around Jerez de la Frontera to argue that rural anarchism was more rational than millenarian. In particular, she has stressed the extent to which anarchist organisational strategies owed their origins to local associationist traditions: by 1870 in Jerez, for instance, there were approximately fifty different societies of artisans, small proprietors and workers.[10]

9. Fusi, 'Movimiento obrero . . . ', pp.206–8.
10. Temma Kaplan, 'The Social Base of Nineteenth-Century Andalusian Anarch-

Although Cadiz was perhaps an atypical region within the province of Andalusia, in general the nature of productive activity was a major determinant of the form that labour protest took. The staple produce of the Andalusian *latifundia* were cereals and olive oil. On average, these crops provided work for between 180 and 250 days in the year, with the worst months for unemployment being from February to April and August to October. In those months in which there was work wage levels were appallingly low, a situation compounded by the desperate need of the *braceros* for any form of income. At harvest times, between June and September, the situation was only slightly ameliorated by the huge increase in demand for labour which temporarily led to higher wages; in general, though, the landless day labourers lived in conditions of extraordinary deprivation and physical hardship. In the late 1880s, conditions in Grazalema, a district in the province of Cadiz, were apparently so desperate that prisoners begged to remain in jail, where they would at least be fed, rather than return home to starve.[11]

A vital concomitant of these conditions was that strike activity was of limited efficacy. For large parts of the year strikes were wholly pointless, since there was no work available. In those periods when there was work, massive labour shortages militated against worker solidarity. Moreover, the lack of opportunity to accumulate any surplus funds during those periods in which there was work rendered strike actions impracticable. Thus, with the exception of the years 1903–4, when special circumstances associated with chronic drought prevailed, agrarian strikes in Andalusia between 1875 and 1914 were both rare and of marginal significance. Between 1875 and 1900, there was only one registered strike — in 1893. The extent of the 1903–4 strike wave is unknown. Between 1905 and 1910, there were 19; between 1908 and 1914, just 13. However, as will be seen, possibilities for effective political or legal redress of grievances were also lacking in the latter years of the nineteenth century. This helps explain the propensity of some landless peasants to turn so readily to violent forms of protest. None the less, it is important to stress that rural anarchism in

---

ism in Jerez de la Frontera', *Journal of Interdisciplinary History* (1975), VI:1, p.58; see also Temma Kaplan, *Anarchists of Andalusia, 1868–1903* (Princeton, 1977). Kaplan is not wholly fair to those she criticises, since her representation of their views in tendentiously reductionist.

11. Kaplan, *Anarchists of Andalusia*, p.162.

Andalusia was more limited than is often thought in the years before the First World War. Terrorist activity in the years after 1875 was basically restricted to the provinces of Cadiz and Seville, while in Cordoba the general pattern of relations between owners and workers was remarkably harmonious until 1903.

The other main centre of anarchist strength in Spain during the late nineteenth and early twentieth century was Catalonia. The Catalan economy was centred around textile production and the wine trade. Between 1860 and 1889, when the French vineyards were devastated by phylloxera, viticulture was of considerable importance in Catalonia. Relations between owners and peasants in this period were largely untroubled on account of *rabassa morta* contracts by which peasants, the *rabassaires*, were granted land on which they planted vineyards and used part of the proceeds to cover their rents. The rents were reasonable, and the tenancy agreements, which remained valid so long as the newly planted vines survived, generally lasted forty to fifty years, a compensation for the initial years of non-production while the vines grew. However, in 1889 the Spanish vines also succumbed to the dreaded phylloxera parasite and the wine trade went into sharp decline. The response by owners was to import American vines; however, these had a life-expectancy of just twenty-five years and took longer to reach fruit-producing maturity than indigenous Spanish vines. Naturally, the traditional *rabassa morta* contracts became considerably less attractive to the *rabassaires*, and when the owners attempted to impose share-cropping agreements as a means to extend their control still further, there emerged serious social conflicts which continued intermittently until the Civil War. However, the *rabassaires*, who enjoyed what was seen as a privileged position, were resistent to political recruitment, and the conflict, after flaring briefly towards the end of the nineteenth century, was kept in check until after the end of the First World War.

More significant from the point of view of anarchist recruitment was the Catalan textile industry, the dominant source of employment in Catalonia. Barcelona was the principal site of industrial production in Spain: by 1900, 15–20% of the entire Spanish industrial population worked in the Catalan capital and its environs. Indeed, Barcelona province, along with Madrid, and the Basque regions of Vizcaya and Guipúzcoa, was one of the four Spanish provinces at the turn of the century where less than 50% of the active population was employed in agriculture. By 1900 barely one million people in

Spain were employed in the industrial sector; of those, 25% were employed in the construction industry, whilst other important sectors were transport (15%), textiles (13%), mining (8%), and metallurgy (6.5%).[12] Conditions of work were normally oppressive, characterised by poor standards of safety and hygiene, as well as lack of job security and risible wages. However, anarchism did not become a mass movement in Catalonia until after the end of the First World War; moreover, its development there was a long and disconnected process. Inevitably, the predominance of industry in Catalonia ensured that the nature of the anarchism which penetrated the north-eastern province differed from that which existed in Andalusia. Thus, whereas the southern anarchists favoured libertarian communism, in Catalonia revolutionary syndicalism held sway.

The issue of why anarchism rather than socialism took root among the Catalan textile hands and became a major social force in the twentieth century remains one of the most puzzling questions in modern Spanish historiography. Some historians, such as Gerald Brenan and Raymond Carr, have pointed to the supposed influence exercised on the Barcelona proletariat by the arrival of violently anarchist southern migrants seeking employment in the Catalan capital.[13] In fact, by 1920 only 0.7% of the population of Barcelona originated from Andalusia. Amongst other reasons adduced to explain anarchist strength in Catalonia have been: the concentration of industry in small factories and the survival of artisanal, familial concerns; the divorce between an industrialised society and semi-feudal state; the brutality of employers and the harshness of labour conditions; frustration at the failure of democratic reforms; and the rejection by the Catalan work-force of modernity and 'capitalist intrusion'. All of these factors may have exercised an influence at given moments in given areas; however, since they were not exclusive to Catalonia, they fail to provide a fully convincing explanation.

In the Basque province of Guipúzcoa, for example, small-scale industrial concentration did not appear to favour the implantation of anarchism as opposed to socialism; similarly, in both the Basque Country and Asturias the disparity between industrial mining sectors and the anachronistic politics of a predominantly agrarian society was no less marked than in Catalonia, yet in these two

12. Fusi, 'Movimiento obrero . . . ', p.214.
13. For example, Carr, *Spain*, p.445; Brenan, *Spanish Labyrinth*.

regions socialism rather than anarchism took root. Basque prosperity was based on the iron mines of Vizcaya. Between 1876 and 1900, the Basque Country underwent an intensive period of industrialisation, based largely on the introduction to Spain of the Bessemer iron-smelting process. High grade Vizcayan ore attracted considerable foreign investment, mainly British, French, German and Belgian, which led to the estabishment of numerous metallurgy companies around the capital, Bilbao, as well as an important shipbuilding industry. Amongst the most notable of these new companies were La Vizcaya and Altos Hornos, both created in 1882, which would merge at the start of the twentieth century. Two further effects were the transformation of Bilbao into a major commercial centre, reflected in the establishment of a flourishing banking trade, as well as a major increase in population as landless labourers poured into Vizcaya in search of work.

Between 1877 and 1900, the population of Vizcaya rose from 189,954 to 311,361. This gave rise to serious social problems, since Vizcaya lacked the basic infrastructures of water supply, sewerage, housing or public services to support such a rapid rise. It was in the mining industry that the difficulties were most acute. To combat the lack of housing, mining companies built wooden '*barracones*', or barrack-type huts, in which the work-force was required to live. Appalling levels of hygiene led to widespread disease and discontent. In 1894, the Vizcayan Health Inspector visited five *barracones* in which there were just 181 beds for 362 men. Unsurprisingly, the mortality rate in Vizcaya was the highest in Spain, averaging 33 per 1,000 between 1878 and 1895. Labour combativity was familiar in Vizcaya, but, despite five general miners' strikes between 1890 and 1910, socialism gained a foothold only with difficulty. Before the First World War, workers in the large factories showed little inclination to affiliate to either political parties or syndicates.

It was a similar story in Asturias, where coal-mining had taken off in the 1860s in reply to the demand generated by railways and the nascent Spanish iron industry. After 1885 three major mining companies emerged: Unión Hullera y Metalúrgica Asturiana (1885), Hulleras del Turón (1891) and Hullera Española (1892). None the less, the population of Asturias remained almost entirely rural, even though local agriculture was never able to support the population. This led both to high levels of migration and to the emergence of the *obrero mixto* (mixed worker), who split his time between the mines and working on the land and became the dominant figure in the mine work-force until the First World War. As late as 1911, between 60 and 70% of the mine work-force was comprised of mixed workers. Not being purely industrial, the mixed worker tended to be resistant both to labour discipline imposed by employers and to attempts at recruitment by labour organisations. As the chief engineer at Hullera Española complained in 1891, it was difficult for the company to impose its will on the workers who were also tenant farmers because 'they are more afraid of losing their land than losing the wage we pay them'.[14]

Although labour protest in the form of absenteeism, the refusal to work overtime and a general resistance to the imposition of labour discipline was widespread in Asturias from the 1870s onwards, the miners proved resistant to the organised labour movement. In regional terms, both socialism and anarchism spread inland from the coast, starting with the dockers and metalworkers of Gijón. Socialism only began to establish a small presence in the mines at the end of the nineteenth century, with only two unions and 200 organised workers in the coalfields in 1900. It was not until the creation of the Sindicato de Obreros Mineros de Asturias (SMA) in 1910 that the definitive organisation of the mine workers began. Unlike the construction workers of Madrid, or the textile workers of Barcelona, the northern miners proved slow to organise politically.

The Spanish state and the labour movement

Such anomalies underline the importance of stressing the specificity of regional variations in the labour process. However, the fact that organised working-class activity became significant rather later in Vizcaya and Asturias than in Andalusia and Catalonia suggests the need to look also at other factors influencing the organisation of the labour movement. One such factor was the development and nature of the Spanish state. The state determined the parameters within which the labour movement was able to organise and operate politically: it provided the framework as well as deciding on the very legality of labour organisations. Its particular significance in Spain lay in the fact that, unlike in Britain and in France, there was

14. Adrian Shubert, *The Road to Revolution in Spain. The Coal Miners of Asturias 1860–1934* (Chicago, 1987), pp.36–8.

no establishment during the nineteenth century of a relatively democratic polity able to adjust to and absorb new social forces. At the same time, however, nor was the ruling class as unambiguously autocratic as that which dominated in, for example, Tsarist Russia. Instead, the Spanish state developed along what might be termed 'Prussian' lines, with the notable difference that industrial capitalism in Spain remained underdeveloped.

To borrow Barrington Moore's formulation, by the last quarter of the nineteenth century a 'reactionary coalition' had become established in Spain between a powerful political oligarchy, made up of the monarchy, landowners and the Church, and a politically weak commercial and manufacturing bourgeoisie.[15] The weakness of the Spanish bourgeoisie is a vital point. In terms of sociopolitical development, the majority of these middle classes were 'Catholic and conservative, imitators in their modest sphere of aristocratic attitudes and without a proud, independent bourgeois culture.'[16] There was no sizeable bourgeoisie in nineteenth-century Spain linked to the development of an industrial economy at the forefront of political transformation. In other words, in Marxist terms, the political revolution which brought about the modern constitutional state in Europe and thereby 'destroyed all the estates, corporations, guilds and privileges which expressed the separation of the people from its community',[17] did not occur in Spain: there was no bourgeois-led revolution, nor even a Spanish variant of the upheavals in 1848.

The roots of the reactionary coalition had been established during the 1830s and the 1850s when Church lands were disentailed as part of an ultimately unsuccessful attempt at fiscal restructuring. These estates were bought up mainly by existing landlords, but also by members of the embryonic commercial and industrial bourgeoisie. However, rather than using their capital to modernise agricultural production and invest in industry, the bourgeoisie allowed itself to be 'co-opted' by the political oligarchy. Attracted by the prestige conferred by land ownership, a substantial proportion of the new

15. The analysis here is based on Barrington Moore Jr, *The Social Origins of Dictatorship and Democracy* (London, 1967), Chapter VIII, pp.433–52, and also on Paul Preston, 'Spain', in Stuart Woolf (ed.), *Fascism in Europe* (London, 1981), pp.329–51.

16. Raymond Carr, *The Spanish Tragedy* (London, 1977), pp.9–10.

17. Karl Marx, 'On the Jewish Question', *Early Writings* (Harmondsworth, 1975), p.232.

haute bourgeoisie was easily persuaded to collaborate in the coalition's basic aim: maintaining the prevailing social system against any reformist threats to agrarian dominance. These threats derived in a rather inchoate manner principally from liberal army officers and from the poorly organised working class. However, the bourgeoisie's lack of genuine revolutionary drive was clearly demonstrated in the period 1868 to 1874; these six years of political chaos culminated in the establishment of an ultimately abortive republic, created more by accident than design. A series of military *pronunciamientos* (risings) and urban riots in Madrid and southern regions combined in 1868 to oust the Spanish monarchy, long discredited by overt corruption, its hypocritically clerico-conservative leanings and its disdain for the politically powerless.

In the ensuing power vacuum, the liberal bourgeoisie let slip its golden opportunity. Rather than take the initiative to institute thorough reforms, the bourgeoisie lost its nerve in a manner which recalled the earlier 1848 risings elsewhere in Europe. Lacking coherent leadership and direction, the working class and peasantry were able to do little more than stage a number of poorly co-ordinated cantonalist risings in the Levante and Andalusia. These were easily put down, but the spectre of proletarian disorder dampened liberal enthusiasm for progress. Unable to establish its authority, the First Republic, formally established in February 1873, was crushed by the army in December 1874. Once more, the bourgeoisie ceded its right to rule in return for the provision of political stability in which to make money. The monarchy was restored in the person of Alfonso XII; reform was abandoned.

The 'Restoration Monarchy' ruled over Spanish political life until 1923. Until 1897 it was dominated by the politician Antonio Cánovas de Castillo, architect of the so-called *turno pacífico* (literally, peaceful turnaround). The idea behind the *turno* was to maintain the configuration of political power in Spain basically unaltered, while presenting a façade of parliamentary democracy. Two political parties, the Conservative and the Liberal, were created to represent the two principal sections of the landed oligarchy, the wine and olive growers of the south and the wheat growers of the centre. These landed classes, whose economic power rested on their *latifundia* estates, were linked to the political centre in Madrid, alongside the Church and the higher-ranking military, through the system of *caciquismo*. *Caciques* were local political bosses who, through a variety of more or less corrupt means, ensured that electoral results approximated to the pre-determined outcomes decided upon in Madrid. Since the only alternatives were Conservative government under Cánovas, or Liberal government under Práxedes Sagasta, it was effectively impossible for other interests to find political expression. The Canovite system, modelled on its founder's admiration for British parliamentary procedures, had little to do with democracy; still less did it cater for the representation of workers' and peasants' interests.

It was within this political context that the Spanish labour movement was obliged to organise during the Restoration Monarchy. Perhaps unsurprisingly, its efforts were beset with difficulties. In early 1869, the Federación Regional Española (FRE), the Spanish branch of the International Working Men's Association (IWMA or First International), had been established in Barcelona following Giuseppe Fanelli's famous mission the previous year. Fanelli's impact derived less from the power of his oratory than from the fact that he brought with him a series of documents concerning the International. Included amongst these were the statutes and programmes not only of the IWMA, but also of Bakunin's International Alliance of Socialist Democracy, which had recently entered the IWMA. The contradictions between the two positions, which were to develop into the struggle between 'authoritarians' and 'anti-authoritarians' within the IWMA, apparently went unremarked by the Spaniards. However, the FRE soon made it clear that it favoured the 'anti-authoritarian' stance of the Bakuninites; its ideological position was propagated by its Barcelona-based newspaper, significantly entitled *La Federación*.

The ideology of the FRE could be described as anarcho-collectivism. In short, it sought the destruction of state power, which would be brought about through revolution once the working class had been made aware of its superior strength and fire-power. In order to achieve this task, the FRE, which rejected party political activity, was organised along the lines of a labour organisation. The basic cell was a local craft union, and all the unions of different crafts within one area joined a local federation. The various local federations converged in the Spanish Federal Committee. The Federation, charged with the task of destroying the bourgeois state, was seen as sacred by the Catalan textile hands who made up its main centre of support. In 1874, however, with the collapse of the First Republic, the FRE was declared illegal along with all other labour movements; not until 1881, under the Liberal administration of

Sagasta, did the political oligarchs of the Restoration Monarchy allow workers' associations legal status. In the intervening period the FRE had effectively collapsed.

In 1881, the FRE was recreated as the Federación de Trabajadores de la Región Española (FTRE) (Workers' Federation of the Spanish Region), organised along the same lines as before. In its first year of existence it claimed some 58,000 members, divided principally between Catalonia and Andalusia. However, the initial success of the FTRE did not last. It was plagued by conflicts between the two regions: the Catalans, in line with their long-standing associationist traditions, were in favour of reformist tactics; by contrast, in Andalusia reformism was usually rejected out of hand by the more desperate and rather more numerous membership, although Kaplan suggests this picture should be qualified in the case of Cadiz.[18] The Andalusians accounted for 66.2% (over 38,000) of the total membership, with their main centres of strength being Malaga, Seville and Cadiz. Just over 50% were day labourers, the rest comprising viticultural workers (16.5% in Malaga and 13% in Cadiz) and members of unspecified '*oficios varios*' (various occupations), probably carpenters, confectioners, shoemakers, masons and the like. It has been calculated that more than half the heads of families in rural Andalusia belonged to the FTRE.[19]

The conflict between Catalan caution and Andalusian radicalism found perhaps its best known expression in the events surrounding the so-called 'Mano Negra', or Black Hand, affair. The 'Mano Negra', supposedly an extremist secret society dedicated to assassinating Andalusian landlords, was 'discovered' by the Civil Guard in 1882 and used as a pretext over the years that followed for harsh repression of the anarchist movement. Although doubts have subsequently been expressed as to the veracity of Civil Guard claims, the FTRE responded to the 'Mano Negra' at its Third National Congress, held in Seville in 1883, by denouncing its members as criminals, assassins and robbers and dissociating itself from them. Whatever the truth of the 'Mano Negra' affair, there were certainly several more or less secret societies, such as the 'Desheredados' (Disinherited), which engaged in violent direct action throughout rural Andalusia during the 1880s. Their existence provided the

---

18. Kaplan, *Anarchists of Andalusia*, pp.124ff.

19. Antonio Calero, *Movimientos obreros en Andalucía (1820–1936)* (Madrid, 1976), pp.26–7.

grounds for concerted state-backed repression which led to the decline of the FTRE and ultimately its collapse in 1888. The 1885 National Congress in Barcelona had been attended by the Federal Committee alone, while the Madrid Congress two years later enjoyed the presence of a mere sixteen delegates. With the FTRE disbanded in 1888, the rest of the century witnessed only sporadic attempts at organisation, a situation perhaps best exemplified by the invasion of Jerez in 1892. Near midnight on 8 January, a band of about 500 labourers marched into Jerez chanting slogans such as 'Long live Anarchy!' and 'Death to the Bourgeoisie!'. Armed mainly with pruning hooks and scythes, the marauders murdered two local clerks before they were easily put to flight by the city's Civil Guard, supported by local inhabitants. Although the insurrection appears to have been carefully planned, its precise aims are obscure; its one unambiguous result was to provide the authorities with a legitimate excuse to engage in further brutal repression of the anarchist movement.

There is a temptation to argue that the violence of Andalusian anarchism as opposed to the Catalan variant derives simply from the greater brutality of daily existence in the southern province and the rigid intransigence of employers. This factor must be accorded importance. However, the image of utopian anarchists locked in struggle with a gratuitously inflexible landed class fearful of social revolution should be tempered. As Josep Fontana has observed, the reality of labour struggles in rural Andalusia often boiled down to a more basic division between a demand on the part of the work-force for better conditions and fear on the part of the employers that their poorly organised agricultural system could not support increased wages without risking bankruptcy.[20] The struggles between labourers and landowners were thus usually more mundane than manichean or millenarian: membership of the anarchist movement did not necessarily imply a commitment to fully-fledged libertarian communism as opposed to a more basic desire to bring about an improvement in living standards. The anarchist movement was able to attract members largely through the lack of any credible or persuasive alternative.

Certainly the socialist movement offered little of obvious relevance of the Andalusian *braceros*. The Partido Socialista Obrero

---

20. Josep Fontana, *Cambio económico y actitudes políticas en la España del siglo XIX* (Barcelona, 1973), pp.186–7.

Español (PSOE) had been founded in Madrid on 2 May 1879, in conditions of illegality, by a small group of men associated with the minority 'authoritarian' branch of the International in Spain. It can hardly be overstressed that the Spanish socialist movement was marked from its inception by painfully slow growth. The majority of its early recruits were Madrid typographers and printworkers, members of the Asociación del Arte de Imprimir, a craft union originally founded in 1871. Later, the PSOE extended its influence to the dockers and metalworkers of Asturias and the Basque Country. However, not until just before the First World War did it manage to attract the mineworkers of these two regions; equally, it was only after 1910 that any significant number of intellectuals started to join the party. Moreover, the PSOE failed to establish an important presence either in Catalonia or in Andalusia, the two most crucial areas of radical potential in Spain. The reasons for this failure represent the reverse side of the coin of anarchist success: they hinge on the organisational strategy of the respective movements. The critical factor is that the PSOE organised as an electoralist political party in a country marked by electoral falsification and mass political demobilisation, whereas the anarchists tended to organise on syndical lines and explicitly rejected participation in parliamentary politics.

There are no precise records of PSOE membership in its earliest years; even the number of people involved in its original consititution is open to dispute. However, on the basis of the PSOE's own figures, presented to congresses of the Second International, the rather partial picture given in Table 6.3 emerges. A further indication of the PSOE's slow growth can be seen in the number of affiliated groups which attended its congresses (see Table 6.4). In Asturias, for example, where the mining industry was to become a socialist stronghold in the twentieth century, the PSOE was unable to organise branches until 1897, although in Vizcaya membership rose from 820 in 1900 to a peak of 1,992 in 1904, before falling to 710 in 1915.

Ideology and organisation in the socialist movement

In addition to its slow growth, a further fundamental feature of the early socialist movement was the poverty of its ideology. The PSOE leaders, above all its founding father, Pablo Iglesias, insisted that the

Table 6.3 Growth of the PSOE, 1891–1912

Year	No. of groups	Membership	Votes	Councillors	Press
1891	39	5 457	5 000	5	4
1893	50		7 000		7
1896			15 000	5	6
1898			20 000		
1900	45		23 000	9	7
1901			25 000	27	
1904	150	10 500	29 000	50	12
1905			23 000		
1907	100	6 000		71	7
1910	198	10 000	45 000		12
1912		13 000			

Source: Carlos Forcadell, *Parlamentarismo y bolchevización* (Barcelona, 1978), p. 27.

Table 6.4 PSOE Congresses, 1888–1915

No. of Congress	Date	No. of groups	Membership
I	1888	16	
II	1890	23	
III	1892	37	
IV	1894	42	
V	1899	55	
VI	1902	82	
VII	1905	144	
VIII	1908	115	
IX	1912	198	13 000
X	1915	238	14 332

Source: Jesús M. Eguiguren, *El PSOE en el País Vasco (1886–1936)* (San Sebastián, 1984), p. 38.

party's political praxis was derived from Marxist theory, even though the theory they espoused was rigid, schematic and derivative, bearing little obvious relation to the socio-economic or political situation in Spain. In turn, the praxis often bore little obvious relation to the theory, thereby giving rise to an ideological confusion which continued to encumber Spanish socialism throughout much of the twentieth century. Essentially, there emerged in the Spanish socialist movement a clear division between consistently revolutionary rhetoric and decidedly reformist practice. In itself, this was both unremarkable and hardly unique; its importance lay in the fact that the rhetoric determined certain parameters within which the PSOE acted politically. In particular, the poor understanding of the nature of state power and social structures in Spain, reflected in the simplistic insistence that the country was divided between the bourgeoisie and proletariat, led to costly political misjudgements. Above all, it fostered a political isolationism which marked the socialist movement until 1909. It is for this reason that the official ideology of the Spanish socialist movement merits attention: paradoxically, its very poverty invested it with peculiar significance.

The reasons for the poverty of Spanish Marxism remain obscure. There are perhaps three main factors which converged and contribute towards an explanation. The first concerns the influence within Spain of mechanistic French interpretations of Marxism. The mouthpiece of the first Spanish Marxists had been *La Emancipación* (1871–3), which moved away during 1872 from the Bakuninite current of the FRE towards a more explicit identification with Marx. Under the prompting of Marx's son-in-law, Paul Lafargue, who had fled to Spain from the Paris Commune in 1871, the editor of *La Emancipación*, José Mesa y Leompart, attempted to keep the FRE faithful to the orientations of the General Council of the IWMA. Mesa's failure in this self-appointed task prompted the creation of the Nueva Federación Madrileña (NFM), supposedly organised on the basis of IWMA statutes. In fact, the NFM failed to supersede the anti-electoral line of the early Spanish workers' movement, an orientation at odds with Marx's emphasis on the need to struggle to win reforms from the existing state. Even if abstentionist attitudes could be justified on the grounds that the Spanish state had not reached the stage at which it was meaningful to seek reform under its auspices, these grounds were not used. Instead, *La Emancipación* rejected electoral activity because it held that 'workers have nothing to do in bourgeois parliaments'.[21]

The early Spanish Marxists had a decidedly limited first-hand knowledge of the works of Marx and Engels. This should be seen as hardly surprising: not only was it difficult to gain access to what was proscribed by the state as subversive literature, but even if central Marxist texts had been available in good translations it is unlikely that the PSOE leaders would have found time to internalise them. The majority of early leaders of the PSOE came from a

21. *La Emancipación*, No.63, 24 August 1872.

working class which enjoyed little leisure time and few possibilities
of acquiring more than basic levels of education; what learning they
had was usually the result of autodidactic efforts. Moreover, Marx's
Das Kapital, for instance, is not a particularly accessible work, nor
indeed would it have provided many obvious clues as to the political
nature of the Spanish state. In the light of these constraints, the early
PSOE leaders not unnaturally turned to the French socialists for
guidance and advice. It was far more likely that the Spanish socialists would have a working knowledge of French than of German or
English, and this fact, together with geographical proximity, contributed to a heavy French influence on early Hispanic socialism.
Moreover, this link was fortified by José Mesa who had left Madrid
for Paris in the early 1870s.

Once in France, Mesa established contact with Jules Guesde and
Gabriel Deville. Increasingly involved with the Parisian circle associated with the journals *Les Droits de l'Homme*, *La Révolution*
and later *L'Egalité*, Mesa became an intermediary between Paris and
Madrid, transmitting to the Spaniards ideas formulated by the
French.[22] In many ways, this was a disaster for the Spanish socialists. Essentially, Guesdist Marxism was reductionist and determin-
istic, characterised by the rigidity and simplicity of most of its
postulates. In turn these derived from a superficial understanding of
some of the fundamental works of Marx and Engels, together with
the survival of ideological influences of pre-Marxist socialism and
an incapacity to relate theoretical perspectives to concrete conditions. The appeal of Guesdist formulations, in which revolution was
seen as both inevitable and on the immediate political agenda, had
much to commend them to the theoretically unsophisticated early
Spanish socialists.

The second reason relates to the manner in which Pablo Iglesias,
the dominant figure within the PSOE from 1879 until his death in
1925, stamped his authority upon the party. Although the potential
for the development of Marxist theory in Spain was anyhow
limited, given the general stagnation of intellectual currents, the
character and actions of Iglesias compounded an already unpromising situation. At the same time, however, he played a vital role in
the organisational formation and development, such as it was, of the

22. Carlos Forcadell, *Parlamentarismo y bolchevización* (Barcelona, 1978), p.37,
makes the important point that *all* European ideological currents which reached
Spain were mediated by French influences.

Spanish socialist movement. Perhaps the fundamental characteristic of Iglesias was pragmatism wedded to a basic mistrust of whatever lay outside his own personal ambit. Thus, he mistrusted not just republican politicians, but also the few intellectuals who, at an early stage, joined the PSOE. Both of these antipathies, it could be argued, incurred heavy costs for the Spanish socialist movement. In many ways, Iglesias personified Spanish socialism. Although, the victim of many personal attacks from anarchists and republicans alike, his almost puritanical commitment to socialist ideals was undeniable. In this he was representative of a tradition which came to mark the Spanish socialists — a tradition of ascetic morality which derived from the socialist ideal an all-embracing code of conduct. Theory played but a small part in the concerns of Iglesias. As Juan José Morato conceded in his largely hagiographic biography of the socialist leader, organisational questions took up so much of his time that there was little left to devote to studying Marxist theory.[23]

The socialist leader's overriding concern with organisational matters went alongside a dismissive attitude towards the role of intellectuals in the PSOE. Indeed, a division between workers and intellectuals was a marked feature of the PSOE in the nineteenth century. As Raymond Carr has stated, 'to Socialists they appeared as individualists whose intellectual aestheticism removed them from practical politics'.[24] An indicative example of this concerns Miguel de Unamuno, the Spanish philosopher and essayist, who was perhaps the major figure who could have acted as a catalyst for the development of Marxist thought in Spain. He became thoroughly disillusioned with the PSOE on account of Valentín Hernández, editor of *La Lucha de Clases* (Bilbao), to which Unamuno was a regular contributor while a member of the party between 1894 and 1897. Hernández's attitude towards intellectuals at times verged on contempt, particularly in relation to the lack of importance he felt they attached to questions of political organisation. Unamuno, for his part, began to see the PSOE as marked by narrow-mindedness and dogmatism, as made evident in his letter of May 1895 to his friend Pedro Múgica:

I'm a convinced socialist, but my friend, those who go by that name here

23. Juan José Morato, *Pablo Iglesias Posse — educador de muchedumbres* (Barcelona, 1977; first published 1931).

24. Carr, *Spain*, p.532.

are impossible; fanatics ignorant of Marx, poorly educated, obsessed by order, intolerant, full of prejudices of bourgeois origin, blind to the virtues and uses of the middle class, unaware of the evolutionary process. In fact they've got everything except any social sense.[25]

Unamuno left the PSOE in disgust in 1897, and it was not until after the 1909 alliance with the republicans that any significant number of intellectuals joined the party.

The third main reason for the poor development of Marxism in Spain was that the First International showed little interest in the Iberian peninsula. While it is true that Marx and Engels themselves demonstrated some degree of interest in Spanish affairs, in general little attention was paid to the Iberian mainland by the Internationalists. After Fanelli's somewhat duplicitous mission in 1868, the representative of the First International in Spain was Paul Lafargue who had arrived in the Iberian peninsula after the collapse of the Paris Commune in 1871. Lafargue, though, was given his role more on account of his happening to be in Spain, and his ability to speak Spanish (he was of Cuban descent), than because of any intimate knowledge of Spanish affairs. Moreover, his abilities as a populariser of Marxism were probably over-estimated on account of his familial connection with the grand master himself. Certainly, his period in Spain cannot be judged a great success, and the Iberian peninsula remained a low priority in the concerns of the IWMA.

The combination of these three factors helps to explain the poverty of early Marxist theory in Spain. This poverty was reflected in two further features of the early socialist movement which require emphasis. First, as if to compensate for their lack of theoretical sophistication, the early socialist leaders devoted major attention to organisational issues. This both confirmed the pre-eminence of Madrid as the centre of the movement, administratively and numerically, and also exacerbated the division between revolutionary rhetoric and reformist practice which was to become so characteristic of the PSOE. Whilst party propaganda predicted imminent violent revolution to be led by the industrial proletariat, party leaders concentrated on maintaining the organisation intact against potential state repression. As a result, the PSOE became a highly centralist party and developed a strict adherence, pitched in

25. Cited in S. Fernández Larraín (ed.), *Cartas inéditas de Miguel de Unamuno* (Madrid, 1972), p.207. The reference to evolutionism reflects the influence of Darwin.

moral terms, to the legal framework of political activity. Much more important, however, the socialist leaders failed to appreciate the need to organise in rural Spain. This can hardly be overstressed: since revolution was seen as the task of the industrial proletariat, the landless peasantry was effectively ignored. It can only be described as extraordinary that, in a country so primordially agricultural as Spain, the socialist movement failed even to elaborate an agrarian programme until 1918, and expended no significant effort in establishing a rural presence until 1930. The only plausible explanation is that the PSOE leaders fell victim to that part of the theory they espoused which was least applicable to Spanish conditions: the inevitable confrontation betweeen the bourgeoisie and the proletariat. Seduced by its simplicity, they failed to appreciate that rigidly stagist Marxism was of limited relevance to the historical moment in which they were operating.

Second, the poverty of Marxism in the PSOE also led to ideological ambiguity within the socialist union movement which was established in 1888, the year of the party's first National Congress. Despite repeated assertions that all reformist actions were useless, and that the inevitable revolution was on its way, Iglesias was consistently concerned to set up a national union structure to regulate political strike actions by the working class. This reached fruition with the founding of the Unión General de Trabajadores (UGT) in August 1888. The UGT represented a logical development of previous initiatives in Spain, associated principally with the FRE, the Asociación General del Arte de Imprimir and the Barcelona-based Federación Tipográfica y de las Industrias Similares. This was reflected in the three main elements of its founding statutes: the absence of any rigid ideological definition, in order to attract workers who were not necessarily socialist; a moderate attitude with regard to union struggles; and organisational centralism. The UGT was to be more successful in the first of these elements than the leaders of the PSOE might have liked. As Juan Pablo Fusi has suggested, the mis-match between UGT membership and support for the PSOE raises the question of whether the UGT before 1931, when the Second Republic was established, was effectively a socialist union at all.[26]

Organisational centralism meant that the UGT was effectively

---

26. Juan Pablo Fusi, 'El movimiento socialista en España (1879–1939)', in *Actualidad Económica* (25 May 1974), 845, p.63.

Table 6.5 Membership of the UGT, 1888–1914

Year	Membership	Year	Membership
1888	3 355	1903	46 574
1890	3 896	1904	56 900
1891	5 304	1905	36 557
1892	8 014	1906	32 405
1893	8 533	1907	32 612
1894	6 279	1908	44 912
1895	6 278	1909	43 562
1896	6 154	1910	40 984
1899	15 264	1911	80 000
1900	26 088	1912	100 000
1901	31 558	1913	127 804
1902	32 778	1914	121 553

Source: Amaro del Rosal, *Historia de la UGT 1901–1939* (2 vols, Barcelona, 1977), Vol. 2, p. 919.

run from Madrid, even though initially its headquarters were in Barcelona, since in reality UGT and PSOE leaders were the same people. Thus, although the establishment of the UGT in Barcelona represented a recognition of Catalonia's importance within the labour movement, this was vitiated by the lack of any real organisational autonomy. The extent of the socialists' failure to penetrate Catalonia can be gauged from the fact that in 1893, 20% of the UGT's paltry membership of just over 8,500 was based in Barcelona; by 1910, when affiliation to the UGT had risen to almost 41,000, there were just 635 members (1.5%) in the Catalan capital. Despite the existence of regionalist problems in both Catalonia and the Basque Country, these were never analysed theoretically as issues with importance for the socialist movement. Instead, regionalism and nationalism were dismissed as purely bourgeois notions.

Like the PSOE, which also held its first Congress in August 1888, the UGT was marked during the rest of the century by slow growth. Its main centres of strength were Madrid, Asturias and Bilbao; indeed, Santos Juliá has suggested that the history of the UGT amounts to the history respectively of the bricklayers, miners and metalworkers in these three areas.[27]

27. Santos Juliá, 'Largo Caballero y la lucha de tendencias en el socialismo español (1923–1936)', in *"Annali" della Fondazione Giangiacomo Feltrinelli* 1983/1984, pp.861–2.

Madrid was the dominant centre of the UGT, and within Madrid the building trade held sway: the Federación Local de Obreros de la Edificación accounted for up to a quarter of the capital's membership, which in turn represented over half the UGT's total membership for much of the period prior to the Second Republic. In 1905, out of a UGT's total membership of just over 36,500, the strongest regions were: Madrid (18,809), Alicante (6,709), Vizcaya (4,464) and Asturias (3,155). Two years later, when total UGT membership had dropped by over 10%, in Madrid it had fallen by just 5%.

The centrality of the Madrid building trade within the UGT had important implications for the union's organisation and activity. As with the PSOE, the issue of organisational cohesion was uppermost. Madrid building workers had to overcome dispersal in small units of production, together with the constant threat represented by a large reserve army of industrial labour ready to take their jobs. The union was conceived above all as a defensive body aimed at protecting its members from the abuses of unscrupulous employers, as well as fostering a sense of identity and unity within the trade. The concomitant of this was that the union leaders, figures such as Iglesias and Francisco Largo Caballero, allocated to themselves exclusive capacity for taking initiatives on behalf of their members. These initiatives were fundamentally concerned with protecting jobs above all else: the favoured tactics were non-confrontational. Cautious and legalistic, the UGT leaders turned unwillingly to strike action only as a last resort when all possibilities of negotiation had failed. Ironically, the UGT looked to the Spanish state as the ultimate guarantor of any progress it managed to achieve: the state was the only entity which could exert authority over the owners and employers once agreements had been reached.

However, it was precisely on account of the activities of the state that the Spanish labour movement had been reduced by the late 1890s to a position of parlous weakness. Torn between reductionist revolutionary rhetoric and essentially pragmatic political practice, the isolationist PSOE was confirmed as marginal to Spanish political life, a position in which it was to remain until the elaboration of an electoral alliance with republican parties in 1909. Despite Prime Minister Sagasta's introduction of a Law of Universal Suffrage in May 1890, which in reality was somewhat circumscribed by the partial continuance of *caciquismo*, the PSOE made little impact in the elections of 1891, 1893, 1896 and 1898, reaching just 20,000 votes in the last of these. This compares with the 1,427,000 votes received by the German socialists in 1899.

The anarchist movement, meanwhile, devastated by the repression unleashed after the Mano Negra affair, had fallen increasingly under the control of extremists who, following Kropotkin and Malatesta, preached anarcho-communism in opposition to Bakuninite collectivism. The division centred around the issue of 'propaganda-by-deed', promoted in particular by Italian émigrés in Barcelona. Following the Valencia Congress of 1888, which saw the formation of the Anarchist Organisation of the Spanish Region, collectivism had effectively collapsed. Bakuninite syndical currents were reduced to a Catalan rump in the Pact of Union and Solidarity of the Spanish Region (officially called the Spanish Federation for Resistance to Capitalism), also formed in 1888. Born in an era of terrorist ascendancy, as practised both by the state and by libertarian anarcho-communists, the Pact of Union and Solidarity was condemned to a sorry existence. Police reprisals, together with repressive legislation, led to its dissolution in 1896. The Anarchist Organisation of the Spanish Region also suffered severely at the hands of the state: by 1898 it had virtually abandoned 'propaganda-by-deed' as a costly and ineffective tactic. The Spanish labour movement as a whole seemed on the verge of collapse.

Roots of revival in the early twentieth century

However, 1898 saw the Spanish state also lurch towards a destabilising crisis. The first cracks in the Restoration Monarchy's *cacique*-based system of *turno pacífico* had started to appear towards the end of the century. Arguably, the seeds of the system's ultimate collapse were sown outside Spain: the 'Cuban Question', which had long been an open sore for Madrid, re-emerged during the 1880s and 1890s despite the 1878 Peace of Zanjón, imposed by General Martínez Campos. A resurgence of Cuban nationalism led to full-scale war breaking out in 1895. The Spaniards were unable this time to quell the nationalists and the struggle, which was both expensive and threatening to become very protracted, was brought to an end by the interested intervention of the United States in 1898. A war of seven months' duration resulted in Spain losing her last remaining colonies outside Africa in the most humiliating of circumstances: the destruction of the entire Spanish fleet was a deeply traumatic experience for the once imperial and still proud nation.

The disaster of 1898 was the catalyst for the appearance in Spain of 'a general *fin de siècle* pessimism which reacted violently against the clichés of parliamentary liberalism'.[28] However, although the stability of the state was severely undermined, the main beneficiaries of the surge of discontent which arose as a result of 1898 were not the socialists or anarchists. Instead, the disaster gave rise to what became known as 'regenerationism'. Associated principally with the polymath Joaquín Costa, regenerationism became something of a national watchword in the early years of the twentieth century. The primordial concern of the regenerationists in regard to politics was to inject morality into a corrupt and discredited system, to rebuild state structures on a more principled and democratic basis, to 'regenerate' the nation. While regenerationist currents would find some echo in the PSOE after the 1909 Republican–Socialist alliance, in the immediate aftermath of 1898 it was conservative proponents of 'revolution from above', such as Antonio Maura, who took up the torch of reform. If galling for the anarchist and socialist leaders, it was none the less a sadly accurate reflection of the weakness of their respective movements at the start of the twentieth century. Indeed, in 1900 less than 5% of the Spanish proletariat was integrated in syndical organisations, and industrial conflicts did not represent a significant political problem. Political organisation amongst the landless labourers of Andalusia, meanwhile, had been effectively disarticulated by state-backed repression.

However, with the new century the overwhelmingly depressing situation of the labour movement began to change. Notably, there was a marked increase in the number of strikes that took place, reflecting the start of a steady growth in membership of the UGT. The colonial struggle had incurred two major costs: its prosecution involved the state in inflationary expenditure, while defeat removed highly profitable export markets for Catalan textiles. With a normalisation in political life, many workers began to join the socialist UGT for defensive purposes. Particularly in Vizcaya, and to a lesser extent in Asturias, the UGT at last began to make inroads, although it still suffered periodic slumps (see Table 6.6). Increasing confidence led to the promulgation of a national general strike by the PSOE in June 1905. However, it received little support from the Spanish work-force, in part almost certainly due to the socialists' poor propaganda network, and passed virtually unnoticed.

28. C.A.M. Hennessy, *Modern Spain* (London, 1965), p.12.

Table 6.6 Growth of the UGT in Vizcaya

Date	No. of sections	Membership
1893	11	491
1901	36	3012
1903	53	4634
1905	66	5191
1907	47	1773
1909	52	2268
1911	60	9295
1915	59	3702

Source: Juan Pablo Fusi, *La política obrera en el País Vasco, 1880–1923* (Madrid, 1975), p. 489.

None the less, Spanish workers continued to exercise growing political muscle. Whereas in 1905 there were 153 strikes in Spain, few of which involved more than 20,000 strikers, by 1913 there were over 300, many involving over 80,000 strikers. Between 1904 and 1913, there were 1,271 strikes, although there were periods of low-level activity, especially from 1905 to 1909. The strikes were clearly concentrated regionally: 25% took place in Barcelona, 12% in Madrid, 8% in Vizcaya and 5% in Valencia. These four areas, together with Asturias, provided 60% of all strikers in this period. Equally, of course, it is clear that large parts of Spain remained relatively untouched by strike activity. It would appear that most strikes, 42% of which between 1905 and 1923 were for higher wages, occurred in periods of relative economic prosperity rather than hardship. Although there were exceptions, most of the UGT strikes in the early twentieth century were motivated by rising expectations.

The relative success of the UGT, at least up to 1905, contrasted with the declining fortunes of the anarchist movement. In both Catalonia and Andalusia the anarchists suffered severe setbacks between 1902 and 1904. In the north-eastern province, the syndicalists had been calling since the turn of the century for a revolutionary general strike as the only possible road to revolution. An attempted general strike in Barcelona in February 1902, however, turned out to be a disaster: it was quickly and easily crushed, leading to widespread disillusionment among the Catalan proletariat with Bakuninite collectivist tactics. A further attempt to stage a general strike the following year was opposed by the UGT, and, significantly, by a few collectivists also, fearful that the strike would fail and lead to the discrediting of the collectivist position. This is precisely what happened. One consequence was a renewed outbreak of terrorist activity, which in turn merely led to further repression being brought down on the anarchist movement in Catalonia. Between 1902 and 1909, Barcelona's union membership was reduced from 45,000 to just 7,000.

Moreover, underlining the increasingly limited impact of the anarchists in Catalonia, the first years of the twentieth century saw a considerable rise in support for the faction of the Radical Republican Party headed by Alejandro Lerroux. An ambitious anti-clerical demagogue, Lerroux offered the Catalan proletariat a purely political solution to their grievances: the replacement of the monarchy with a republic. The success of Lerroux is doubly significant: grounded in legalist adherence to parliamentary procedures, notwithstanding the violence of his rhetoric, it suggests both that there was no innate propensity within the Catalan proletariat towards anarchist solutions, and also, by extension, that there were no structural obstacles to socialist penetration in Catalonia. Furthermore, it prompted the suggestion from within the PSOE that an alliance with the republicans should be considered. Iglesias, however, remained inflexible: the socialists, he insisted, must demonstrate their moral superiority whilst concentrating on spreading the Marxist message untainted by any spurious compromise. This was a costly miscalculation, for while Lerroux won nearly 75% of the vote in Barcelona at the 1903 general election, the socialist vote collapsed to just 3%. The socialists signally failed to capitalise on the decline of Catalan anarcho-syndicalism.

If the anarchist movement had effectively collapsed in Catalonia by 1904, the position was equally bleak in the southern province of Andalusia. Sporadic and poorly co-ordinated strike actions by libertarian communists against landowners broke out in 1900 and culminated three years later with an attempted general strike in the province of Cordoba. The strike was short-circuited by the granting of concessions by employers in order to protect their harvest, which promised to be abundant. However, once the harvest had been collected, the employers reneged on their earlier agreement and lobbied the state for protective measures against pre-harvest strike actions. The following two years were marked by disastrous droughts. A wave of strikes in 1905 motivated by sheer desperation came to nothing: by the end of the year the organised anarchist movement had more or less collapsed in Andalusia. In its place, there was a renewed outburst of rather desperate isolated acts of violence which sought unsuccessfully to recapture the spirit of 'propaganda-by-deed'. For the decade before the First World War, rural anarchism in Andalusia remained very much on the defensive.

The reversals suffered by the anarchist movement in both Andalusia and Catalonia led, perhaps paradoxically, to the recrudescence of collectivism. In Barcelona, the influence of French revolutionary syndicalists like Pouget and Griffuelhes inspired the creation in 1904 of a new federation of working-class associations which became known as Solidaridad Obrera (Workers' Solidarity). In 1907 it started publishing a weekly newspaper of the same name, expanded its operation to encompass the entire region of Catalonia, and ultimately spawned the Confederación Nacional del Trabajo (CNT) in 1910. Solidaridad Obrera was conceived of initially as a pure syndicalist union, organised around immediate demands to be achieved through collective bargaining. However, it soon evolved, on the basis of the French model, a theory of direct action linked to a philosophy of the daily struggle, thereby differentiating itself from its more apocalyptic Bakuninite precursors of the 1870s. At its First Congress, held in Barcelona in early September 1908, Solidaridad Obrera brought together 143 delegates representing over 90 local federations and societies. Although still small, the new federation was to lay the basis for the resurgence of anarcho-syndicalism in Catalonia. It was also the moving force behind Barcelona's so-called Tragic Week of July 1909, a watershed in the history of the Spanish labour movement.

The spark which ignited the events of the Tragic Week was the government's ill-considered call-up of Catalan reservists for a minor campaign in Morocco. Resentful at what was seen as an unnecessary and unjustifiable imposition of political authority by Madrid, Solidaridad Obrera issued a strike call towards the end of July, which was supported by the Federación Socialista de Cataluña, as the PSOE had been long opposed to Spanish colonial involvement in North Africa. In Barcelona the strike degenerated into an urban riot of extreme intensity. Throughout all Catalonia, but particularly in the capital, the Catholic Church became the target of pent-up resentment over its position as pillar of the established order. Many churches and convents were sacked and burned, and several religious lost their lives in the disturbances. The repression unleashed in response by government forces under the hardline Governor-

General, Juan de la Cierva, was ferocious: 175 workers were shot in the streets, and many executions followed. The most important of these was that of the anarchist Francisco Ferrer, who almost certainly had little to do with the events of the Tragic Week. The European outcry at Ferrer's execution forced the Prime Minister's resignation. However, more important from the point of view of the Spanish labour movement, the Tragic Week reconfirmed the anarchists as the leaders of any revolutionary movement in Catalonia.

The repression which followed the Tragic Week forced Solidaridad Obrera to cancel a national congress planned for later in 1909. However, in late October of the following year Solidaridad organised a National Workers' Congress in Barcelona, attended by 114 local federations and societies, from which emerged the CNT. In September 1911, the CNT held its First Congress with a claimed membership of 26,571 divided into 140 syndicates. The formation of the CNT marked the start of a bitter struggle with the UGT which would continue on and off until the Civil War. In the immediate aftermath of the CNT Congress, however, the struggle was forced into abeyance: the CNT was declared illegal by a Barcelona judge following its involvement in a general strike almost certainly triggered by the government. In 1912 the assassination by an anarchist of the Prime Minister, José Canalejas, brought down vicious repression on the CNT which was forced into clandestinity, in theory organised by a secret National Committee which in practice was unable to meet. Not until 1915 was the CNT able to reorganise following its legalisation the previous year by the Liberal administration of the Conde de Romanones. Thereafter, as is well known, the anarcho-syndicalist union became a major force in Spain.

For the socialist movement, events in Catalonia sounded a clear warning. In danger of being marginalised by the pincer movement of the anarchists on their left and the republicans on their right, the PSOE had to reconsider its tactical stance. The result of the reconsideration was the Republican–Socialist electoral alliance, established at the end of 1909. Fusi has argued that in fact such an alliance had already become a reality in various regional sectors of the PSOE, most notably in the Basque Country during the provincial elections of 1907.[29] While the Tragic Week acted as the immediate

---

29. Fusi, 'Movimiento socialista . . . ', p.65.

catalyst, the question of an alliance had been posed earlier by Vicente Barrio, secretary of the UGT, at the party's VIII Congress in 1908. Barrio was particularly concerned at the continued failure of strike actions, and at the success of the Radical Republican, Alejandro Lerroux, who had been able to capitalise on anti-government feeling. Complaints against Madrid *laissez-faire* policies were hardly new, but under the dynamism of Lerroux, republicanism in a radical and demagogic guise had experienced a resurgence, tapping the growing social and political unrest in Barcelona. The success of Lerroux stood in stark contrast to the ineffective efforts of the PSOE, and highlighted the costs of previous failures to organise effectively in the Catalan capital.

Caught within the confines of an interpretative scheme which could not have been simpler — the proletariat was right, the bourgeoisie was wrong — Pablo Iglesias increasingly found himself not just unable to explain the failure of socialism in Spain to develop in line with his messianic pronouncements, but also faced with ever greater challenges to his political line from within the PSOE. His response, predictably pragmatic, was the Republican–Socialist Conjunction, agreed upon on 7 November 1909. The Conjunction was of major political significance, for it marked the end of the socialist movement's rigidly isolationist stance. It also transformed the party into a national force for the first time in its history.

Following the 1909 Conjunction both the PSOE and the UGT experienced an impressive increase in membership, the latter expanding threefold between 1910 and 1912. In large measure this was due to the UGT's penetration amongst the mineworkers of Asturias and Vizcaya. Until 1911, mining sections in the UGT had been almost insignificant, never representing more than 8% of the total membership. Although both provinces had seen several miners' strikes over the preceding thirty years, neither had a strong organisational tradition among the working class. However, in 1910 the Sindicato de Obreros Mineros Asturianos (SMA), affiliated to the UGT, was established by Manuel Llaneza, a socialist who modelled the new union on those of northern France. Llaneza's main aim was to avoid decentralisation: locals were not autonomous, and they could act only with the blessing of the executive committee. The SMA established a presence in Asturias remarkably quickly (see Table 6.7).

A number of early successes, particularly in 1911 at the Fábrica de Mieres and the Hulleras del Turón, led to a vigorous response from

Table 6.7 Membership of the SMA, 1911–15

Year	Membership	Percentage of work-force
1911	1 800	11.7
1912	10 000	62.2
1913	8 653	48.6
1914	10 000	54.8
1915	12 867	64.5

Source: Adrian Shubert, *The Road to Revolution in Spain* (Chicago, 1987), p. 112.

the mining companies. The number of company police was increased, and efforts were made to stimulate the formation of rival Catholic syndicates, although these proved ultimately of little impact.

Similarly, in Vizcaya there was a notable increase in the number of miners affiliated to the UGT. However, the growth of the socialist movement also saw an increase in internal dissent, as Pablo Iglesias' personal dominance declined. Between 1910 and 1914 bitter divisions over the issue of trade union tactics developed within the PSOE, leaving it severely weakened on the eve of the Great War. Iglesias consistently propounded the twin line of propaganda efforts supported by carefully organised local strikes, but remained steadfastly opposed to all revolutionary initiatives. In fact, strike actions by the UGT in some areas were becoming increasingly independent of the PSOE's central apparatus. In Vizcaya powerful miners' leaders such as Eladio Fernández Egocheaga and Facundo Perezagua contested the PSOE's centralism and characteristic caution. Perezagua had clashed with the PSOE leadership in 1910 over the miners' strike in the Basque Country, and later the railworkers' strike of 1912 which started in Catalonia and extended to cover large areas of Spain. The most bitter clash, though, came over the 1913 Rio-Tinto miners' strike, which Perezagua and Egocheaga wanted to convert into a general strike with the ultimate aim of radicalising the socialist movement. Iglesias, in collaboration with Manuel Llaneza of the SMA, opposed this move for fear of the PSOE's tactical line being undermined. The upshot was the expulsion of the two Basque leaders from the UGT and PSOE. However, the division was merely a precursor of arguments which would eventually lead to the split of the PSOE in 1921 over the question of the Third International.

Overall, it must be concluded that the organised labour movement in Spain before the First World War was marked by a general pattern of sporadic growth and limited impact, punctuated by the occasional spectacular, if short-lived, challenge to state power. Within this grim panorama, the anarchist movement enjoyed greater success, albeit fluctuating, than did the socialist movement. The reason for this lies with the respective organisation and ideology of the two movements. The anarchists were both more flexible in terms of ideology and more adept in terms of organisation than were their socialist rivals. This allowed them to establish a presence in the two regions with most radical potential: Catalonia and Andalusia. There was nothing pre-ordained about this. With a different organisational structure and a less rigid ideological outlook, there is no reason why the socialist movement could not have penetrated these two regions also. Therefore, perhaps the question of anarchist strength in Spain requires reformulation. Rather than seek the reasons for the success of anarchism, it is maybe more pertinent to analyse the failure of Spanish socialism, for it is this which really sets apart the history of the organised labour movement in Spain from the general European pattern.

BIBLIOGRAPHY

Note: This Bibliography contains only English-language titles; however, there is a wealth of relevant recent research which has been published only in Spanish. I would be happy to supply detailed references for students wishing to consult this corpus.

M. Bookchin, *The Spanish Anarchists. The Heroic Years 1868–1936* (New York, 1977)

F. Borkenau, *The Spanish Cockpit* (London, 1937)

G. Brenan, *The Spanish Labyrinth* (Cambridge, 2nd edn, 1950)

R. Carr, *The Spanish Tragedy* (London, 1977)

—— *Spain 1808–1975* (Oxford, 2nd edn, 1982)

J. Harrison, *An Economic History of Modern Spain* (Manchester, 1978)

C.A.M. Hennessy, *The Federal Republic of Spain, 1868–1875* (Oxford, 1962)

—— *Modern Spain* (London, 1965)

R. Herr, *An Historical Essay on Modern Spain* (Berkeley, 1971)

E.J. Hobsbawm, *Primitive Rebels* (Manchester, 1971)

J. Joll, *The Anarchists* (London, 2nd edn, 1979)

T. Kaplan, 'The Social Base of Nineteenth-Century Andalusian Anarchism in Jerez de la Frontera', *Journal of Interdisciplinary History* (1975), VI, pp.1, 47

—— *Anarchists of Andalucia, 1868–1903* (Princeton, 1977)

R.W. Kern, *Liberals, Reformers and Caciques in Restoration Spain, 1875–1909* (Albuquerque, N. Mex., 1974)

—— *Red Years/Black Years. A Political History of Spanish Anarchism, 1911–1937* (Philadelphia, 1978)

F. Lannon, *Privilege, Persecution, and Prophecy. The Catholic Church in Spain 1875–1975* (Oxford, 1987)

E. Malefakis, *Agrarian Reform and Peasant Revolution in Spain* (New Haven, Conn., 1970)

S. de Madariaga, *Spain: A Modern History* (London, 1942)

K. Marx and F. Engels, *Revolution in Spain* (New York, 1939)

J. Nadal, 'The Failure of the Industrial Revolution in Spain, 1830–1914', in C.M. Cipolla (ed.), *The Fontana Economic History of Europe*, Vol. 4 (Glasgow, 1973)

P. Preston, 'Spain' in S. Woolf (ed.), *Fascism in Europe* (London, 1981)

J. Romero Maura, 'The Spanish Case', in D.E. Apter and J. Joll (eds), *Anarchism Today* (London, 1970)

—— '*Caciquismo* as a Political System', in E. Gellner and J. Waterbury (eds), *Patrons and Clients* (London, 1977)

A. Shubert, *The Road to Revolution in Spain. The Coal Miners of Asturias 1860–1934* (Chicago, 1987)

X. Tusell Gomez, 'The Functioning of the Cacique System in Andalusia, 1890–1931', in S.G. Payne (ed.), *Politics and Society in Twentieth-Century Spain* (New York, 1976)

J.C. Ullman, *The Tragic Week* (Cambridge, Mass., 1967)

P. Vilar, *Spain. A Brief History* (Exeter, 2nd edn, 1977)

G. Woodcock, *Anarchism* (Harmondsworth, 1975)

ABOUT THE CONTRIBUTORS

JOHN DAVIS is Chairman at the Centre for Social History at the University of Warwick. His research interests are in Italian social and economic history 1750–1914 and he is currently working on social change in Southern Italy during the Napoleonic period. Publications include: *Gramsci and Italy's Passive Revolution* (1979); *Merchants, Monopolists and Contractors: Economy and Society in Bourbon Naples 1815–60* (1981); and, most recently, *Conflict and Control: Law and Order in 19th century Italy* (1988), a general survey of Italian social and political history from the *ancien regime* to the First World War.

DICK GEARY is Head of German Studies at the University of Lancaster, and a Research Associate at the Institute for the Study of European Labour History at the Ruhr University, Bochum. His research interests have been in the history of German Social Democracy and he is currently working on unemployment in Germany between the wars. Publications include: *European Labour Protest, 1848–1939* (2nd edn. 1984); *Karl Kautsky* (1987); and, as editor with Richard J. Evans, *The German Unemployed* (1987).

PAUL HEYWOOD is Lecturer in Politics and Assistant Director of the Centre for Contemporary Spanish Studies at Queen Mary College, University of London. His research interests have been in Marxism and the Spanish Socialist Movement between 1879 and 1936. He has published various articles on the left in Spain, and is currently working on a study of the Socialist Party and Defence Policy.

ROGER MAGRAW is Lecturer in History at the University of Warwick. He is currently preparing a work on the social history of the French working class from c.1815–c.1940. Publications include: 'The Conflict in the Villages: Popular Anticlericalism in the Isère 1852–1870', in T. Zeldin (ed.), *Conflicts in French Society* (1970); 'Pierre Joigneaux and Socialist Propaganda in the French countryside 1849–51', *French Historical Studies*, vol.x, no.4 (1978); *France 1815–1914: The Bourgeois Century* (1983); and 'Popular anticlericalism in nineteenth-century rural France' in J. Obelkevich, L. Roper and R. Samuel (eds.), *Disciplines of Faith* (1987).

GORDON A. PHILLIPS is Senior Lecturer at the University of Lancaster. His research interests have included the National Transport Workers' Federation and he is currently working on a social history of the blind in Britain. Publications include: *The General Strike* (1979); and *Casual Labour: The Unemployment Question in the Port Transport Industry, 1880–1970* (with Noel Whiteside: 1985).

CHRISTOPHER READ is Lecturer in History at the University of Warwick and has been Visiting Scholar at the universities of Harvard and Columbia and at the Soviet Academy of Sciences in Moscow. His research interests lie in the Russian Revolution. Publications include *Religion, Revolution and the Russian Intelligentsia* (1979) and various contributions to journals on Russian social history. His study of Bolshevik cultural policy, 1917–25, *Politics and Culture in Revolutionary Russia*, is due to be published shortly.

INDEX